THE EDITORS: JOSEPH, WILLIAM AND DON CARLOS SMITH

First Edition

JONATHAN NEVILLE, MS, JD

Other LDS nonfiction by Jonathan Neville

The Lost City of Zarahemla
Brought to Light
Moroni's America
Moroni's America (Pocket edition)
Letter VII: Oliver Cowdery's Message to the World about the Hill Cumorah
Whatever Happened to the Golden Plates?
Why Mormons Need the Book of Mormon
Moroni's History (2018)

———

LDS fiction by Jonathan Neville

Before the World Finds Out
The Joy Helpers
Moroni's Keys
Among All Nations
In Earthly Things

———

Blogs
http://www.lettervii.com/
http://bookofmormonwars.blogspot.com/
http://mormonmesomania.blogspot.com/
http://bookofmormonconsensus.blogspot.com/
http://thefifthmission.blogspot.com/

THE EDITORS: JOSEPH, WILLIAM AND DON CARLOS SMITH

First Edition

JONATHAN NEVILLE, MS, JD

The Editors: Joseph, William, and Don Carlos Smith
Copyright © 2016, 2017 by Jonathan Neville
First Edition

This is a work of nonfiction. The author has made every effort to be accurate and complete and welcomes comments, suggestions, and corrections, which can be emailed to **lostzarahemla@gmail.com**.

All opinions expressed in this work are the responsibility of the author alone.

6-20-17

ISBN-13: 978-1545050798
ISBN-10: 1545050791

Front cover inset: printing tools at the Nauvoo Printing Shop. Photo by the author.
Back cover inset: the author in the Nauvoo Printing Shop. Photo by Ryan Fisher.

DIGITAL
LEGEND
Toll Free 1-877-222-1960

www.digitalegend.com

To open-minded people everywhere, with deep appreciation for everyone involved with the Joseph Smith Papers project.

Table of Figures

TABLE OF CONTENTS

--->>> <<<---

Preface

How do we know what Joseph Smith actually taught?

Much of what is attributed to Joseph in books and lesson manuals was not written by him. Joseph relied on scribes and clerks to write what he dictated (or directed to be written). We have originals of some of these documents and original copies of others, but many of the most widely known teachings of Joseph Smith are found only in the printed pages of the 1842 *Times and Seasons*.[1]

From February 15 through October 15, 1842, Joseph Smith was listed in the boilerplate at the end of the *Times and Seasons* as editor, printer, and publisher. Ever since, people have assumed this meant Joseph wrote, or at least approved of, every unattributed article in the paper. (*Attributed* articles include those signed by the author. *Unattributed* articles are those published (i) anonymously, (ii) over the signature of "Ed." for Editor(s), and (iii) over fake names, or pseudonyms.)

The Joseph Smith Papers project has made a tremendous amount of material available that was previously inaccessible, or even unknown. It is completely understandable that scholars, authors, and Church leaders would assume that unattributed material in the 1842 *Times and Seasons*, published while Joseph was the named editor, originated from him. However, we have more information now than we've ever had before—not only Joseph Smith's actual writings, but important information about cultural and historical context. Digital databases make searching and comparing much easier. When we assemble the data with a fresh look and different perspectives, we can discover new connections and draw new inferences.

We can ask and answer new questions.

The assumption that Joseph Smith wrote or approved of unattributed articles has had significant doctrinal implications. One of the best known is the Mesoamerican theory of Book of Mormon geography. That theory

---

[1] *The Times and Seasons* was the official Church newspaper in Nauvoo, Illinois, from November 1839 through February 1846. For the first year, it was published monthly. Beginning in November 1840, it was published twice a month.

originated with anonymous articles in the September and October 1842 *Times and Seasons* that linked the Book of Mormon to discoveries of ruins in Central America. If Joseph Smith wrote or approved the articles, the theory goes, we should examine archaeological and other evidence from that area to vindicate Joseph Smith.

I think this attribution to Joseph is a historical mistake that should be corrected for future generations.

Another issue raised by an unattributed article is the role of women in the Church. That article, titled "Try the Spirits," is addressed in my book *Brought to Light*.

In this book, I examine the evidence regarding Joseph's actual role as editor. I propose he was merely the nominal editor; i.e., he was editor in name only, with little if any hands-on participation in actual editing (or writing). Instead, he let others produce the paper. I also propose that, in response to the Central American articles in September and October, Joseph realized that having his name on the paper gave it an unwarranted imprimatur of authority. Consequently, he formally resigned. The next issue, dated November 15, showed John Taylor as editor.

Although technology has changed dramatically, the lessons learned in the early days of the Church apply to us today. We can learn a lot from studying the work of the early LDS authors and editors.

One important lesson was expressed by Oliver Cowdery. When he announced his resignation from the *Messenger and Advocate*, he wrote:

> **a man is responsible to God for all he writes. If his communications are not according to the truths of heaven, men may follow incorrect principles,** and digress, step after step from the straight path, till arguments, persuasions and facts, are as unheeded as the idle vision, when darkness and death rivet their destructive chains to be beaten off no more.

I share Oliver Cowdery's sense of duty for what I write, and I'm eager to stand corrected on any points I make in this or any of my other books and articles. The views expressed in this book are my responsibility alone.

I encourage your feedback and your further research, should you be inclined to embark—or continue on—the never-ending pursuit of truth.

Church History Timeline—1805-1846

1805 – Joseph Smith (JS) born 23 December in Sharon, Vermont

1820 – JS First Vision near home in Palmya, New York

1823 – JS visited by angel Moroni, views plates, 21-22 September

1827 – JS marries Emma Hale in Jan, obtains plates 22 September

1828 – Martin Harris (MH) takes transcript of characters to New York; JS translates plates with MH as scribe; MH loses the manuscript

1829 – JS translates plates with Oliver Cowdery (OC) as scribe; JS and OC receive Aaronic Priesthood from John the Baptist and baptize one another; JS and OC receive Melchizedek Priesthood from Peter, James and John; 3 and 8 witnesses view plates

1830 – Book of Mormon published; Church organized; first missionaries sent to Lamanites (American Indians)

1831 – LDS gather to Kirtland; New Jerusalem in Missouri revealed

1832 – W.W. Phelps publishes first Church newspaper, *The Evening and the Morning Star*, in Independence, Missouri

1833 – Printing press destroyed, LDS flee to Clay County

1834 – First Stake organized in Kirtland; Zion's Camp leaves Kirtland for Missouri, returns to Kirtland

1835 – In Kirtland, Quorum of the Twelve Apostles (Q12) organized; First Quorum of Seventy organized; D&C canonized; OC writes history of the Church in a series of letters, published in the Kirtland LDS newspaper *Messenger and Advocate* and copied into Joseph's personal journal

1836 – Kirtland Temple dedicated; JS and OC visited by the Lord, Moses, Elias, and Elijah, who confer Priesthood keys

1837 – First mission to outside the U.S. and Canada (England); David Whitmer is Church leader in Missouri, with WW Phelps and John Whitmer; JS and Sidney Rigdon leave Kirtland for Missouri

1838 – Phelps, John Whitmer, David Whitmer, Oliver Cowdery excommunicated; Gov. Boggs issues extermination order; JS imprisoned in Liberty Jail, Missouri

1839 – LDS move to Illinois; JS escapes from Missouri; *Times and Seasons*

(T&S) published in Nauvoo; JS visits Washington, DC and Philadelphia

1840 – Most of Q12 in England on mission; *Millennial Start* published; 3rd edition of Book of Mormon published; Nauvoo receives a charter.

1841 –OC's church history letters republished in *Times and Seasons*; *Gospel Reflector* published in Philadelphia and also reprints the OC letters; Orson Hyde dedicates Holy Land; Q12 return from England

1842 – Relief Society organized; JS becomes editor of T&S; Wentworth Letter (Articles of Faith), Joseph Smith-History and Book of Abraham published in T&S; First temple endowments in Nauvoo; *Wasp* published

1843 – Nauvoo grows; temple built

1844 – JS martyred; Q12 assume leadership

1846 – LDS leave Nauvoo for Utah

Joseph Smith's family

Figure 1 - Joseph Smith's family

Name	Dates of birth/death and place of death
Joseph Smith Sr.	12 July 1771 – 14 Sept 1840 (Nauvoo)
Lucy Mack	8 July 1775 – 14 May 1856 (Nauvoo)
Unnamed son	1796 (Vermont)
Alvin Smith	Feb 1798 – 19 Nov 1823 (Palmyra)
Hyrum Smith	9 Feb 1800 – 27 Jun 1844 (Carthage)
Sophronia Smith	16 May 1803 – 22 July 1876 (Fountain Green)
Joseph Smith, Jr.	2 Dec 1805 – 27 Jun 1844 (Carthage)
Samuel Harrison Smith	13 Mar 1808 – 30 July 1844 (Nauvoo)
Ephraim Smith	13 Mar 1810 – 24 Mar 1810 (Vermont)
William B. Smith	13 Mar 1811 – 13 Nov 1893 (Osterdock, IA)
Katherine Smith	28 July 1813 – 2 Feb 1900 (Fountain Green)
Don Carlos Smith	25 Mar 1816 – 7 Aug 1841 (Nauvoo)
Lucy Smith	18 July 1821 – 9 Dec 1882 (Colchester, IL)

Early Church Publications Timeline

1832-33 – *The Evening and the Morning Star*, Independence, Mo. W.W. Phelps, Editor.

1833-34 – *The Evening and the Morning Star*, Kirtland, Ohio. Oliver Cowdery, Editor.

1834-37 – *Latter Day Saints' Messenger and Advocate*, Kirtland, Ohio. Oliver Cowdery, John Whitmer, Warren A. Cowdery, Editors.

1837-38 – *Elders' Journal*, Kirtland Ohio and Far West, Mo., Joseph Smith, Editor.

1839-46 – *The Times and Seasons*, Nauvoo, Illinois, Don Carlos Smith, Ebenezer Robinson, Robert B. Thompson, Joseph Smith, John Taylor, Editors.

1840-1970 – *The Latter-day Saints' Millennial Star*, Manchester, England, P.P. Pratt, Editor (followed by many others).

1841 – *The Gospel Reflector*, Philadelphia, Pennsylvania, Benjamin Winchester, Editor.

1842-3 – *The Wasp*, Nauvoo, Illinois, William Smith and John Taylor, Editors.

1843-45 – *Nauvoo Neighbor*, Nauvoo, Illinois, John Taylor, Editor.

1844-45 – *The Prophet*, New York, New York, George T. Leach, William Smith, Samuel Brannan, Editors.

Figure 2 - Daguerrotype of Nauvoo, 1846

Chapter 1: Publishing the Restoration

→⇒ ⇐←

IN A CHURCH FOUNDED ON A BOOK—THE BOOK OF MORMON—it should be no surprise that writing, editing, and publishing would play a critical role in early Church history. It was not easy work. Many of the earliest revelations addressed the inherent challenges and difficulties the early Latter-day Saints faced as they sought to do the Lord's will and publish the news of the Restoration to the world.

In our day, when anyone can easily write and publish anything to the entire world through the Internet, the practical realities of publishing in the early 19th century are easily overlooked. Publishing as a Mormon in the early days of the Church superimposed the added burdens of poverty, isolation, and extreme persecution onto what was already a very difficult occupation.

Even before he obtained the original set of plates from Moroni, Joseph Smith faced tremendous opposition to the work. When he finally was able to translate the text in the relatively safe environment of Harmony, Pennsylvania, months of effort were wasted when Martin Harris lost the only copy of the hand-written manuscript of the first translation.

This was a significant setback in temporal as well as spiritual terms.

The loss of 116 pages of good paper alone was significant. We don't give a moment's thought to such basic requirements as obtaining paper on which to write the translation, but for Joseph Smith, paper was not easy to come by. Joseph Knight, whose horse and carriage Joseph took to the Hill Cumorah to obtain the plates, later supported the translation. He wrote that he gave "Joseph a little money to buy paper to translate." He "let him have some little provisions and some few things out of the store, a pair of shoes, and three dollars in money to help him a little."[2]

---

[2] Knight, Joseph, Sr. *Reminiscences*, no date. CHL. MS 3470. For an introduction to Joseph Knight and a transcript of *Reminiscences*, see Dean Jessee, *BYU Studies Quarterly*, 17:1 (1977): http://scholarsarchive.byu.edu/cgi/viewcontent.cgi?article=1819&context=byusq.

These details help put Joseph's circumstances in perspective.

Joseph Smith was never much of a writer.[3] He made sporadic journal entries from November 1832 through December 1835 and wrote several letters and notes, but the total word count of everything he wrote in his own handwriting (his holographic work) is only around 16,000 words. (By comparison, the entire Pearl of Great Price is about 13,000 words. The Book of Ether alone is about 17,000 words.)

Much of Joseph's holographic writing is mundane. There are brief journal entries ("the sabath went to meeting &c."), simple notes to others (he wrote to Newel K. Whitney seeking wood to burn in his office stove), and letters to Emma about his travels. Some of the material is significant, such as his letters to Emma from Liberty Jail. But overall, we rely almost entirely upon the work of his scribes and other observers to know what Joseph Smith, Jr., said and did.

It is always possible that additional holographic writings may surface, but based on what we presently have, we can reach some conclusions. Joseph wrote very little of his own history. So far as we know, he never wrote the words *Mormon, Moroni, Cumorah, Bible, Aaron,* or *Melchizedek* in his own handwriting. Only once did he refer to the "new testament." There are no holographic doctrinal expositions, quotations from scriptures, or references to books he read. We don't have original copies of many items published over his signature, such as the Wentworth letter or D&C 127 and 128, so we don't know if he originally wrote or dictated those, or merely approved the work of others who had put his thoughts (or theirs) onto paper.

One might assume that a person with such rudimentary writing skills would not care much for publishing books and newspapers, but for Joseph Smith, publication was essential and urgent. The first two editors in the Church—W.W. Phelps and Oliver Cowdery—were called by revelation. With them, Joseph arranged for the publication of the first Church

---

[3] A compilation of all the known writings in Joseph's own handwriting is included in Appendix 4. Most of these are available in the Joseph Smith Papers (JSP) here: http://www.josephsmithpapers.org/site/documents-in-joseph-smiths-handwriting

newspaper—*The Evening and the Morning Star*—as early as 1832. This paper was published in Independence, Missouri.

Publishing a newspaper in the early 1800s involved three main functions: writing, editing, and printing. Each presented its own challenges. *The Evening and the Morning Star*, for example, consisted largely of extracts from other newspapers, from other Christian writers, and from the Book of Mormon or other latter-day revelations. W.W. Phelps, the editor while the paper was published in Independence, wrote relatively short editorials, including comments on the extracts. Presumably he read widely to find pieces that would be relevant and acceptable to Mormon readers. He'd have to edit them to assure conformity with Mormon points of view. The physical reality of printing on the old hand presses was a labor-intensive work that detracted from the writing and editing roles.

The Evening and the Morning Star ceased publication in Missouri after little more than a year when a mob destroyed the printing office on 20 July 1833 because of an editorial about slavery that Phelps published. Joseph sent Oliver to the East coast to purchase another printing press, which was set up in Kirtland in a printing office owned by Frederick G. Williams that was located behind the Temple. Oliver Cowdery assumed the role of editor. He resumed publication of *The Evening and the Morning Star* from December 1833 through September 1834.

In October 1834, Oliver began publication of the *Latter Day Saints' Messenger and Advocate*. The first item in the first issue is an Address by Oliver that reflects his sense of responsibility as Editor, a topic discussed in Chapter 2.

In May 1835, John Whitmer took over as editor, only to see Oliver reprise the role in March 1836 when Whitmer moved to Missouri.

Oliver was listed as Editor beginning with the April 1836 edition. Then, in February 1837, Oliver's brother Warren became the named editor when Joseph Smith and Sidney Rigdon purchased the printing press. The final issue of the *Messenger and Advocate* was published in September 1837.

As writers, editors, and publishers, Phelps and Cowdery accomplished miracles and greatly pushed the work forward, yet both were forced out of the Church (along with the entire Whitmer family). Warren Cowdery joined other dissenters. The stresses and pressures of publishing may have played an role in the estrangement of these men from the Church. As mentioned in the Preface, Cowdery felt a heavy burden to produce, regularly and in abundance, articles that would build testimony and spread the Gospel. Phelps and the others undoubtedly felt the same burden.

Joseph Smith was well aware of challenges and opportunities inherent in publishing, but he insisted on moving the work forward because he had been commanded by revelation to do so. It may have been the loss of Cowdery and Phelps, two of his closest associates and important Church leaders, that led Joseph Smith to bring the publishing effort even closer to himself. He had assigned his brother Don Carlos to learn the trade in Kirtland from Oliver Cowdery. When the conflict with Warren Cowdery led to the discontinuation of the *Messenger and Advocate*, a new paper was started: the *Elders' Journal*.

Don Carlos became editor of the *Elders' Journal*, although Joseph Smith was listed as editor. (Despite his lack of interest—and ability—in writing, Joseph was listed as Editor during two short-term stints, one at the *Elders' Journal* and one at the *Times and Seasons*.)

Only two issues of the *Elders' Journal* were published in Kirtland: October and November 1837. Persecution there stopped publication—the printing shop was burned. The *Elders' Journal* resumed in a more rudimentary style in Far West, Missouri, for two issues in 1838 (July and August). Conflict between the Saints and the Missourians prevented further publication. The printing press was buried to protect it from enemies.

After the Saints were expelled from Missouri, they eventually moved to Nauvoo, where the *Times and Seasons* began publication in 1839[4] with Don Carlos as editor and Ebenezer Robinson as co-editor. The history of the *Times and Seasons* is addressed in more detail throughout this book.

Before he died, Don Carlos had published a prospectus for a weekly newspaper to be titled *The Nauvoo Ensign and Zarahemla Standard*. The death of Don Carlos led his successor, Ebenezer Robinson, to announce the new paper would not be published after all. However, Joseph's brother

---

[4] Elias Smith and Hiram Clark returned to Far West to recover the press and type, which had been buried before the Saints left. They brought the equipment to Nauvoo where it was used for several years at *The Times and Seasons*.

William decided to revive it. He arranged to edit and publish a weekly Nauvoo paper, albeit under a different name: *The Wasp*. The first issue was published on April 16, 1842.

Beginning on December 10, 1842, John Taylor was listed as editor and publisher of the *Wasp*. In April, 1843, John Taylor discontinued the *Wasp* when he started publishing the *Nauvoo Neighbor*. The new paper was double the size of the *Wasp* and included religious material as part of its role as "a good samaritan."[5]

William moved away from Nauvoo and eventually became editor and publisher of a paper called *The Prophet* in New York (see Chapter 5).

The first document Joseph Smith published was the Title Page of the Book of Mormon. He had it printed separately in late May or early June of 1829 as part of his copyright application.[6]

The Title Page was part of the audacious publishing project: the translation and publication of the Book of Mormon, which consumed the time and effort of Joseph Smith from September 1827 through March, 1830, when the printing was complete.[7] When he first obtained the plates, Joseph may have thought he was supposed to find someone who could help him translate the strange characters. That may have been the reason he copied the characters on a slip of paper and sent Martin Harris to find an expert who could read them. Only when Harris returned from New York did Joseph realize the translation was entirely up to him.

But how to do it?

He had the interpreters from the cache in the Hill Cumorah that also contained the plates, but these were Jaredite; they were too big and

---

[5] "Prospectus of a Weekly Newspaper Called the Nauvoo Neighbor," *Times and Seasons* 4, no. 10 (April 1, 1843): 145-46, online at http://www.centerplace.org/history/ts/v4n10.htm

[6] Chapter 9 of my book *Whatever Happened to the Golden Plates?* discusses the copyright application in more detail. The original printed title page is available in the Joseph Smith Papers at http://www.josephsmithpapers.org/paper-summary/title-page-of-book-of-mormon-circa-early-june-1829/1#historical-intro

[7] An excellent explanation of the printing process is in the December 1972 *Ensign*, online at https://www.lds.org/ensign/1972/12/the-book-of-mormon-goes-to-press?lang=eng.

cumbersome for him to use easily. At some point, he figured out how to accomplish the translation by using a seer stone he'd had for some time. Based on the known historical sources, Joseph apparently alternated between the two devices. Many authors have addressed the translation process.[8] In my view, Joseph translated the Harmony plates primarily with the interpreters, but when he gave these plates to the messenger before leaving Harmony, he also returned the interpreters. I think he used the seer stone exclusively to translate the small plates of Nephi at the Whitmer home in Fayette.

Whether he used the interpreters or the seer stone, the process was the same. When he was in tune with the Spirit, Joseph would see words appear on the stone and he would read them to a scribe.

This procedure raises the question, why a scribe? Joseph used several scribes, including his wife Emma, her brother, Martin Harris, Oliver Cowdery, and John Whitmer. But why a scribe? If he read the words off the stone, couldn't he have simply written them down himself?

Theoretically, he could have.

So far as we know from the text, neither Mormon nor Moroni used a scribe when they compiled the record on the plates. Nephi didn't use a scribe. Nor did his successors. It's interesting that although the Old Testament and New Testament refer to scribes over 100 times, the word never appears in the Book of Mormon.

Why didn't Joseph write out the words?

I propose two reasons.

First, he was not adept at writing. Perhaps he found the task difficult or laborious, or maybe he was self-conscious about his lack of education. His penmanship is not poor, which suggests training and practice, but from the documents we have today, it appears that throughout his lifetime, he wrote very little. Nowhere did he write about many of the significant events in his life. Joseph seemed to dislike the process of writing for whatever reason.

For example, the first substantive entry in Letterbook 1[9] is *History*, circa

---

[8] I discuss this in Chapter 9 of *Whatever Happened to the Golden Plates?*

[9] Letterbook 1, "consisting of ninety-three manuscript pages, preserves copies of early church-related communications dated 14 June 1829 through 4 August 1835. The transcribed text is in the handwriting of JS, Frederick G. Williams, Orson Hyde, and Oliver Cowdery."

Summer 1832, of which Joseph wrote only about half in his own handwriting. Next is a copy of a letter Joseph wrote to W.W. Phelps on 27 November 1832. (We don't have the original of the letter.) The copy in Letterbook 1 starts in the handwriting of Frederick G. Williams and alternates with Joseph's handwriting in midsentence. This suggests Joseph didn't have the patience or desire (or time) to copy even his own letters entirely.

A second reason for using a scribe was the need for a witness to the work. By having someone else listen to his dictation and write the words, Joseph had a witness who could testify that, in fact, the translation was accomplished by the power of God and not by Joseph reading from a manuscript written by him or someone else.

All of the scribes claimed Joseph was reading words from a seer stone or the ancient Nephite interpreters.

Another relevant aspect of the translation is that Joseph did not supply punctuation. This is further evidence of its ancient origins. The Bible Joseph grew up with was fully punctuated. Everything he might have read during his life in western New York in the early 1800s would have been punctuated. Yet when he dictated the text to Oliver Cowdery, there was no punctuation. Ancient languages did not use punctuation. Possibly Joseph knew that, but even so, how strange it must have seemed for him to dictate word after word without indicating when a sentence stopped or began. For Oliver, a schoolteacher, it must have seemed stranger still.

Nor did Joseph edit as he went. He dictated without going back to make changes.

From the outset, the restored Gospel had a mission that encompassed the entire world. The Title Page of the Book of Mormon contains the ambitious declaration that the purpose of the book

is to show **unto the remnant of the house of Israel** what great things the Lord

---

Historical Introduction, Letterbook 1, JSP. The original document of History starts here: http://www.josephsmithpapers.org/paper-summary/letterbook-1/7.

hath done for their fathers; and that they may know the covenants of the Lord, that they are not cast off forever—And also to the convincing **of the Jew and Gentile** that Jesus is the Christ, the Eternal God, **manifesting himself unto all nations**—And now, if there are faults they are the mistakes of men; wherefore, condemn not the things of God, that ye may be found spotless at the judgment-seat of Christ.

In the context of the western New York in 1830, printing 5,000 copies of the Book of Mormon seemed a foolhardy business decision. That's one reason Joseph Smith had such difficulty finding a printer who would take on the project. Financially, the Book of Mormon didn't do well. Martin Harris mortgaged his farm for $3,000 to pay for the printing and, when sales did not cover the cost, he lost his farm. Now, a single original 1830 edition book can sell for $100,000 or more.

Correcting the historical mistake that led people to attribute to Joseph Smith the unattributed articles in the *Times and Seasons* is also useful to see how Joseph effectively managed a situation that was difficult from both personal and public perspectives.

I hope this book builds faith and brings LDS people closer to a consensus about these issues. I hope it will lead to new insights about the Book of Mormon as well as Church history.

The information has significant implications for millions of people around the world who accept the Book of Mormon as scripture (and, in another sense, for those who reject the book as scripture), but it may also impact billions of others who know little to nothing about the issue—so far.

I recognize there will continue to be differences of opinion. History is a subjective interpretation of limited evidence that consists largely of subjective records, but our interpretations often change in light of new information.

Chapter 2: Actual vs. Nominal Editors

THE SCOPE OF JOSEPH SMITH'S ACTIVITY AS EDITOR of the *Times and Seasons* in 1842 has never been clear. Was he a "hands-on" editor who wrote unattributed editorials (signed "Ed." or left anonymous)? Or, if he didn't write these editorials, did he explicitly or implicitly approve of them? Could he have been merely a nominal editor who left the operations and content of the *Times and Seasons* to others?

Joseph's *Journal*, kept on a daily basis (with few exceptions) throughout 1842, gives a detailed look at his activities, including his involvement with the *Times and Seasons*. In chapter 4, I go through the *Journal* in detail. It is critical to notice what the *Journal* says and what it doesn't say.

Before considering Joseph's authorship of unattributed articles, it is important to recognize the collaborative nature of much, if not most, of what Joseph Smith specifically took credit for. The translation of the Book of Mormon itself required collaboration between Joseph Smith and a series of scribes, including Martin Harris, Emma Smith, and Oliver Cowdery. Joseph's translations of the Bible and the Book of Abraham also involved collaboration.

It was no secret that Joseph relied on others to help him write. The Lord himself recognized how important collaboration was. D&C 124:12 states, "And again, verily I say unto you, let my servant Robert B. Thompson help you to write this proclamation, for I am well pleased with him, and that he should be with you." Thompson died seven months later without having written the proclamation—it was eventually written by Parley P. Pratt in 1845[10]—but the scripture shows that, at least this occasion, Joseph needed help to write.

In fact, according to the Joseph Smith Papers,

---

[10] Alex D. Smith, "Organizing the Church in Nauvoo," *Revelations in Context*, online at https://history.lds.org/article/doctrine-and-covenants-organizing-nauvoo?lang=eng.

The majority of the time, Joseph Smith relied on scribes and clerks to compose, copy, or take down his dictation of the thousands of pages attributed to him, including sacred texts, correspondence, journals, histories, administrative records, and other documents.[11]

Just as there is no record of Joseph *writing* any of the unattributed material in the 1842 *Times and Seasons*, there is also no record of Joseph *dictating* any of that unattributed material. The absence of a historical record regarding Joseph's authorship is corroborated by evidence that *someone else actually wrote* the unattributed editorials. It was not an oversight by his clerks and scribes that they never mentioned Joseph writing this material; their record is accurate. He simply didn't write the unattributed articles.

With the historical facts clear, there is still room for different interpretations. People can still discuss whether, and to what degree, Joseph *approved* of the unattributed material. People can also have different views as to whether, and to what degree, we should deem the material to be Joseph's own teachings, even though he didn't write or dictate it.

In most cases, it probably doesn't matter who wrote the unattributed editorials in the *Times and Seasons*. So long as the doctrine is sound, does it make a difference whether the original author was Joseph Smith, Wilford Woodruff, John Taylor, William Smith, W.W. Phelps, Benjamin Winchester, or someone else?

Probably not.

But in other cases it makes a big difference.

There are several problems in assessing authorship in the *Times and Seasons*. In other contexts, subject matter expertise might be a clue to authorship, but in 1842 Mormonism, everyone was writing about the same general subject matter. All the candidate authors wrote extensively about the scriptures and how to interpret and apply them. The candidates shared similar experiences and the same basic beliefs about the Restoration and Joseph's role as Prophet. They all wrote in a literary culture that was not

---

[11] Documents in Joseph Smith's Handwriting, Joseph Smith Papers, online at http://josephsmithpapers.org/site/documents-in-joseph-smiths-handwriting.

strict about citing sources and distinguishing between direct quotations and paraphrasing. There are few holographic samples, and even fewer holographic samples intended for publication; people writing personal letters tend to have a different style and vocabulary than when writing for publication.

The unattributed articles also feature indications of multiple authorship and editing, which further blurs distinguishing characteristics. And yet, each candidate had some unique characteristics, such as word choice, theme, and type of argument, that help to distinguish them from the others.

In this book I include examples of known edits, where I compare an original manuscript with the published version. These give us a glimpse into the kinds of wording and grammar changes that result from revisions, whether by the original author or by an editor (or editors).

The most famous examples of what could be called editing by Joseph Smith are the revisions of the Book of Mormon itself for the 1837 and 1840 editions. He changed some terminology, grammar, punctuation and spelling, but there are no detailed records about whether it was Joseph or his collaborators who originally suggested each change. Joseph Smith's new translation of the Bible, which he mostly dictated to others, also gives us insights into his editing process.

In both of these cases, Joseph perceived editing as an inspired activity. He was making changes to scripture, after all. Whether, and to what extent, Joseph ever edited newspaper articles is unknown. The assumption that he did so is a matter of circumstance and conjecture, not historically supported fact.

There was little question about who edited and wrote unattributed articles at *The Evening and the Morning Star*. W.W. Phelps was essentially a one-man show in Independence in 1832 and 1833. When Oliver Cowdery revived the paper in Kirtland starting in December 1833, he, too, was clearly in charge. He signed his first editorial and created boilerplate with his name.

Figure 3 - Boilerplate, EMS, Dec. 1833

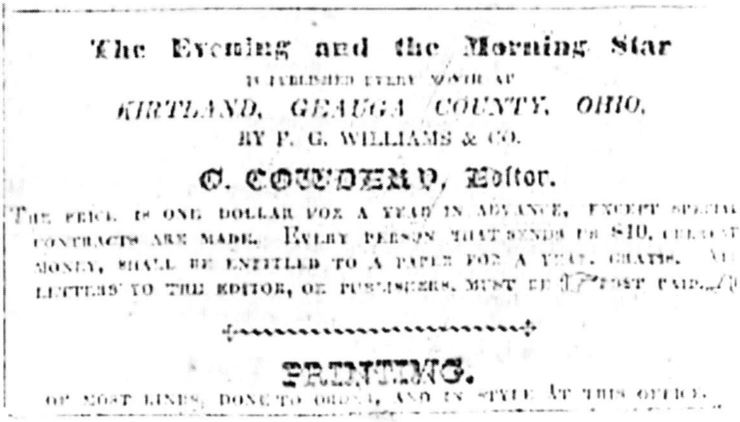

When Oliver started the *Messenger and Advocate* in October 1834, the boilerplate also showed him as Editor.

Figure 4 - Boilerplate, M&A, Oct. 1834

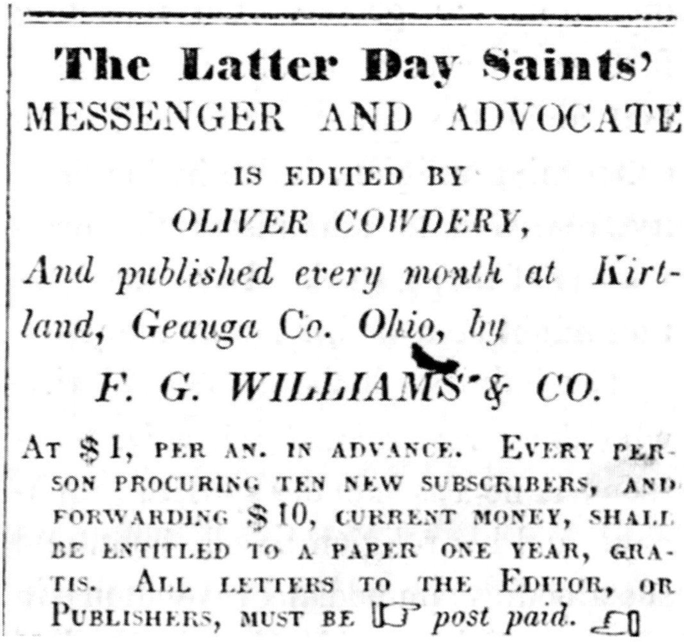

Although he was listed as Editor, Oliver also signed the inaugural editorial in the October 1834 issue separately, as he did other articles published while he served as editor. Letters published in the paper were addressed to "O. Cowdery."

The Cowdery boilerplate remained through the May 1835 issue, but was changed for the June issue when John Whitmer became editor.

Figure 5 - Boilerplate, M&A June 1835, p. 144

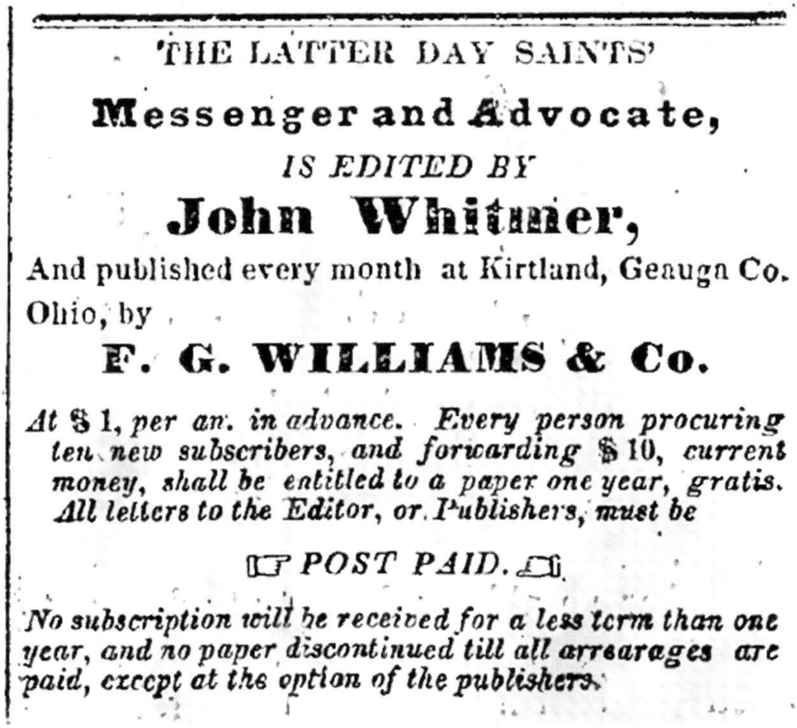

THE LATTER DAY SAINTS'

Messenger and Advocate,

IS EDITED BY

John Whitmer,

And published every month at Kirtland, Geauga Co. Ohio, by

F. G. WILLIAMS & Co.

At $ 1, per an. in advance. Every person procuring ten new subscribers, and forwarding $ 10, current money, shall be entitled to a paper one year, gratis. All letters to the Editor, or Publishers, must be

☞ *POST PAID.* ☜

No subscription will be received for a less term than one year, and no paper discontinued till all arrearages are paid, except at the option of the publishers.

Whitmer served as editor through the March 1836 issue. When Oliver took over the editorship again in April 1836, the boilerplate was changed accordingly. Notice that this time, only the spacing between sections of the boilerplate and the name of the editor were changed.

Figure 6 - Boilerplate, M&A, April 1836, p. 304

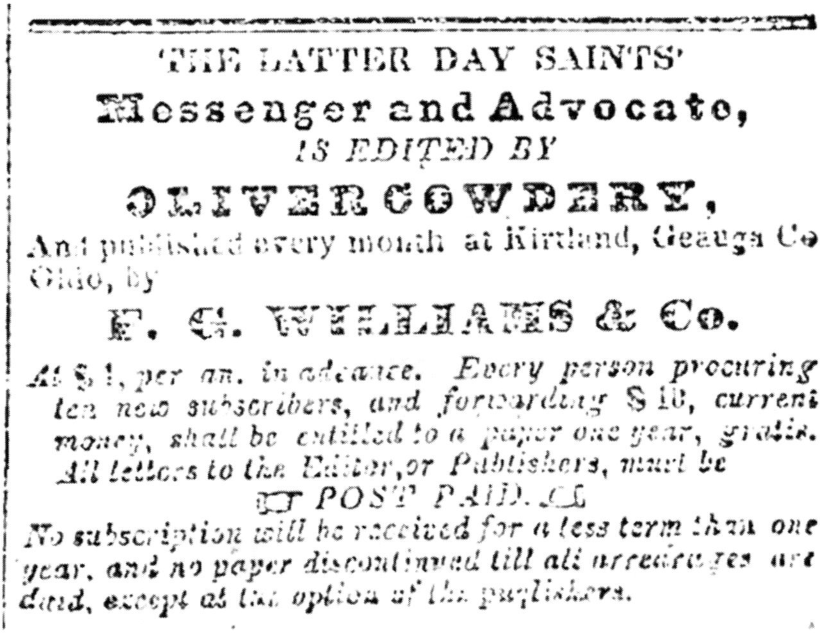

This history of changing boilerplate language, on its face, tends to support the idea that the named editor is the actual editor. However, that conclusion does not appear to accurately reflect what took place at the *Messenger and Advocate.*

As previously noted, Oliver Cowdery took over as the named editor beginning with the April 1836 issue. The boilerplate remained the same in each issue through November 1836. No boilerplate was used in December or January. Oliver's brother Warren took over as named editor beginning with the February 1837 issue, with this notice:

NOTICE.

The late firm of O. Cowdery & Co. is this day dissolved by mutual consent. The entire establishment is now owned by Joseph Smith, Jr. and Sidney Rigdon.

W. A. Cowdery takes the editorial chair, and in matters of business relative to the Messenger and Advocate, or any other pertaining to their printing office or book bindery, acts as their agent.

14

All letters by mail, relating to the business of the office must be addressed to W. A. Cowdery, postage paid; none others will receive attention, except at his discretion.

Instead of the boilerplate at the end of each issue, Warren inserted the following boilerplate about half way through each issue (a midplate). In the February 1837 issue, it is on page 457, which was incorrectly numbered in that issue as page 445.[12]

Figure 7- Boilerplate, M&A, Feb. 1837, p. 457

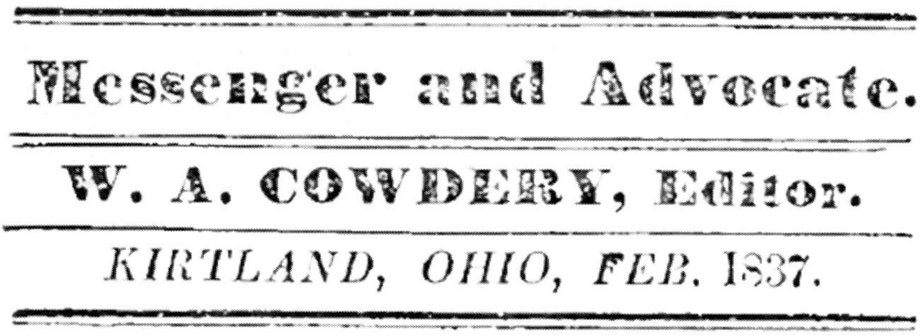
Messenger and Advocate.
W. A. COWDERY, Editor.
KIRTLAND, OHIO, FEB. 1837.

However, when Warren wrote his valedictory in the final issue of the *Messenger and Advocate* in September 1837, page 569, he explained what was going on behind the scenes. "The editorial charge of the Messenger and Advocate has rested more or less on us for a period of sixteen months past, but **nominally it has rested solely on us, but eight months**."

What did he mean by "nominally" here?

Eight months covers the period of February through September 1837—the period during which the boilerplate showed him as editor. The period of sixteen months goes all the way back to June 1836. From June 1836 through November 1836, the boilerplate showed Oliver Cowdery as editor.

Using the editorial "we" for himself, Warren here claims he had been the acting editor of the newspaper since June 1836, although he was the named (or nominal) editor only since February 1837. Warren's distinction between

[12] Online: https://archive.org/stream/latterdaysaintsm01unse#page/n461/mode/2up.

the nominal and the real or acting editor was not reflected in the boilerplate. Consequently, the boilerplate identification of the editor of a newspaper may reflect the nominal, but not the actual, editor.

To further complicate matters, the *Messenger and Advocate* published Oliver Cowdery's "Valedictory" in August 1837—just a month before Warren Cowdery wrote his own "Valedictory" in the final issue of the newspaper. Both valedictory statements are included in Appendix 4.

In his Valedictory, Oliver made the following statement that describes the burden felt by editors of Church-related material. I include it here to keep in mind the heavy responsibility that rested on the actual editors of these early Church newspapers.

> When this last reflection rises in the mind, **the heart almost sinks within this bosom**, lest in consequence of some darkness over the intellect, or some deep anxiety and concern, occasioned by inevitable and irresistible [sic] pecuniary embarrassment, **I may have dropped an item, or left unintelligible some important fact, which has occasioned an incorrect understanding on matters of eternal life.**[13]

---

[13] Oliver Cowdery, "Valedictory," *Messenger and Advocate*, Vol. III, No. 11, August 1837, p. 547.

Chapter 3: Don Carlos Smith as Editor

JOSEPH SMITH KNEW THAT A FAVORABLE MEDIA OUTLET was essential for the success of the Church. Not only were newspapers antagonistic toward the Church, but anti-Mormon books and pamphlets proliferated and called for responses. Church publications were essential to support missionary efforts, to educate the Saints about doctrine, and even to manage Church affairs throughout the United States and England.

The first two editor/publishers Joseph appointed were W.W. Phelps and Oliver Cowdery. Both men were excommunicated for a period of time. Joseph seems to have recognized he needed someone he could trust, so he turned to his brothers, starting with Don Carlos.

Don Carlos Smith was the seventh son and ninth named child of Lucy Mack and Joseph Smith Sr. (Later in life, he signed letters as "D.C. Smith" and "Don C. Smith.") He was born on March 25, 1816, in Norwich, Windsor County, Vermont, making him ten and a half years younger than Joseph Smith.

Little is known of his youth, but he was present at the first conference of the Church, which was held at the Peter Whitmer Sr., home in Fayette, New York, on June 9, 1830. Although he is not listed in the one-page minutes,[14] he was baptized that day by David Whitmer in Seneca Lake, about 3.5 miles away. He was also "ordained to the Priesthood" when he was fourteen, but the exact date is not known.[15]

---

[14] Minutes, 9 June 1830, list only a dozen men by name, but a later account reported about 30 members attended, along with other believers and investigators. The Minutes are online at http://www.josephsmithpapers.org/paperSummary/minutes-9-june-1830

[15] The most complete biographical information is included in Joseph Smith History, vol. C-1, addenda, which is reproduced in Appendix 2 of this book.

From the outset, he was deeply involved in the Church. Here are some examples from Joseph Smith's history (Appendix 2 of this book):

- The evening after the plates of the Book of Mormon were shewn to the eight witnesses, a meeting was held, when all the witnesses, as also Don Carlos bore testimony to the truth of the Latter Day dispensation

- He accompanied his father to visit his grandfather and relatives in St. Lawrence Co: N.Y., in August 1830. During that mission he convinced Solomon Humphrey Jr., a licensiate of the Baptist order, of the truth of the work.

- He was one of the 24 Elders who laid the corner stones of the Kirtland Temple.

- He served missions to Pennsylvania, New York, Kentucky, and Tennessee. His account of some of these missions is included in Appendix 2.

Don Carlos married Agnes Coolbrith, eight years his senior, in Kirtland, Ohio, on July 30th, 1835. They had three daughters, the youngest of whom was born March 10, 1841, just five months before Don Carlos died. Her given name was Josephine Donna Smith, but she became known later in life as Ina Coolbrith.

Five months after Don Carlos died, his wife Agnes married Joseph Smith (January 1842). After Joseph died in Carthage, she married George Albert Smith, cousin of Joseph and Don Carlos. However, she did not accompany the Saints to Utah. Instead, Agnes married William Pickett, a Mormon lawyer and printer in St. Louis, Missouri. They had twin boys (named Don Carlos and William). In 1851, they moved to Utah, where William practiced law with George Albert Smith until he was cited for contempt of court. He moved to California, leaving the family in Utah for about a year before returning to accompany them to northern California.[16]

The family eventually settled in Southern California, where Josephine (Ira) became known, according to a letter she wrote to Joseph F. Smith, as "the Los Angeles poetess, Ina Smith (niece of the Prophet)." Ira eventually became a popular poet who worked with Bret Harte and Jack London, among many others. Mark Twain and Alfred Lord Tennyson recognized her

---

[16] The best account of Agnes' life I've found is in Todd Compton, *In Sacred Loneliness: The Plural Wives of Joseph Smith*, (Signature Books, 1997).

work, and she became the first California Poet Laureate. The public didn't know of her Mormon origins until after her death.[17]

Agnes reportedly wrote a letter to her nephew, Joseph F. Smith, acknowledging the "household of Joseph."

Joseph Smith's *Journal, 1832-1834*, includes this entry under the date of 22 November 1833: "my brother [Don] Carlos Smith came to live with me and also Learn th[e] printing art."[18] Joseph's history (Appendix 2) includes this note about Don Carlos: "In the fall of 1833 he entered the office of Oliver Cowdery, to learn the art of printing."

Don Carlos apparently worked in the printing shop throughout the Kirtland publishing runs of *The Evening and the Morning Star* and the *Messenger and Advocate*. He took over the Kirtland press when the *Elders' Journal* commenced publication in October 1837. The Prospectus for the *Elders' Journal* claimed it would be edited by Joseph Smith. However, it also informed readers that "All letters whether for publication or other purposes, sent to the office must be directed to DON C. SMITH."[19]

In his History, 1838-1856, Joseph indicated that Don Carlos ran the *Elders' Journal* for its first two issues that were published in Kirtland.

> On the commencement of the publication of the *Elders Journal* in Kirtland, he took the control of the establishment until the office was destroyed by fire in December 1837, when in consequence of persecution he moved his family to New Portage.[20]

This comment could be interpreted to mean Don Carlos ran only the business and printing work. However, Peter Crawley indicates that Don Carlos "actually did the editorial work for these two numbers" of the *Elders'*

---

[17] A summary of Ira's life is at https://en.wikipedia.org/wiki/Ina_Coolbrith.

[18] Online at http://www.josephsmithpapers.org/paper-summary/journal-1832-1834/30.

[19] Sidney Rigdon, "Prospectus," *Messenger and Advocate*, Vol. III, No. 11, August 1837, p. 547.

[20] See Appendix 2 and http://www.josephsmithpapers.org/paper-summary/history-1838-1856-volume-c-1-addenda/12.

Journal.[21] This conclusion is consistent with the notice requiring letters to be addressed to Don C. Smith, and I agree with it for these reasons.

It also seems unreasonable to infer that Joseph Smith had the time, interest, and aptitude to actually edit the *Elders' Journal*. Joseph's name appeared on both sets of boilerplate—the newspaper used both a midplate similar to that used by Warren Cowdery and an endplate similar to the one used by Oliver Cowdery. However, the endplate required that letters be directed to DON C. SMITH, a departure from the custom of directing letters to the named editor.

Don Carlos had to deal with a practical problem. Sidney Rigdon and Joseph Smith purchased the printing shop from Oliver Cowdery with notes. Rigdon explained what happened next when he testified at the High Council trial of Oliver's membership (held in Far West on April 12, 1838):

> Sidney Rigdon testifies that in January 1837 Oliver Cowdery offered to sell out his share in the printing office at Kirtland Ohio, which they Joseph Smith jr & Sidney Rigdon bought and gave their notes, after which say in the spring following he wished to get a press & some of the type which they granted him on conditions that he should give up the notes above refered [sic] to, he then went into the office and took whatever he pleased & so completely stripped the office, as he (Rigdon) was informed by D. C. Smith, that there was scarcely enough left to print the "Elders Journal," whereas, before there was a sufficient quantity to print a weekly and monthly paper, the book of Covenants, Hymn Book, Book of Mormon &c. but the notes he did not give up.[22]

This suggests that Don Carlos was resourceful in printing the newspaper, as he would be later in Nauvoo when he started the *Times and Seasons*.

The printing press that Oliver obtained from the Kirtland printing shop was transported to Far West. John Whitmer purchased it in August 1837. In April 1838, it was sold to Edward Partridge and the High Council resolved to resume publication of the *Elders' Journal*. Two issues were printed in July

---

[21] Peter Crawley, *A Descriptive Bibliography of the Mormon Church*, Volume 1, Item 39, online at https://rsc.byu.edu/archived/descriptive-bibliography-mormon-church-volume-1/entries-1-100.

[22] Lyndon W. Cook and Donald Q. Cannon, *Far West Record*, (Deseret Book Company 1983), April 12, 1838, p. 168, online at http://gospelink.com/library/document/25254.

and August 1838, but then violent opposition forced the Saints to leave Far West. The printing press and type were buried for protection.

Don Carlos resumed his publishing career in Nauvoo in 1839. Peter Crawley describes the sequence of events.

> The history of the *Times and Seasons* begins in April 1839, when Elias Smith, Hiram Clark, and others unearthed the Far West press and type and hauled them to Nauvoo. In June a council of the First Presidency and other Church leaders gave this press to Ebenezer Robinson and Don Carlos Smith with the understanding that they would publish a magazine—named by the council *Times and Seasons*—which would promote the interests of the Church. Robinson and Smith were to bear all of the expense of this undertaking and to keep all of the profits.
>
> Ebenezer Robinson was exactly two months younger than Don Carlos Smith and also an experienced printer. Born in New York, May 25, 1816, he began his printing career at age sixteen at the Utica *Observer*. Three years later, although not a Latter-day Saint, he moved to Kirtland and obtained work at the Mormon print shop. He was baptized by Joseph Smith in October 1835 and in the spring of 1837 moved to Far West. The following year he resumed his career as a printer at the Mormon press in Far West. When the Saints were driven out of northern Missouri in November 1838, he spent a short time in prison, and then joined the immigration to Illinois. For two and a half years he ran the printing business in Nauvoo, until he sold it to the Church in February 1842....
>
> Robinson and Smith set up their press in the basement of a former warehouse on the bank of the Mississippi. Here during June and July they cleaned the press and type. After purchasing a new font with $50 borrowed from Isaac Galland and some paper with another $50 borrowed from a friend, they struck off a prospectus and began to print the first number of the *Times and Seasons*, dated July 1839. After printing two hundred copies, both took sick with swamp fever, and this stopped all printing activity for four months. In the mean time, they received a few subscriptions which enabled them to move the press to a small, new, one-and-a-half-story frame building on the northeast corner of Water and Bain streets. By November they had recovered enough to begin again on the magazine. With the help of a newly hired young printer Lyman Gaylord, they reissued the first number of the *Times and Seasons*, now dated November 1839.

Together Robinson and Smith edited and published the first fifteen numbers (November 1839–December 1, 1840). On December 14, 1840, they dissolved their partnership, with Robinson taking over the job and book printing, and Smith continuing to edit and publish the *Times and Seasons*. Smith edited the next nine numbers alone, whole numbers 16–24 (December 15, 1840–April 15, 1841). With the issue of May 1, 1841, Robert B. Thompson joined the magazine, and together they edited whole numbers 25–31 (May 1, 1841–August 2, 1841). On August 7, 1841, Don Carlos Smith died, and Ebenezer Robinson rejoined the magazine as co-editor with Thompson and as publisher. This partnership lasted for just one issue, whole number 32 (August 16, 1841), because Thompson died twenty days after Smith. Robinson continued as sole editor and publisher for whole numbers 33–41 (September 1, 1841–January 1, 1842).[23]

Working conditions in the printing shop were difficult. Typesetting was laborious and tedious. Conditions were damp and crowded. Don Carlos undoubtedly felt the same pressure of editing and publishing the paper that Oliver Cowdery had described in his Valedictory. Not only was he responsible for the paper, but he had been elected as a Nauvoo city councilman and was a brigadier general in the Nauvoo Legion, as well as president of the high priests at Nauvoo.

On June 3, 1841, Don Carlos wrote a letter[24] to Joseph asking his brother to sell land he had just purchased. The letter gives additional insight into the relationship between the brothers and living conditions in Nauvoo at the time. At one point he writes

Bare with me Joseph while I write—I have no opportunity to converse with you—you are thronged with business—all the time (almost) in the narrows, straining the last link, as it were, to get out of this & that Pinch &c. &c. all this I know, I am not ignorant of it—I have been, and now am in the <same> mill—

---

[23] Crawley, *Descriptive Bibliography*, Item 60.

[24] http://www.josephsmithpapers.org/paper-summary/letter-from-don-carlos-smith-3-june-1841/1

when I'll get through the hopper I know not, one thing I do know, and that is this when I got into the hopper in this place I was owing in Kirtland and elsewhere about $200,00 <or more and w[hole in page] not worth a red cent. [25]

It is quite striking that the two brothers are both in Nauvoo but Don Carlos had no opportunity to talk with him because Joseph is "thronged with business." This detail seems to be typical of Joseph's life in Nauvoo. People constantly sought his attention, and he had myriad problems to solve and projects to supervise. The demands on his time must be considered when evaluating the feasibility of Joseph himself acting as editor, printer and publisher of the *Times and Seasons* in 1842.

Don Carlos explained his financial situation and his plan to start a weekly newspaper.

I feel anxious to enlarge the printing business by publishing a weekly news paper, and I think it will do well, if it should, it will be very valuable.

When W.W. Phelps began publishing *The Evening and the Morning Star* in Independence, Missouri, he also published the *Upper Missouri Advertiser*, a weekly focused on secular news and commerce. These two papers set a pattern that would be followed in subsequent Church publications; i.e., a monthly religious paper and a weekly secular paper. Oliver Cowdery published the *Northern Times* in 1835 along with the *Messenger and Advocate* in Kirtland.

As he indicated in his letter to Joseph, Don Carlos sought to emulate the same model by adding *The Nauvoo Ensign and Zarahemla Standard* to the *Times and Seasons*. He solicited subscriptions and began plans for the second paper, but Don Carlos' death halted the Zarahemla paper.

In April 1842, Don Carlos' concept of a second Nauvoo paper was implemented by his brother William Smith when he started *The Wasp*, which is discussed in Chapter 5.

Don Carlos had a relatively brief tenure as editor of the *Times and*

----

[25] The entire letter is in Appendix 3.

Seasons before his death, but he showed great initiative, ability and ambition even in the face of exceptionally difficult circumstances. Joseph Smith's confidence in his brother was well placed.

For the first year, the *Times and Seasons* was published monthly, just as *The Evening and the Morning Star* and the *Messenger and Advocate* had been. Each twelve months was called a "Volume" of the newspaper, starting in November 1839. Each issue was a "Number." You can see the entire run of the *Times and Seasons* online, starting with Volume 1, Number 1 (November 1839), here: http://www.centerplace.org/history/ts/v1n01.htm.

The place of publication was listed as "Commerce, Illinois" in the first six numbers of Volume 1. Beginning with Volume 7 (May, 1840), the masthead shows "Nauvoo, Illinois" instead.

Each issue of the paper was sixteen pages long, set in double columns. A typical issue contained about 12,000 words, which includes about 60,000 characters and 10,000 spaces. Each character and space had to be set individually (except for boilerplate such as the masthead and the endplate).

In the last issue of Volume 1 (October 1840), Don Carlos announced an expansion of the newspaper. He and Robinson added additional staff to publish the *Times and Seasons* twice a month, a practice that continued until the Saints left Nauvoo. Some interesting passages are in **bold** below.

PROSPECTUS

FOR THE SECOND VOLUME OF THE TIMES & SEASONS.

To our Patrons and Friends: As this number closes the first volume of this paper, we feel anxious to say a few words to our kind friends who have felt willing to extend the helping hand, and patronize us in the commencement of our undertaking; and sustained the press in its infancy.

It is a well known fact, that we commenced this paper under the most adverse circumstances possible, as the press and type had just been resurrected from the bowels of the earth, in the State of Missouri, where it had been necessary to deposit [deposit] them, during the war carried on against us by

Lilburn [Lillburn] W. Boggs **and his unholy gang of Land Pirates,** consequently they were not fit for use, until made so at a heavy expense; and **having been robbed of all we had, therefore we were not in a situation to put it in that situation we should wish;** however, notwithstanding all these difficulties we have been enabled, by the blessing of heaven, to worry through with one volume, and now propose, commencing the second; and as it has, we trust, passed its infancy, and is now approaching to childhood, we think it all important that it should increase in strength, and vigor, therefore **we shall publish it hereafter twice each month, to gratify the request and desire of many of our subscribers who are anxious to learn of the mighty spread of truth oftener than once each month.**

The great ascessions [ascensions] making to the church, and the introduction of the benign gospel of peace, into new places, and other nations; also the great demand for publications from every part of America, renders it altogether necessary for us to issue our periodical oftener than formerly. We should be pleased to publish our paper weekly, as **we have an abundance of matter for the instruction of the saints, as President Joseph Smith jr. is furnishing us with essays on the glorious subject of the priesthood, also giving us extracts of the new translation to lay before our readers,** of the second volume,-but our circumstances will not permit us to publish oftener than twice a month, as we are but a child yet, and you are aware that a child must creep before it can walk, and walk before it can run; so we, having passed our infancy, must content ourselves by walking the coming season, not saying what we will do the following year; but leave that to the destiny of Heaven, and the good will of our friends and the saints.

We shall endeavor to make the second volume as interesting and instructive as possible, not sparing any pains on our part to give, as early as can be, all important information concerning the church at home or abroad. It will contain essays on the following subjects; the gospel, the priesthood and the gathering of Israel. We shall also give a synopsis of the general news of the day.[26]

As promised, the next issue contains an "Extract from the Prophecy of Enoch." The "essay on the glorious subject of the priesthood" is actually the first letter about Church history written by Oliver Cowdery to W.W. Phelps

---

[26] http://www.centerplace.org/history/ts/v1n12.htm.

(a reprint from the *Messenger and Advocate*). Presumably Joseph gave these letters to his brother to publish as essays on the Priesthood. In ensuing issues of the *Times and Seasons*, Don Carlos would go on to reprint all of Oliver's letters, including Letter VII.

As an indication of the challenges faced by the editors, the first number of Volume 2 on November 1, 1840, contains an apology from Don Carlos and Robinson to their readers for delays in the paper:

> We wish to say for the benefit of our readers, that having accomplished our business in Cincinnati, and returned home, we now feel justified in assuring our friends, that hereafter the paper shall be issued from our office by the times specified. The delays which have occurred heretofore, are not altogether our fault; as we have ascertained that several times, after the packages have been lodged in the Post office, it has been several days, and some times, weeks, before they were forwarded; and in many instances, after they were forwarded, they never arrived to the places of destination. For these delays we can not be accountable; but situated as we are, (being publishers,) if there is any delay, we have to bear the blame of it; as it is most generally supposed, if a number is not received in season, that it was not issued as soon as it should have been; which we have to acknowledge, has been the case in some instances, during the publishing of the past volume: occasioned by circumstances to us unavoidable. But as the sickly season is past, and we have made large additions to our establishment, also, having obtained a great supply of paper, sufficient for six or eight months, we mean that no pains shall be spared on our part to have the paper printed regularly in future.[27]

This issue also includes warming to readers that gives useful insight into day-to-day life in Nauvoo.

LOOK OUT FOR THIEVES!!

This place has been infested of late with a gang of thieves, insomuch [inasmuch] that property of almost all kinds, has been unsafe unless secured with bolts and bars; cattle and hogs have been made a free booty. The community are awake to

---

[27] http://www.centerplace.org/history/ts/v2n01.htm.

ferret them out, and have already made some inroads among them; the measures that are taking, have created a general alarm among the midnight pilagers, and they are making tracks as fast as possible. As it is very possible that some may escape JUSTICE, and palm themselves upon an unsuspecting community, we give this notice as a timely warning, that all may be on the look out. We sincerely hope that all those who escape justice here, will soon be overtaken in their wickedness-ALTON is a suitable place for all such characters.

Under the editorship of Don Carlos, the *Times and Seasons* became a highly influential and important publication in the Church. Because its pages were filled mainly with extracts, minutes, and letters, we don't see a lot of Don Carlos' personal writing. One database of Church historical documents contains only two entries for Don Carlos, both from the *Times and Seasons*.[28] It is impossible to tell how much of the commentary such as the two passages quoted above was written by Don Carlos individually or by Robinson or someone else.

Don Carlos was only 25 years old when he died of a respiratory disease, possibly pneumonia. His obituary is included in Appendix 3.

When Don Carlos died, the news spread quickly. Benjamin Winchester left his mission in Massachusetts as soon as he heard Don Carlos had died. He returned to Philadelphia and wrote a letter to Joseph Smith, expressing his condolences and offering himself as a replacement at the *Times and Seasons*. This is the letter I discussed in *The Lost City of Zarahemla*.

In the letter, Winchester writes,

> If I could get any thing to do in Nauvoo for a livelihood I should like it very much. There is much printing to do in Nauvoo and as I am somewhat acquainted with that business perhaps you could get me a situation of that kind.[29]

---

[28] See https://bcgmaxwell.wordpress.com/church-historical-documents-corpus/early-lds-authors/don-carlos-smith/.

[29] Benjamin Winchester, *Letter*, Philadelphia, PA, to JS, Nauvoo, IL, 18 Sept. 1841.

As if this request for a job was not clear enough, Winchester offers another hint.

> I never regretted the death of any man more than that of Don Carlos and I said 'who can fill his place.'

As I explained in *Lost City*, page 56, "Winchester knew Don Carlos from the Kirtland days. Winchester was ordained an Elder ten days after Don Carlos was ordained a High Priest. Don Carlos worked in the Kirtland printing shop under Oliver Cowdery, which ultimately led to his work at the *Times and Seasons*. Like Winchester, Don Carlos went on a mission to Pennsylvania and New York. Surely they had friends in common. Don Carlos had published letters and other material Winchester had sent to the *Times and Seasons*. No doubt Winchester's condolences are sincere, but at the same time, he is not shy about his hopes to be the one to fill his place."

When Winchester arrived in Nauvoo on October 31, 1841, he received a severe rebuking from Joseph Smith. Nevertheless, he began working at the *Times and Seasons*. From October 15 through February 15, every issue of the newspaper included a letter or article written by Winchester.

As I've discussed in *Lost City* and *Brought to Light*, Winchester had substantial influence on the *Times and Seasons* during 1842.

From the historical record available to us, we can see that Don Carlos worked closely with his brother Joseph and presented a considerable amount of material that blessed the lives of the Saints and helped move the work forward. Joseph's confidence in Don Carlos was well justified.

Available in JSP here: http://bit.ly/16TVURB.

Chapter 4: Joseph Smith as Editor

THIS CHAPTER ANALYZES WHAT IS KNOWN ABOUT JOSEPH SMITH'S role as editor of the *Times and Seasons* from 15 February through 15 November 1842.

Joseph Smith's formal association with the *Times and Seasons* in 1842 is well known. The *Times and Seasons* had been published in Nauvoo continuously since November 1839. Don Carlos Smith and Ebenezer Robinson were the original editors, but Don Carlos became the sole editor in December 1840 when Robinson left to begin printing books instead.

Don Carlos was a natural choice for this position—primarily because his printing mentors had left the Church by the time the Saints settled Nauvoo. A July 20, 1831, revelation (Section 57) had specified that William W. Phelps "be established as a printer unto the church." In fulfillment of that revelation, Phelps founded the first Mormon newspaper, the *Evening and Morning Star*, in Independence in 1832. The revelation also provided for an assistant:

> let my servant Oliver Cowdery assist him, even as I have commanded, in whatsoever place I shall appoint unto him, to copy, and to correct, and select, that all things may be right before me, as it shall be proved by the Spirit through him.[30]

When mobs destroyed the press in Independence, *The Evening and the Morning Star* moved to Kirtland, eventually succeeded by the *Latter Day Saints' Messenger and Advocate* (1834-37). Phelps and Cowdery collaborated on both papers. Don Carlos learned the art of printing at age 17 when he worked with Oliver Cowdery at the print shop in Kirtland, beginning in the

---

[30] D&C 57:13

fall of 1833.[31]

In the midst of dissention and apostasy, Don Carlos published two issues of the *Elders' Journal* in Kirtland in the fall of 1837 before losing the printing press to an apostate faction.[32] Two more issues of the *Elders' Journal* were published in Far West on a different printing press before a Missouri mob attacked. This time, the press was saved by being buried.

By the time the Saints moved to Nauvoo, both Phelps and Cowdery were out of the Church, so it made sense for Don Carlos to start the newspaper. E. Robinson described the background in a column he wrote in *The Return*, May 1890:

> At a council of the First Presidency and other authorities of the church, early in June [1839], it was decided to let Don Carlos Smith, and the writer, (as we were practical printers,) have the printing press and type which had been saved from the mob in Missouri, by having been buried in the ground and a haystack placed over it, and that we should publish a paper for the church, or a church paper, at our own expense and responsibility, and receive all the profits arising therefrom. The council named said paper *Times and Seasons*. Accordingly we undertook the task, and after purchasing fifty dollars worth of type on credit, from Dr. Isaac Galland, and cleaning the Missouri soil from the press and type that had been saved, and hiring from one of the brethren, fifty dollars in money, which we sent for paper, we issued the prospectus for the *Times and Seasons*, and sent it to brethren residing in different states.
> (Heretofore, in "Items of personal history," when speaking of myself, have used the pronoun we, as is customary with editors, but having formed a copartnership with Don Carlos Smith, it seems necessary that a change be made in the manner of expression, therefore hereafter, when speaking of our company affairs, will use the term we, but when speaking of myself, individually, will use the pronoun I

---

[31] JS History, vol. C-1, addenda, 12, online in the JSP at http://josephsmithpapers.org/paperSummary/?target=X623274D1-44FF-4315-BD94-3FEE59F93729, Following the destruction of W.W. Phelps' printing press in Independence, Missouri, Cowdery continued the publication of Phelps' *The Evening and the Morning Star* in Kirtland starting in December 1833 and published *The Saints' Messenger and Advocate* from October 1834 through September 1837.

[32] Ibid. Publication of the *Elders' Journal* on a different printing press resumed in Far West, Missouri, in July and August 1838 before the printing press was buried in the ground to be saved from the mob. This press was later reclaimed and used for the *Times and Seasons*. See discussion later in this article.

and my. The reader must not consider it egotism at the frequent appearance of these terms, as it cannot well be avoided.)

The only room that could be obtained for the printing office, was a basement room in a building formerly used as a warehouse, but now occupied as a dwelling, situated on the bank of the Mississippi River. The room used for the printing office had no floor, and the ground was kept damp by the water constantly trickling down from the bank side. Here we set the type for the first number of the paper, which we got ready for the press in July, and had struck off only some two hundred copies, when both Carlos and the writer were taken down with the chills and fever, and what added to our affliction, both our families were taken down with the same disease. My wife was taken sick the very next day after I was, which sickness continued ten months. This was a year of suffering for the citizens of the place, as it was estimated at one time, there was not one well person to nearly ten that were sick. Five adults died out of one family in one week.[33]

Before our sickness we had wet down paper sufficient for two thousand copies of *the Times and Seasons*, which paper mildewed and spoiled. Afterwards another batch of paper was wet down by Francis Higbee, who thought he could print the papers, but he failed and that paper was lost.

Subscriptions for the paper soon commenced coming in, in answer to the prospectus, and the two hundred copies sent out, which enabled us to provide for our families; and also to have a small, cheap frame building put up, one and a half stories high, the lower room to be used for the printing office, and our friends moved myself and wife into the upper room, or chamber, in the latter part of August. We were moved upon our bed, and a portion of the time in those days, neither of us was able to speak a loud word. This was a happy change for us, as it gave a clean sweet room to dwell in, and the benefit of near neighbors, it being in town.

Although Robinson formally left the *Times and Seasons* in November 1840, he had spent most of June through October getting the Book of Mormon published in Cincinnati.[34] As of December 1840, Don Carlos was the sole editor for five months. This job, already difficult, became more so because he started publishing two issues a month in November 1840, just

---

[33] E. Robinson, "Items of Personal History of the Editor," The Return, Vol. 2. No. 5., Davis City, Iowa, May 1890, p. 258, available online at http://www.sidneyrigdon.com/RigWrit/M&A/Return1.htm

[34] Ibid, pp. 259-262.

before Robinson left. Perhaps that increased load was a factor in Robinson's decision.

Help arrived in May 1841, when Robert B. Thompson became an additional editor at the *Times and Seasons*. The work was still difficult; "Don Carlos died from a respiratory disease with pneumonia-like symptoms" [35] likely caused by long hours in the cold, damp conditions Robinson described. Robinson returned as editor to help Thompson, but then Thompson died just twenty days after Don Carlos, leaving Robinson as the sole editor. On December 13th, Robinson recruited Wilford Woodruff to "help him in writing & in other business,"[36] but to no avail. Instead, Robinson hired Gustavus Hills as an assistant editor, making the announcement in the January 15, 1842, issue of the *Times and Seasons*.

Less than two weeks later, on January 28th, Joseph Smith announced a revelation that the Quorum of the Twelve should take control of the newspaper:

A Revelation to the twelve concrning [sic] the Times and Seasons.

Verily thus saith the Lord unto you my servant Joseph. go and say unto the Twelve That it is my will to have them take in hand the Editorial department of the Times and Seasons according to that manifestation. which Shall be given unto them by the Power of My Holy Spirit in the midst of their counsel Saith the Lord. Amen[37]

On February 3, Wilford Woodruff recorded a slightly broader version of the revelation: "A Revelation was given a few days since for the Twelve to obtain the printing establishment of E. Robinson & govern the printing of the Times & Seasons & all the church publications." Note 108 in the Joseph

---

[35] Richard Lloyd Anderson, "Joseph Smith's Brothers: Nauvoo and After," *Ensign*, September 1979.

[36] Wilford Woodruff, *Journal*, December 13, 1841 (Typescript version edited by Scott G. Kenney, Signature Books, 1983) Vol 2, p. 141. (referenced herein as Woodruff, *Journal*, followed by the page number).

[37] 28 January 1842, *Journal*, December 1841-December 1842, available online at http://josephsmithpapers.org/paperSummary/journal-december-1841-december-1842?p=18&highlight=times%20and%20seasons#!/paperSummary/journal-december-1841-december-1842&p=18

Smith Papers provides helpful background and explains the sequence of events and who was involved:

> According to Wilford Woodruff, "After consulting upon the subject the quorum appointed Elders J Taylor & W Woodruff of the Twelve to Edit the Times & Seasons & take charge of the whole esstablishment [sic] under the direction of Joseph the Seer." The contract with Ebenezer Robinson for the sale of the printing office was closed one week after this revelation was received. Under the new arrangement, JS would function as editor of the Times and Seasons, with Taylor assisting him in writing and Woodruff overseeing "the Business part of the esstablishment."[38] [sic]

Despite Woodruff's observation that he and Taylor were appointed to edit the paper, only Joseph is listed as Editor, Printer and Publisher on every issue from 15 February through 15 October 1842 (with the exception of the 1 August issue).

Robinson sold his printing operation in February and published his Valedictory as Editor of the *Times and Seasons* on February 15, 1842. He introduced the new Editor with this paragraph:

> Under these circumstances I now take leave of the editorial department of the Times and Seasons, having disposed of my entire interest in the printing establishment, book-bindery, and stereotype foundery [foundry], and they are transferred into other hands. The Editorial chair will be filled by our esteemed brother, President Joseph Smith, assisted by Elder John Taylor, of the Quorum of the Twelve, under whose able and talented guidance, this will become the most interesting and useful religious journal of the day.

Robinson's comments point out that there was more to the printing office than just the *Times and Seasons*; the printing establishment, book-bindery, and stereotype foundry were also important businesses. The printing establishment handled a variety of projects separate from the newspaper. The book-bindery was important because when people purchased books, they were loose pages that had to be bound separately. The

---

[38] Ibid, Note 108, citing (Woodruff, *Journal*, 3, 4, and 19 Feb. 1842; JS, Journal, 4 Feb. and 2 Mar. 1842.)

stereotype foundry created metal plates for material that included graphics or was repeated often in the newspaper, such as advertisements, the masthead—and the identification of the Editor.

Managing the paper, by itself, was no small task. The *Times and Seasons* was published twice a month, on the 1st and 15th, and a typical issue contained around 14,500 words. On top of editing and writing duties, the entire issue had to be manually typeset, character-by-character, and then proofread from a sample print run. Once corrected, the type was inked by hand, a process that required considerable skill and had to be repeated for each copy. The newsprint had to be dampened and set into the galley and slid under the press where the operator would pull the spring-loaded handle and press the paper onto the type. Then the paper had to be extracted and dried on a rack before it could be hung on overhead racks for a day or so before each issue could be assembled and mailed out. The total number of copies printed of each issue is unknown, but Wilford Woodruff reported in his Journal on March 19, 1842, that "We struck off about 500 No of the 10 No 3 vol of Times and Seasons."

Robinson's introduction fails to mention Woodruff. This may be because Woodruff was not to be involved with editing despite his appointment by the Twelve; perhaps the terminology used by the Twelve did not mean "editing" per se, but more broadly meant whatever duties were necessary to produce the newspaper. Maybe Robinson ignored Woodruff because he resented him for not accepting the offer to join the paper in December. At any rate, Woodruff was the most active of the three new editors. His daily journal shows him working at the print shop almost daily, with the exception of the last two weeks in March and the first week in June when he was sick, and an extended absence from July 28-September 26 when he went to St. Louis for supplies and became ill. In his journal on February 19, Woodruff explained that "it has fallen to my lot to take charge of the business part of the establishment." He wrote only one signed article for the *Times and Seasons* while Joseph was the named editor. It was published 15 April (T&S 3:12) and titled "SABBATH SCENE IN NAUVOO." The article describes a discourse by Joseph Smith on the subject of Baptism and describes the events of the day.

Also on February 19, Woodruff wrote, "Joseph the Seer is now the Editor of that paper [the *Times and Seasons*] & Elder Taylor assists him in writing." The phrase "assists him in writing" is vague. It could mean Taylor helped Joseph write and edit material for the paper, or it could mean Taylor helped Joseph write correspondence and official documents related to Joseph's roles as Mayor, General of the Nauvoo Legion, President of the Church, etc., as well as his legal affairs, including the numerous real estate transactions and his petition for bankruptcy in April 1842.

When Robinson introduced John Taylor, he also didn't specify in what way Taylor would "assist" Joseph. In fact, the February statements by Woodruff and Robinson, plus one entry in Joseph's journal from March 9[39], are the only mentions of John Taylor's involvement with the *Times and Seasons* until late September 1842, when Taylor met with Joseph to discuss moving a printing press across the river. The September meeting, discussed later in this article, notes that Taylor had recovered from a serious illness. It is not known when that illness began or how it affected his involvement, if any, at the *Times and Seasons* between March and September.

Joseph's formal resignation as Editor of the *Times and Seasons* in the 15 November 1842 issue announced that John Taylor had taken over; the 15 November issue "commences his [Taylor's] editorial career." This seems an odd choice of words if, in fact, Taylor had been editing the paper since March. One possible explanation for the lack of references to Taylor's editing activity is that his involvement with the printing shop pertained to other activities, such as the book bindery, or writing responses to letters received at the paper.

Until November 1842, Taylor never signed any articles in the *Times and Seasons*, unlike William Law, a counselor in the First Presidency, who signed two articles. Taylor's journal, if he kept one during 1842, is not extant, but other records show him participating with the Quorum of the Twelve in various meetings and activities. For example, on 22 July, the Nauvoo City Council appointed Taylor, along with William Law and Brigham Young, to "a special Committee, with the Recorder [James Sloan] to assist, to prepare a

---

[39] Joseph's journal records, "Examining copy for the Times & Seasons presented by Taylor & Bennet [John C. Bennett]"

Petition to lay before the Governor of this State."40 The Petition was signed the same day. As Joseph Smith was Mayor of Nauvoo at the time, perhaps this is the kind of writing activity he engaged in to "assist" Joseph.

Following Robinson's Valedictory in the February 15, 1842, issue, the new editors introduced themselves with this paragraph:

TO SUBSCRIBERS.

It will be noticed in the above communication of our much respected friend, E. Robinson, Esq. that the paper is no longer printed, and published by that gentleman; but that it has fallen to our lot to issue this valuable and interesting periodical, and to take the Editorial chair.

We esteem our predecessor for the honorable course that he has taken in the defence [defense] of righteousness, and in the support of truth. He has done honor to the cause he espoused; he has stood firm in the day of adversity; and when foes frowned, and persecution raged, in the midst of pecuniary embarassments [embarrassments], (growing our to our persecutions in Missouri,) he hss [has] boldly, nobly, stood in the cause of freedom, of liberty, and of God; he has gone forward with a steady course; he has stemmed every torrent, braved every danger, and borne [born] down all opposition: and amidst accumulated difficulties, truth has triumphed, error and misrepresentation has been frowned down; and bigotry, superstition, and ignorance have hid their hoary heads in shame.

The "Times and Seasons" is now read with interest in almost every city throughout the length, and breadrh of this vast republic, -it has crossed the great Atlantic; and through it multitudes of the inhabitants of England are made acquainted with what is transpiring in the far famed "West."

We siucerely [sincerely] give Mr. Robinson this meed of praise and as he is now retiring from the field, crown him with those laurels which under God he has fairly, and honorably won.

As it regards ourselves we have very little to say, but shall leave it for the future to unfold; and for a discerning public to judge. The important events that are daily transpiring around us; the rapid advance of truth; the many communications that we are receiving, daily, from elders abroad; both in this country, in England, from the continent of Europe, and other parts of the world; the convulsed state of the nations; the epistles and teachings of the Twelve; and the revelations which we are receiving from the most High, will no doubt furnish us with material to make this paper interesting to all who read it, and whilst we solicit

---

40 Nauvoo Minutes, 22 July 1842, Kindle location 3656.

the patronage, and support of our friends, we pray that the God of Israel may inspire our hearts with understanding and direct our pen in truth. Ed.

This introduction was written in first person plural but signed with a singular "Ed." The new editors did not explain the lack of personal signatures here, a somewhat surprising omission for an introduction. In the November 15, 1842, issue, when Joseph Smith wrote his own Valedictory and John Taylor assumed the role of Editor, both men personally signed their respective comments. Thereafter, Taylor discontinued the use of articles signed as "Ed." until February 1843. (The "Ed." signature had been used sparingly prior to March 1842.)

Whatever the reason, the generic "Ed." signature became characteristic of the paper during Joseph's editorship—it was found in nearly every issue between March and November—and it was used whether the editorial was written in first person singular or plural, as it was here.

It is also important to note that this was not Joseph Smith's first foray into editing a newspaper. The *Elders' Journal*, published in 1837-1838, also included a notice that it was "Edited by Joseph Smith Jr."[41] Despite this designation, Joseph Smith's History discusses the involvement of Don Carlos: "On the commencement of the publication of the Elders' Journal in Kirtland, he [Don Carlos] took the control of the establishment until the office was destroyed by fire in December 1837, when in consequence of persecution he moved his family to New Portage."[42] Consistent with this biographical detail, Erastus Snow and Wilford Woodruff both wrote to Don Carlos at the Elders' Journal. Woodruff wrote, "My object in addressing you at this time, is to forward you a list of the names of some of our friends from the several Islands of the sea, who wish you to send them your valuable paper, vis: the *Elders' Journal*."[43] Although Joseph Smith was the named

---

[41] *Elders' Journal*, Vol. 1, No. 1, October 1837, p. 16. Available online at https://archive.org/stream/eldersjournalkir01unse#page/14/mode/2up

[42] *History, 1838-1856*, volume C-1 Addenda, 7 August 1841, available online at http://josephsmithpapers.org/paperSummary/?target=X623274D1-44FF-4315-BD94-3FEE59F93729

[43] *Elders' Journal*, November 1837, p. 17, available online at https://archive.org/stream/eldersjournalkir01unse#page/14/mode/2up

editor, the Prospectus for the *Elders' Journal* directed readers to send mail to Don Carlos. This arrangement suggests that Joseph's concept of the role of named editor was not hands-on; the *Elders' Journal* set a precedent for Joseph's name appearing as Editor while one of his brothers did the work.[44] After all, according to Joseph's own handwritten journal, Don Carlos had come to Kirtland specifically to live with Joseph and "also Learn the printing art."[45]

Regarding the *Times and Seasons*, apart from his assumption of the title "Editor," there is little evidence that Joseph Smith actually did much editing after the Book of Abraham was published in March. Joseph's journal and other records describe his 1842 activities in court proceedings (civic and church), his constant involvement with real estate and financial matters, his many speeches and time spent in council and instructing various individuals and groups, his focus on temple work (he first presented the endowment on May 4), his work with the Nauvoo Legion, the Nauvoo Lodge of Free Masons, and the Nauvoo City Council (he was elected Mayor of Nauvoo on May 19th), and much more, including organizing the Relief Society in March and going into hiding to avoid arrest and extradition to Missouri. But neither his journal nor any contemporary accounts mention him involved with editing the *Times and Seasons* after March 1842.

Joseph Smith's journal became a relatively reliable source of information starting in December 1841 when Willard Richards was appointed. The Joseph Smith Papers explain his involvement:

> Richards arrived in Nauvoo in August 1841 after a four-year mission to England. Joseph Smith found him to be "a man after his own heart, in all things, that he could trust with his business" and appointed him temple recorder and "Scribe for the private office of the President" on 13 December 1841. Richards began "the

---

[44] The Historical Introduction to the *Elders' Journal* in the JSP papers simply states, "It is unknown how labor was divided on the newspaper or how much immediate responsibility JS had for the content." http://josephsmithpapers.org/paperSummary/elders-journal-october-1837

[45] Joseph Smith, Journal, 1832-1834, 22 November 1833, available online at http://josephsmithpapers.org/paperSummary/?target=JSPPJ1_d1e3981

duties of his office" immediately, apparently writing the first entry of Joseph Smith's journal on the day of his appointment. Richards kept the journal for the remainder of Smith's life, with the exception of the period from 30 June through 20 December 1842, when he moved his wife and son from Massachusetts to Nauvoo. During Richards's absence, William Clayton kept the journal, with occasional assistance from Eliza R. Snow and Erastus Derby. References in the journal to the recorder, scribe, or secretary always refer to Richards; the other scribes did not make reference to themselves.[46]

Joseph's daily journal recorded only seven references to the printing office between March 10 and November 15—and none of them mention editing activities. Two entries in September refer to moving a printing press across the river to start another newspaper, a project that would become significant in connection with William Smith, as discussed later in this article.

Of course, not every activity the Prophet engaged in was recorded in his journal. It is possible he spent a lot of time reading, writing, and editing. What the journal does reflect, however, is direct and frequent involvement with the *Times and Seasons* in March when the Wentworth letter and the Book of Abraham were being prepared and published. In May and June, Joseph transacts business and meets in council at the printing shop. He has a letter copied, hears letters read, drops off poetry, and visits in the evening with the night watch to see the *Wasp*. But at no time after March does his journal report a single instance of him writing, editing, or even previewing the *Times and Seasons*.

Journal entries regarding the printing office.

23 February 1842 – Wednesday – visited the printing office & gave R. Hadlock instructions concerning the cut for the altar & gods in the Records of Abraham, as designed for the Times and Seasons.[47]

24 February – Thursday – Thursday 24. Attending to business at the general office. P.M. was explaining the Records of Abraham to the Recorder. Sisters Marinda and Mary and others present to hear the Explanations.

---

[46] http://josephsmithpapers.org/intro/introduction-to-journals-volume-2.

[47] Joseph Smith, Journals, Vol. 2, February 23-4, 1842, p. 36, available at josephsmithpapers.org

1 March 1842 – Tuesday – During the fore-noon, at his office & the printing office correcting the first plate or cut of the Records of father Abraham, prepared by Reuben Hadlock for the Times and Season[s] and in council in his office in the P.M. and in the evening with the Twelve & their wives at Elder Woodruff's.

2 March 1842 – Wednesday – Read the Proof of the "Times and Seasons" as Editor for the first time. No 9th of Vol 3d in which is the commencement of the Book of Abraham.

4 March 1842 – Friday – Exhibiting the Book of Abraham in the original to Bro Reuben Hadlock so that he might take the size of the several plates or cuts & prepare the blocks for the Times & Seasons & also gave instruction concerning the arrangement of the writing on the Large cut illustrating the principles of Astronomy. (in his office) with other general business.

8 March 1842 – Tuesday – Commenced translating from the Book of Abraham for the 10 No of the Times and Seasons—and was engaged at his office day & evening. [48]

9 March 1842 – Wednesday – Examining copy for the Times and Seasons presented by [John] Taylor & Bennet [John C. Bennett],—and a variety of other business in the Presidents office in the morning. In the afternoon continued Translation of the Book of Abraham, called Bishop Knight & Mr. Davis &c with the Recorder. & continued translating & revising. & reading letters in the evening Sister Emma being present in the office.

10 March 1842 – Thursday – a great variety of other Business. The President retired to the Printing office with his Lady with the twelve who had been at the office.

10 May 1842 – Tuesday – Transacted a variety of business at the Store, printing office &c.

16 May 1842 – Monday – Transacting business at the store until 10 AM – Then at home & in the P.M. at the printing office with Bro. Young, Kimball, Richards &c in council.

22 May 1842 – Sunday – At home, called at the Editors office to have letter copied for Quincy Whig, denying the charge of killing Ex Governor Boggs of Missouri as published in the Quincy Whig.

28 May 1842 – Friday – walked to the store with Emma and did some business in the city, called at 8 in the evening at the printing office with the night watch to see the *Wasp*.

4 June 1842 – Saturday – At the printing office in the morning. Heard the

---

[48] Joseph Smith, Journals, Vol. 2, March 8–9, 1842, p. 42, available at josephsmithpapers.org

Letters from the Grand master Jonas D King & Mr Helme about Bennets expulsion from the Lodge in Ohio.

12 June 1842 – Sunday – Home. Brought some poetry to printing office & got some newspapers.

11 July 1842 – Monday – With Mr. Hunter in the A.M. and in the P.M. was at the printing office reading mail papers. Bought a horse of Wilson Deputy Sheriff.

21 September 1842 – Wednesday – In the large room over the store. In the P.M. had a visit from Elder John Taylor one of the quorum of the Twelve who is just recovering from a severe attack of sickness. He counseled Elder Taylor concerning the printing office – removing one Press to Keokuk &c.

22 September 1842 – Thursday – At home. Arranging with Jacob Remick concerning moving printing press to Keokuk; buying paper &c.

[Note: this is the last mention of the printing office in Joseph's journal until after November 15th, when John Taylor formally assumed the editorship of the *Times and Seasons*.]

The entry on 22 May is particularly significant. Although Joseph's journal reports that he called at the Editor's office, the letter for the *Quincy Whig* was published in the *Wasp*, not the *Times and Seasons*. This raises an inference that the "editor" Joseph referred to was the editor of the *Wasp*— William Smith—not John Taylor (and certainly not himself).

The entry on 28 May is curious. The May 28th issue is the one that contained Joseph's letter for the *Quincy Whig*, so it's natural that he would want to see how it looked in print. But why would Joseph visit the printing office with the night watch to see the *Wasp*? One possibility is he was so busy during the day the only chance he could get to see the *Wasp* was in the evening. Perhaps he knew that the print run would be too wet during the day to read it. Another possibility is that Joseph was avoiding William, with whom he had a history of conflicts. Hence the late evening visit with the night watch. Regardless of the reason for the night visit, if Joseph was actively editing the *Times and Seasons*, it seems likely he would have had access to proof the *Wasp* before it was printed.

Editorial oversight.

One incident reinforces the inference of Joseph's non-involvement raised by his Journal entries. On January 23, 1842, Joseph's journal records a disciplinary action he took against a man identified as "A Lits."

January 23 Silenced Elder Daniel Wood, of Pleasant Vale for preaching that the church should unsheath [sic] the Sword—and also silenced Elder A, Lits for preaching that the authorities of the church were done away.—&. And sent the Letters by the hand of Elder William Draper Junior who preferred the charges; & cited A Lits to appear before the High council of Nauvoo forthwith.— & published the same in the Times and Seasons. in the name of Joseph Smith. P.C.J.C.L.D.S. and B Young P.Q.T.—W. Richards Clerk.[49]

Joseph's journal also shows that on March 9th he was examining copy for the *Times and Seasons* presented by John Taylor and John C. Bennett. This would have been the copy prepared for the March 15th edition that included the Book of Abraham and the first installment of the History of Joseph Smith. Pursuant to Joseph's direction from January, the 15 March 1842 *Times and Seasons* published the following just above the boilerplate identifying Joseph Smith as editor.

NOTICE.

Elder A. Lits is requested to come to Nauvoo immediately, to answer to chargers [sic] which may be preferred against him.

Four months later, however, the 15 July 1842 *Times and Seasons* featured this notice which appears directly above the new boilerplate identifying Joseph Smith as editor. (The stereotype was changed beginning with the July 1st issue. The wording was changed slightly to avoid the unnecessary repetition of Joseph's name.)

NOTICE.

A notice appeared in the paper some few weeks ago advertizing [advertising] Elder A. Lits to return to Nauvoo. The notice was inserted by some officious

---

[49] Joseph Smith, Journal, 23 January 1842, p. 36

person without authority; we know of no person by that name, but suppose that Elder William A. Lits is the person intended; if so, he is in perfect good standing in the church, and there are no charges preferred against him.

It seems highly unlikely that if Joseph Smith was personally editing the paper in July, he would have forgotten he ordered the publication of the original notice back in January and published the notice on March 15. The March 15 issue is the only one for which there is a record of Joseph actually examining the copy. It contained the second installment of the Book of Abraham and Joseph's signed introduction to the "extract from my journal" that constituted the History of the Church; surely he would have been aware of the contents of this issue.

The editor of the July 15th edition characterized the Lits insertion in the March 15th edition as the work of "some officious person." This phrase indicates that the editor was unaware of Joseph's action in "silencing" Elder A. Lits in the first place, and apparently did not realize that Joseph had specifically examined copy presented by John Taylor for the March 15th edition.

This evidence suggests not only that someone else was editing the July 15th edition of the *Times and Seasons*, but that whoever the editor was, he didn't seek approval or review from either John Taylor, Brigham Young, Willard Richards or Joseph Smith. But he did feel authorized to state that William A. Lits was in good standing.

This was not the first example of lax—or puzzling—editorial oversight. The 15 April 1842 *Times and Seasons* includes a famous error in the "History of Joseph Smith." In what is now Joseph Smith—History 1:33 in the Pearl of Great Price, the angel who visited Joseph was misnamed in the *Times and Seasons*: "He called me by name, and said unto me that he was a messenger sent from the presence of God to me, and that his name was Nephi."

This error was later noted in the History of the Church:

In the original publication of the history in the *Times and Seasons* at Nauvoo, this name appears as "Nephi," and the *Millennial Star* perpetuated the error in its republication of the History. That it is an error is evident, and it is so noted in the manuscripts to which access has been had in the preparation of this work.[50]

Orson Pratt and Joseph F. Smith also noted this error and advised John Taylor about it by letter dated 18 December 1877.

> The contradictions in regard to the name of the angelic messenger who appeared to Joseph Smith occurred probably through the mistakes of clerks in making or copying documents and we think should be corrected. . . . From careful research we are fully convinced that Moroni is the correct name. This also was the decision of the former historian, George A. Smith.[51]

April was still in the time frame when the record shows Joseph was most active in editing the *Times and Seasons*, yet this serious error was published, without correction in subsequent issues, and republished in the Millennial Star. Although the Pratt/Smith note attributes the error to "the mistakes of clerks," the episode raises a question about the editing process. Did Joseph actually proofread every word in the *Times and Seasons*? Did he actually proofread every word even in his own history? Based on this example, it appears not—even during the period when he was most closely involved with the *Times and Seasons*. In addition, the Pratt/Smith note was sent to John Taylor. There's no record that Taylor remembered the error or had any explanation apart from what Pratt and Smith came up with. For example, Taylor didn't respond by explaining that he and Joseph were aware of the error and decided not to correct it for some reason. This suggests that Taylor was no more actively editing the *Times and Seasons* in April 1842 than Joseph Smith was.

A related question is why the error was not corrected by Joseph himself. He apparently did not proofread the paper before publication; it is also possible that no one called it to his attention after publication. Maybe he didn't think the mistake was serious enough to publish a correction. In fact, an earlier incident suggests that Joseph and his associates may have chosen

---

[50] Joseph Smith, *History of The Church of Jesus Christ of Latter-day Saints*, 7 volumes, edited by Brigham H. Roberts, (Salt Lake City: Deseret Book, 1957), 1:11–12, footnote 2

[51] Letter, Orson Pratt and Joseph F. Smith to John Taylor, 18 December 1877; cited in Dean C. Jessee, ed., *The Papers of Joseph Smith: Autobiographical and Historical Writings* (Salt Lake City: Deseret Book, 1989), 1:277, nt. 1

not to correct the error because they didn't want to call attention to it.

Two wedding announcements published in the 15 February issue (the one in which Robinson announced his resignation and introduced Joseph and John Taylor as the new editors) caused a stir among Joseph's enemies:

> Married-In this city on the 6th inst. by the Rev. Erastus H. Derby, Mr. Gilbert H, Rolfe, to Miss Eliza Jane Bates, all of this city.
>
> On receipt of the above notice, we were favored with a rich and delightful loaf of cake by no means below the medium size; which makes us anxious that all their acts through life may be justified; and when life wanes and they find a peaceful abode in the "narrow house," may the many outs and ins they have made, leave to the world an abundant posterity to celebrate their glorious example.
>
> Married-In this city by Pres't. Hyrum Smith, Mr. J. W. Johnson to Miss Elizabeth Knight, all of this city.
>
> The above notice was accompanied with the usual Printer's fee, (a nice piece of bridal cake,) for which we tender our sincere thanks, and our best wishes for the future prosperity of the happy pair. Ed.

There are several details to note about these announcements. Beginning with its second issue in December 1839, the *Times and Seasons* had regularly published wedding notices and obituaries, but this practice ended after the 1 March 1842 edition. That change may have been prompted by the fallout from these particular wedding announcements, or may have been a reflection of the transition away from local news (which would be covered in the Wasp beginning in April). The "Ed." signature following the wedding announcement appears to be a comment from the Editor—except both potential Editors, Joseph Smith and E. Robinson, later claimed they didn't know about them. This incident illustrates the ambiguity of the signature. (This is only the third instance of the "Ed." signature in the third volume of the *Times and Seasons*. The first instance was in the January 15th issue, probably by Gustavus Hills since the article involved music and Hills was Professor of Music at the University of Nauvoo. The second instance was the signature below the introduction titled "TO OUR SUBSCRIBERS" discussed above.)

The 15 February issue of the *Times and Seasons* is also the first to conclude with the boilerplate declaring Joseph Smith's roles as editor, printer, and publisher.

These wedding announcements would have been long forgotten but for two things: the editor of a competing newspaper, the Warsaw Signal, claimed outrage that the Prophet would publish such a wedding notice, and the *Times and Seasons* published a lengthy explanation and apology on 15 March:

TO THE PUBLIC.

Lest wrong impressions should obtain abroad, detrimental to the interest and influence of President Joseph Smith, respecting a marriage notice, which appeared in the Times and Seasons, of the 15th of February ult. I deem it a privilege to make a short statement of facts concerning the matter, which, I am confident, will entirely exonerate that gentleman from all blame or censure, which may have been put upon him on account of the publication of said notice. On the 6th of Feb. I gave possession of the establishment, to Willard Richards the purchaser on the behalf of the Twelve; at which time my responsibility ceased as editor. On the 7th this marriage took place, and the notice was written by one of the hands in the office, and put in type by one of the boys, without, undoubtedly, any expectation of its being printed. At this time it was not fully decided whether President Smith should take the responsibility of editor, or not, therefore that paper went to press without his personal inspection; and as this article was standing in type with the other matter, *it found its way into the paper unnoticed*, as both the person who wrote it, and the boy, together with either journeymen, had been discharged by the purchasers, also, *the proof reader did not observe it*, as the words used were printer's phrases and he was not looking for any thing indecorous or unbecoming. The *first time Pres't Smith or myself saw the article, was after the papers had been struck off, when it was too late to remedy the evil. We both felt very sorely mortified, at the time;* but I am fully persuaded that the kind readers of the Times will cheerfully overlook whatever fault there may be, as that was the first time any such thing ever appeared in the columns of this paper, and not attribute any blame to Pres't Smith, as he is not guilty in the least, and had no knowledge of the thing until it was too late.

I will here take the liberty to state that from an intimate acquaintance of near seven years with Pres't. Joseph Smith, I never yet have seen a single indecent or unbecoming word or sentence, from his pen, but to the reverse; therefore I can with all confidence, assure the patrons of this paper, that they have nothing to fear, but every thing to hope for, in the exchange of editors.

E. ROBINSON. (italics added)

For the Times and Seasons.
Nauvoo, March 14, 1842.
PRESIDENT JOSEPH SMITH:-
Dear Sir: I see, in the last 'Warsaw Signal,' a very wanton and ungentlemanly attack upon yourself, made by the editor of that paper. The editor's article, however, is in perfect keeping with his feel and natural spirit for calumniating the innocent and oppressed. I have, for some time past, been a constant reader of that paper, and feel myself perfectly safe in saying, that scarcely a single number of it has ever been issued, that was not surcharged with epithets of the foulest and basest character, perpetrated against a high-minded and intelligent portion of community, and fabricated by himself--or some individual equally as corrupt-- to answer his own wicked and nefarious purposes.

What I allude to, more particularly, is his remarks relative to a marriage notice which appeared in a former number of the Times and Seasons, charging you with being its author. *I should have remained silent upon this subject, had he made the attack upon any individual but yourself.* But justice to your character renders it an imperious duty for me to speak *and exonerate you from the false imputations of the editor.* Therefore, be it known to that gentleman--if his heart is not wholly impervious to declarations of TRUTH--that the little notice that has so much ruffled his very chaste and moral feelings emenated [emanated] from the pen of no individual other than--myself(!) "Urekah [Eureka]! Urekah!!" Then I would say to the sagacious editor of the Signal-

"Hush, babe, lay still and slumber!

I speak knowingly when I say, that notice went in the Times and Seasons entirely without your sanction, and you knew nothing of its existence until that edition had been 'worked off' and circulated the proof sheet not being examined by you.

After this declaration, I hope the editor of the Signal will do you the justice to exculpate you from the wholesale charges which I have been, in some degree, the means of calling upon your head; and, if he must blame any person for the notice, let his anathemas, like an avalanche, flow upon me-I will bear the burthen [burden] of my own foibles.

With sentiments of respect,

I remain, Sir, your ob't serv't,

L. O. LITTLEFIELD. (italics added)

These comments reveal important details about the operations of the newspaper. Robinson refers to five people, not including Joseph Smith, who were involved: 1) the author of the notice (Littlefield); 2) the "boy" (the boy who cleans the ink off the letters at the end of the day); 3) two journeymen (presumably the typesetters and printers); 4) the proof reader (possibly Hills); and 5) Robinson himself, as editor. All five "had been discharged by the purchasers." Both Robinson and Joseph Smith discovered the announcement after the papers had been printed. (Littlefield notes the papers had been distributed before Joseph discovered the problem.) Robinson claims he and Joseph were "sorely mortified" but took no action, presumably deciding that the scandal would not be worth the expense of reprinting. They published no explicit apology in the succeeding issue on March 1st, although Joseph tried to distance himself from the problem when he published a short disclaimer, explaining that he had nothing to do with the matter:

> This paper commences my editorial career, I alone stand for it, and shall do for all papers having my signature henceforward. I am not responsible for the publication, or arrangement of the former paper; the matter did not come under my supervision. JOSEPH SMITH

Ever since, this effort to distance himself from the wedding announcement (without specifically calling attention to it) has been taken out of context and expanded, without justification, to imply Joseph's endorsement of everything in every issue published over the boilerplate showing Joseph as Editor, a point discussed further below.

It was only after the Warsaw Signal called attention to the wedding announcement that Joseph Smith (or whoever was actually editing the *Times and Seasons*) realized Joseph's initial disclaimer was inadequate. The editor felt it necessary to publish Robinson's explanation and Littlefield's apology. Had the *Times and Seasons* not responded to the *Warsaw Signal*, it is unlikely anyone except for the relatively few local readers of the *Warsaw Signal* would have ever paid attention to the wedding announcement. The *Warsaw Signal* has been long forgotten—copies of its response to the wedding announcement are not even available. But by responding in the very issue that contains a significant portion of the Book of Abraham, the *Times and Seasons* elevated the issue to the point where not only other newspapers of the time circulated it, but readers today, 173 years later, still analyze the wedding announcement and its repercussions.

This experience may have deterred future corrections of errors such as the "angel Nephi" mistake.

Example of editing.

To the extent that Joseph Smith actually functioned as editor, there is little evidence of the process he used. The Wentworth Letter is the only known example from this time period of Joseph presumably editing a document. The letter was published in the 1 March 1842 *Times and Seasons* under the headline "CHURCH HISTORY." Joseph wrote it at "the request of Mr. John Wentworth, editor and proprietor of the Chicago Democrat."

Some of the Wentworth letter was taken verbatim from Orson Pratt's pamphlet, *An Interesting Account of Several Remarkable Visions, and of the Late Discovery of Ancient American Records,* published in 1840 in Edinburgh, Scotland. However, Joseph Smith made some significant edits to Pratt's manuscript.

According to the Joseph Smith Papers,

> No manuscript copy has been located, and it is not known how much of the history was originally written or dictated by JS. "Church History" echoes some wording from Orson Pratt's [pamphlet]. Pratt's summary of church beliefs, upon which JS drew for the list of thirteen church beliefs in "Church History," was in turn based on a theological summary written by Parley P. Pratt. Other individuals may have been involved in compiling the essay, including Willard Richards, who wrote extensively as JS's scribe during this period. Because William W. Phelps revised and expanded the text of "Church History" a year later in answer to a request from editor Israel Daniel Rupp, it is possible that Phelps helped compose the original essay.[52]

It's interesting that the Joseph Smith Papers note doesn't suggest John Taylor as a possible contributor to the Wentworth letter, even though he was working at the *Times and Seasons* in March. Nor do they mention Joseph's brothers, Hyrum and William, who would be natural sources for details and

---

[52] Joseph Smith Papers, "Church History," 1 March 1842, Histories, Vol. 1, p. 491-2, available online at http://josephsmithpapers.org/paperSummary/church-history-1-march-1842?p=1&highlight=wentworth%20letter

corrections about his history.

Although the historical record does not provide sufficient information to know whether or how much Phelps or Richards participated in the composition of the Wentworth letter, the comparison to Pratt's pamphlet does suggest that Joseph did not dictate the Wentworth letter as an original composition. In some cases, much of the Pratt language is retained; in others, it is completely replaced with a significant change in meaning.

This example of Joseph Smith's editing shows he was careful, precise and concise—all qualities that take time. He did not quote Pratt's work or even give Pratt attribution; he published the entire piece as his own. Yet he was sensitive to having his own work edited or extracted. He introduced the letter with this comment: "Mr. Wentworth says that he wishes to furnish Mr. Bastow, a friend of his, who is writing the history of New Hampshire, with this document. As Mr. Bastow has taken the proper steps to obtain correct information, all that I shall ask at his hands is that he publish the account entire, ungarnished, and without misrepresentation."[53]

Joseph Smith as Author

The *Times and Seasons* published only eleven documents signed by Joseph Smith while he was listed as Editor, not counting various affidavits, official statements related to his civic offices, and official orders to the Nauvoo Legion that he signed as Lieutenant General. Some of these documents are as short as a sentence or two, and some are in combination with others (the First Presidency and Quorum of the Twelve). One attribute common to all eleven is the assertion of his authority in an official capacity or biographical sense; i.e., these are pieces no one else could have taken credit for. However, as the Wentworth letter demonstrates, another attribute common to many of these is the participation of scribes and clerks in composition.

March 1, 1842 (T&S 3:9):

---

[53] Ibid. It's interesting that despite Joseph's request that the entire letter be published, the version of the letter published in Chapter 38: The Wentworth Letter in the 2007 lesson manual, *Teachings of the Presidents of the Church: Joseph Smith*, edited out part of the Wentworth letter, including some of the sentences in the comparison table in this article.

- The Wentworth Letter (discussed above and in Chapter 9)

- To Subscribers "This paper commences my editorial career, I alone stand for it, and shall do for all papers having my signature henceforward. I am not responsible for the publication, or arrangement of the former paper; the matter did not come under my supervision." JOSEPH SMITH

- A 246-word letter "To the Brethren in Nauvoo City, Greeting" regarding the organization of work on the temple. (Signed by JOSEPH SMITH, Trustee in Trust)

March 15 (T&S 3:10):
- A 102-word letter to John C. Bennett: "General Bennett: Respected Brother:-I have jut [sic] been perusing your correspondence with Doctor Dyer on the subject of American Slavery, and the students of the Quincy Mission Institute, and it makes my blood boil within me to reflect upon the injustice, cruelty, and oppression, of the rulers of the people--when will these things cease to be, and the Constitution and the Laws again bear rule? I fear for my beloved country--mob violence, injustice, and cruelty, appear to be the darling attributes of Missouri, and no man taketh it to heart! O, tempora! O, mores! What think you should be done? Your Friend, Joseph Smith."

- Introduction to History of Joseph Smith: "In the last number I gave a brief history of the rise and progress of the Church, I now enter more particularly into that history, and extract from my journal. JOSEPH SMITH"

June 1 (T&S 3:15)
- TO THE EASTERN CHURCHES: TO THE EASTERN CHURCHES
"Elder Willard Richards, Recorder for the Temple and my private Secretary, (accompanied, perhaps, by some others of the Twelve) will soon leave Nauvoo, for New York and the Eastern States, for the purpose of receiving funds, for the building of the Temple, which are now much needed; and for the transaction of business in general for the church. I hope the brethren will be diligent in preparing their tithings, for remittance by Br. Richards, and speed him on his journey that he may quickly return to his labors in this place. J. SMITH."

June 15 (T&S 3:16)
    - Notice. "The subscribers, members of the First Presidency of the church of Jesus Christ of Latter Day Saints, withdraw the hand of fellowship from

General John C. Bennett, as a christian, be [sic] having been labored with from time to time, to persuade him to amend his conduct, apparently to no good effect."(signed by Joseph Smith, Hyrum Smith, Wm. Law, nine of the Quorum of the Twelve, and the three Bishops of the Church)

July 1 (T&S 3:17)
- A 2,200-word letter "TO THE CHURCH OF JESUS CHRIST OF LATTER DAY SAINTS AND TO ALL THE HONORABLE PART OF THE COMMUNITY" regarding the character of John C. Bennett (signed by Joseph Smith). [discussed below]

July 15 (T&S 3:18)
- A Notice: "This may certify that Br. Benjamin Winchester is restored to his former fellowship and standing in the Church. He was suspended, according to previous notice, for neglect of council; but learning that he is disposed to abide by the laws of the church, we give him the hand of fellowship. We would say to Elder Winchester that it would be well for him to locate himself in another city immediately; and then it will be well with him, if he will be faithful and true to the great cause." (signed by Joseph Smith, Hyrum Smith, and Wm. Law, and eight of the Quorum of the Twelve, including Wm Smith, W. Woodruff, and John Taylor)

September 15 (T&S 3:22)
- A letter dated September 1st, 1842, "To all the Saints in Nauvoo" which became Section 127 of the Doctrine and Covenants. (Signed JOSEPH SMITH)

October 1 (T&S 3:23)
- A "Letter from Joseph Smith" dated September 6, 1842, addressed "To the Church of Jesus Christ of Latter Day Saints, Sendeth Greeting" which became section 128 of the Doctrine and Covenants. (Signed JOSEPH SMITH)

In addition, there are two unsigned sets of documents that later became canonized as scripture. These share the attribute of the signed documents; i.e., Joseph communicates with authority and clarity as Prophet and President of the Church.

- The Book of Abraham, published in the *Times and Seasons* on March 1, March

15, and May 16.[54]

- The History of Joseph Smith, published in installments starting on March 15 and continuing throughout the year and into 1843. This History includes many of the Sections of the Doctrine and Covenants, as well as the Joseph Smith – History now contained in the Pearl of Great Price.

This output, while impressive considering everything else the Prophet was doing during this time, reflects a small percentage of the original writing in the *Times and Seasons*. Although much of the content of the *Times and Seasons* consisted of reprints of articles, letters, and news from the exchange papers, many issues contained material first published in its pages. For example, in addition to the History, the April 1 issue includes a 415-word report about the organization of the Ladies' Relief Society, signed "ED," and a 5,400-word article titled "TRY THE SPIRITS" that contains numerous outside references, also signed "Ed."

When evaluating the pieces Joseph signed (or published above his printed signature), it is important to realize that his signature alone did not mean he actually wrote the piece. Wilford Woodruff wrote a letter to Parley P. Pratt on June 12, 1842, in which he mentioned how busy Joseph was:

> I had your letter read you sent Joseph it was a good one I don't know whether it was answered or not, I have never seen Joseph as full of business as of late he hardly gets time to sign his name.[55]

If Joseph hardly gets time to sign his name, how could he have time to write the material he signed? And how would he have time to write material he didn't even sign?

It should not be surprising that Joseph had others write for him; letters

---

[54] "A Fac-Simile from the Book of Abraham" and "A Translation," Times and Seasons, Mar. 1, 1842, 703–6, available at josephsmithpapers.org; "The Book of Abraham," Times and Seasons, Mar. 15, 1842, 719–22, available at josephsmithpapers.org; and "A Fac-Simile from the Book of Abraham" and "Explanation of Cut on First Page," Times and Seasons, May 16, 1842, 783–84.

[55] Wilford Woodruff, letter to Parley P. Pratt, June 12, 1842, from Nauvoo, CHL, available online at https://dcms.lds.org/delivery/DeliveryManagerServlet?dps_pid=IE1738096 (Woodruff letter to Pratt).

published over Joseph's signature in the *Times and Seasons* in 1843 and 1844 were actually written by W. W. Phelps.[56] One historian observed, "Because of his lack of formal education, Joseph Smith depended on others to do most of the actual writing of both the sources and the completed history. More than two dozen scribes and writers are known to have assisted him."[57]

Of the above listed items from 1842, the Wentworth letter, as previously mentioned, was probably edited by Joseph, but Phelps and/or Richards likely assisted with the composition.

The 2,200-word letter dated July 1, 1842, regarding Dr. Bennett may also have been written by someone else. Joseph's journal makes no reference to his writing such a letter (although the recorder was sick from June 17 to June 24 and did not take notes). Bennett had made his last defense at the Nauvoo Masonic Lodge on June 16th and Joseph responded in a public speech about Bennett on June 18. In his journal on that date, Wilford Woodruff records, "Among other subjects he spoke his mind in great plainness concerning the iniquity & wickedness of Gen John Cook Bennet [sic] & exposed him before the public." Joseph famously never spoke from a prepared text; the letter published in the July 1 *Times and Seasons* could have been written from notes made during Joseph's speech. There are word choices, phrases, and overall style that suggest Phelps as author. In addition, Phelps had been working on Joseph Smith's history, writing it in first person from Joseph's perspective. (Questions of authorship are discussed in section three of this article.)

The excerpt from "History of Joseph Smith" in the April 1 issue is about 1,400 words long, approximately 10% of the entire issue. It is not clear how much, if any, of this history was originally written by Joseph himself; the manuscript source for the *Times and Seasons* history is in the handwriting of James Mulholland. According to the Joseph Smith Papers, "the relationship of author and scribe was conflated, making it difficult to distinguish between Joseph Smith's contribution and that of his scribes."[58] The "angel Nephi"

---

[56] Brown, Ghostwriter, p. 44-51.

[57] Howard C. Searle, "History of the Church (History of Joseph Smith)," *Encyclopedia of Mormonism* (Brigham Young University, Provo, Utah 2007), available online at http://eom.byu.edu/index.php/History_of_the_Church_%28History_of_Joseph_Smith%29

[58] Histories, Volume 1, Joseph Smith Histories, 1832-1844, p. 202.

example discussed above suggests that not only did Joseph Smith not write it himself, but he did not always closely review the material in his History that was written by others. Joseph's journal rarely mentions his History, but when it does, it shows him reading it, not writing it. On August 14, for example, he reads the history with Emma (discussed below).

W.W. Phelps, "took over the responsibility of writing and compiling the multivolume manuscript JS history" after Robert B. Thompson died in August 1841.[59] Phelps wrote to Parley P. Pratt on June 16, 1842, that he was undertaking "the largest amount of business that I have ever undertaken, since I have been in the church."[60] He told Pratt he had been assigned "to write and compile the History of br. Joseph, embracing the entire history of the church. It will occupy my time and talents for a long time, should nothing intervene."

Phelps was the only known scribe working on the history between August 1841 and December 1, 1842, but he wrote very little during this period. On December 1, 1842, Phelps left Nauvoo to get paper and supplies in St. Louis. By that point, he had written from the bottom of page 75 (where Thompson had stopped in August 1841) to the end of page 130,[61] concluding mid-sentence with Section 58 ("for behold, it is not meet that I should command in all things,"). This brought Joseph's history up to August 1831. Phelps' part of the history is published in the *Times and Seasons* beginning with the September 1, 1843, issue ("Accordingly, they were both baptized...").[62] The bulk of the sixty-five pages Phelps produced (pages 75-

---

[59] Note 566 to 1 December 1842, *Journal, December 1841-December 1842*, JSP, p. 171.

[60] Letter from W. W. Phelps, 1842, *Parley P. Pratt correspondence*, Church History Library (The Church of Jesus Christ of Latter-day, Saints, Salt Lake City, Utah).

[61] Dean C. Jessee, "The Writing of Joseph Smith's History," *BYU Studies* 11:4, p. 441, available online at https://byustudies.byu.edu/showtitle.aspx?title=4976. See also "Historical Introduction" to History, 1838-1856, volume A-1 [23 December 1805 – 30 August 1834]. The last page Phelps wrote is available here: http://josephsmithpapers.org/paperSummary/history-1838-1856-volume-a-1-23-december-1805-30-august-1834#!/paperSummary/history-1838-1856-volume-a-1-23-december-1805-30-august-1834&p=136

[62] http://josephsmithpapers.org/paperSummary/history-1838-1856-volume-a-1-23-december-1805-30-august-1834?p=244#!/paperSummary/history-1838-1856-volume-a-1-23-december-1805-30-august-1834&p=81

130) consists of copies of revelations Joseph received (D&C Sections 33-58:26a). Some of these Phelps had published nine years earlier in the *Evening and Morning Star*;[63] all of them were included in the Book of Commandments that Phelps published in 1833. One wonders how much effort Phelps expended in copying these revelations for the third time into Joseph Smith's History.

Phelps did add some of his own editorial comments to the History. Before Phelps left for St. Louis on December 1, 1842, Joseph "Called on W. W. Phelps to get the historical documents &c. After which he commenced reading and revising history."[64] In Phelps' absence, Willard Richards began work on the project. On 1 and 2 December, Joseph dictated notes A, B, and C to Book A-1. These notes appear on pages 131-133. Page 134 is blank. The narrative Phelps had started continues on page 135, in Phelps' handwriting, through page 157. Presumably he added this material after he returned to Nauvoo.

The three Addenda and other corrections to the text (such as the deletions on pages 118 and 129) appear to be Joseph's first editorial input on Phelps' material, and they are significant.

For example, on page 129, Phelps wrote a section that was subsequently edited:

> The first Sabbath after our arrival in Jackson county, brother W[illiam] W Phelps preached to a western audience, over the boundary of the United States, wherein were present specimens of "all the families of the earth:"— ~~Shem, Ham, and Japheth;~~ for there were several of the ~~Lamanites~~ <Indians> ~~as descendants of Shem~~; quite <a> respectable number of Negroes ~~as descendants of Ham~~; and the balance was made up of citizens of the surrounding country, and fully represented ~~their~~ them ~~great progenitor, Japheth.~~ <selves as pioneers of the west.>

Although the history is written in the first person from Joseph's perspective, this passage—dated 19 June-July 1831—appears to be Phelps'

---

[63] A detailed list is available in "Revelations Printed in The Evening and the Morning Star," *Joseph Smith Papers*, available online at http://josephsmithpapers.org/bc-jsp/content/jsp/pdf/rev-in-evening-morning-star.pdf

[64] 1 December 1842, *Journal, December 1841-December 1842*, JSP, p. 171.

own recollection of the events and interpretation of the genealogy of the people they encountered. Phelps had written a letter from Independence on 23 July 1831 that was published in the Ontario Phoenix on September 7, 1831. In it, he wrote: "The people are proverbially idle or lazy, and mostly ignorant; reckoning no body equal to themselves in many respects, and as it is a slave holding state, Japheth will make Canaan serve him, while he dwells in the tents of Shem."[65]

One might infer that Phelps' letter reflected something he learned from Joseph Smith, and that the history he wrote reflected Joseph's ideas, except that Joseph edited out Phelps' writing about genealogy. The passage on page 129 was published in the *Times and Seasons* on March 1, 1844, with the Phelps' material deleted as shown above. This indicates that Joseph Smith did not accept the deleted language.

However, the version eventually published in History of the Church (after Joseph Smith's death) was Phelps' original—a version that has been quoted in Church manuals[66] and cited for the proposition that Joseph Smith "noted parenthetically that Negroes were 'descendants of Ham.'"[67] The historical evidence shows first, that Phelps, not Joseph Smith, wrote this section of the History, and second, that even when Joseph edited Phelps' work, later historians reverted to the Phelps version.

All of this suggests that after Joseph assigned Phelps to take over the history after Thompson's death in 1841, he did not write any of it himself. He apparently didn't review Phelps' work until December 1842, which suggests the history he read with Emma in August may have been either 1) the portion published in the *Times and Seasons* or 2) the portion Mulholland and Thompson had written before Phelps started work.

Joseph had another good reason for having others write for him: he

---

[65] W. W. Phelps, "Extract of a Letter from the late Editor of this paper," *Ontario Phoenix*, September 7, 1831. This issue of the paper may be viewed online at http://www.sidneyrigdon.com/dbroadhu/NY/wayn1830.htm#090731

[66] "Section 58 The Land of Zion," in *Doctrine and Covenants Student Manual* (2002), 119-124, available online at https://www.lds.org/manual/doctrine-and-covenants-student-manual/section-50-59/section-58-the-land-of-zion?lang=eng

[67] Lester E. Bush, Jr., "Mormonism's Negro Doctrine: a historical Overview," *Dialogue* 8 (Spring (1973), (republished in *Dialogue*, April 4, 2012), pp. 15, 51n24, available online at https://www.dialoguejournal.com/2012/mormonisms-negro-doctrine-an-historical-overview/

simply lacked time.

Opportunities to write.

As previously noted, articles in the *Times and Seasons* that were unsigned or signed simply as "Ed." have been attributed to Joseph Smith because of the boilerplate designating him as editor. However, even the pieces specifically signed by Joseph were composed, at least in part, by others; therefore, it seems unlikely that Joseph would have also had time to compose material he didn't sign.

Some have attributed Joseph's reliance on scribes and clerks to his lack of formal education, but another factor likely was his demanding schedule. The historical record indicates that Joseph had few opportunities to write. He had a full-time job as Mayor of one of the largest cities in Illinois (and the fastest-growing); he had a full-time job as President of the Church; he had a full-time jobs as land developer, building contractor, General of the Nauvoo Legion, and more. He spent time counseling with church and civil leaders, meeting with lawyers, speaking to numerous groups, riding his horse into the country, hiding from authorities, etc. The historical record reflects this busy schedule. When Wilford Woodruff wrote the letter to Parley P. Pratt on June 12, 1842, he mentioned Joseph's intentions for the Book of Abraham:

> The Saints abroad manifest much interest in the Book of Abraham in the T & Seasons [sic] it will be continued as fast as Joseph gets time to translate….[68]

Contrary to these expectations, Joseph never published anything more from the Book of Abraham beyond the material he had already published by the time Woodruff wrote this letter. This suggests Joseph never found the time to translate. Woodruff's description matches up well with the limited writing opportunities reported in Joseph's journal, which reports only a few instances of him writing during 1842. As discussed above, he does not even mention writing his own history.

---

[68] Wilford Woodruff, letter to Parley P. Pratt, June 12, 1842, from Nauvoo, CHL, available online at https://dcms.lds.org/delivery/DeliveryManagerServlet?dps_pid=IE1738096 (Woodruff letter to Pratt).

31 March 1842 – Thursday – In council at his office with Elders [Brigham] Young, [John] Taylor &, & wrote an Epistle to the Female Relief Society and spake to the Society in the afternoon.[69]

11 May 1842 – Wednesday – dictated various letters & business.

14 August 1842 – Sunday – Wrote the following orders to Major Gen. Wilson Law. … This letter was put into the hands of Sister Emma with a charge to deliver it to Gen. Law tomorrow. [The letter is included in his journal.]

16 August 1842 – Tuesday – Wrote a letter to sister Emma giving her instructions how to proceed in case he had to go to the Pine Country. Also wrote a letter to Wilson Law asking his opinion about the appearance of things and the best course to be pursued. [Note: These letters are included in his journal.] I… record the following blessing from the mouth of the president himself. [Later, Joseph's scribe writes, "On the same day that the foregoing letter was wrote [sic] to Major Gen. Law, President Joseph wrote one to Mrs Emma in the following To Wit," and this letter is included in the journal]

23 August 1842 – Tuesday – This day president Joseph has renewed the subject of conversation, in relation to his faithful brethren, and friends in his own words; which I now proceed to record as follows [Note: at one point, Joseph says "I am now recording in the Book of the Law of the Lord," meaning his scribe was writing down what he spoke. At the conclusion, the scribe writes, "After writing so much president Joseph left off speaking for the present but will continue the subject again."[70]]

4 September 1842 – Sunday – President Joseph sent the following letter to William Clayton by brother Erastus H. Derby. The president wrote it and requested it to be read before the saints when assembled at the Gove near the Temple for preaching which was done according to his request. [Note: this is the letter published in the *Times and Seasons* on 15 September which became Section 127. The letter is dated 1 September.]

---

[69] This speech was reported in the Minutes by Eliza R. Snow. It was never published in the *Times and Seasons*.

[70] Journals, Volume 2, December 1841 – December 1842, JSP, p. 119.

7 September 1842 – Wednesday – Early this morning Elder [George J.] Adams and brother [David] Rogers from New York visited president Joseph and brought several letters from some of the brethren in that region… president Joseph…concluded to write him [General J. A. Bennett] an answer. [He also] wrote—or rather dictated a long Epistle to the Saints which he ordered to be read next Sabbath. [Note: This is the letter published in the 1 October edition, now Section 128.]

8 September 1842 – Thursday – This A.M. president Joseph dictated the following letter to Gen. James Arlington Bennett.

12 September 1842 – Monday – At home all day in company with brothers Adams & Rogers, and councilling [sic] brother Adams to write a letter to the Governor.

The inclusion of specific writing (and dictating) activities does not mean Joseph couldn't have also written things not mentioned, such as the items he personally signed as listed above, but it does raise an inference that if Joseph was writing, someone was noting that fact. The few items Joseph's journal actually shows him writing are all accounted for; e.g., the letters are included in his journal. None of the unsigned or "Ed." articles attributed to Joseph are even mentioned in his journal—whether as things he wrote or as things he read. There are no manuscripts showing he prepared his public addresses; the only records of his public teachings are in the journals and histories kept by others. This evidence makes it difficult to support any proposition that Joseph wrote things he didn't specifically take credit for, that were not mentioned in his journal, and that no one else commented on.

Opportunities to read.

Many of the unsigned articles attributed to Joseph include quotations, excerpts and other indications of outside research. This style contrasts with what he wrote and spoke before and after his editorship at the *Times and Seasons*. Throughout his life, it was uncommon for Joseph to rely on outside authority, apart from the scriptures.[71]

---

[71] An example of this is noted in Samuel Brown, "The Translator and the Ghostwriter:

If Joseph had cited other authors, he would have had to read their work. The historical record shows that, while he was the named editor of the *Times and Seasons* in 1842, Joseph's opportunities to read were rare. His journal notes several opportunities to read in January 1842—he read on the 15th, 18-19, 21, 26, and 30th—but the only book he read was the Book of Mormon. From March through November, only four opportunities to read are noted specifically in his journal. (Other dates when he read correspondence for business were noted above.)

25 April 1842 – Monday – Reading, meditation &c. mostly with his family

29 June 1842 – Wednesday – Held a long conversation with Francis Higby... Heard the Recorder Read in the law of the Lord. Paid taxes. Rode out in the city on business with Brigham Young.

14 August 1842 – Sunday – Spent the forenoon chiefly in conversation with sister Emma on various subjects, and in reading this history with her. Both felt in good spirits and were very cheerful. (This comment that Joseph *read* his history with Emma is consistent with the assignment W.W. Phelps had accepted to *write* that history.)

19 August 1842 – Friday – This evening President Joseph had a visit from his Aunt Temperance Mack. Spent the day mostly in conversation and reading.

The reading opportunities reflected in these journal entries, such as they are, do not constitute the type of concentrated study that would be required to write doctrinal expositions of the type that appear in the anonymous *Times and Seasons* articles. Of course, Joseph could have had other opportunities to read and study, but the journal's specific mention of times he spent reading suggests otherwise.

Joseph Smith and W. W. Phelps," *Journal of Mormon History* 34:1 (Winter 2008): 26-7, which notes the disparity between the King Follett Discourse and Joseph Smith's political material that was written by W.W. Phelps. (Brown's article is referred to herein as Ghostwriter. Brown revised the article in Dimensions of Faith: a Mormon Studies Reader, Stephen C. Taysom, ed., (Signature Books, Salt Lake City, Utah, 2011), p. 259, but the JMH version is accessible online at http://digitalcommons.usu.edu/mormonhistory/vol34/iss1/1/

Conclusions about Joseph as author and editor in 1842.

Despite the historical record, some authors have insisted that Joseph Smith actually wrote articles he didn't sign. Others claim that because he was the named editor, Joseph knew about and approved everything that was published in the *Times and Seasons*. Both views should be reconsidered in light of the evidence that Joseph was a multi-faceted leader and manager who lacked sufficient time to write or edit to the extent required to produce the *Times and Seasons*. As Woodruff pointed out, Joseph barely had time to even sign his name. On the few occasions when Joseph did write and edit material, he relied largely on his scribes and clerks. (In the third section of this article, Joseph's role as author will be addressed in more detail.)

Even when Don Carlos announced that Joseph had given him

Some scholars who have looked at the 1842 *Times and Seasons* articles have assumed that there are only three candidates for the role of editor and/or author of the anonymous material: Joseph Smith, Wilford Woodruff, and John Taylor. Overlooked is the fact that another newspaper was being published in the same print shop: the *Wasp*. Its editor, William Smith, was the Prophet's younger brother and a member of the Quorum of the Twelve. Therefore, allowing William to edit the *Times and Seasons* would be consistent with the January revelation requiring the Twelve to take over Church publications.

Chapter 5: William Smith as Editor

AS EXPLAINED IN *THE LOST CITY OF ZARAHEMLA*, William Smith founded the *Wasp* in April, 1842, in Nauvoo as a newspaper focused on local issues. His brother Joseph was the named editor and publisher of the *Times and Seasons*. In March through May, it is likely that Joseph actually worked on the paper, particularly when it was publishing extracts and woodcuts from the Book of Abraham. But later in the Spring of that year, other duties took on greater urgency, and Joseph became merely the nominal editor.

It is important to remember that the *Wasp* and the *Times and Seasons* were published from the same offices on the corner of Water and Bain Streets,[72] using the same printer and paper. They were even mailed out together.[73] The two papers were essentially one operation. This explains how the *Times and Seasons* could be published continuously through the summer and fall of 1842, despite the serious illnesses and absences of Woodruff, Taylor, and Joseph Smith during much of that time. In the absence of these putative editors, William Smith was running the printing press and publishing both the *Wasp* and the *Times and Seasons*.

That said, the evidence indicates that Wilford Woodruff remained involved, particularly with the business aspects of the printing shop. It is less clear what role John Taylor played; some editorials appear to have been written by him, but when he took over as Editor upon Joseph's resignation in November 1842, Joseph wrote that the event marked the commencement of Taylor's editorial career, which suggests he may not have been all that involved as an editor prior to the time when William Smith was forced to

---

[72] Jerry C. Jolley, "The Sting of the Wasp: Early Nauvoo Newspaper—April 1842 to April 1843," *BYU Studies* 1982.

[73] The 16 July 1842 edition of *The Wasp* includes this comment from the *Quincy Whig*: "The mail yesterday, brought us the Nauvoo papers, the "Times and Seasons," and "The Wasp." of the 1st inst."

leave. It seems likely that Taylor was involved more with the printing shop than the newspaper prior to that time.

It is also important to remember that 1842 was not the first time that Joseph acted as the nominal editor of a newspaper that was actually managed by one of his brothers. Joseph had arranged for his younger brother Don Carlos to "Learn the printing art"[74] in Kirtland before giving him responsibility for his own paper—the *Elders' Journal*.

Don Carlos edited both the *Elders' Journal* and the *Times and Seasons*. After Don Carlos died, Joseph announced the revelation to have the Twelve take over the *Times and Seasons*. With William Smith editing *The Wasp* and acting as editor of the *Times and Seasons,* Joseph satisfied the letter of the revelation and continued his pattern of having one of his brothers edit the Church newspapers.

As acting editor of the *Times and Seasons*, William Smith was responsible for many of the articles signed as "Ed." A related question is the authorship of the many anonymous articles published in 1842.

Some of these articles appear to have been edited; i.e., someone wrote the first draft, and someone else edited it before publication. Obviously this is common practice at newspapers. Intrusive editing can make it more difficult for anyone to determine the identity of the original author and what parts were edited. The situation is even more complex when there are multiple editors. This type of collaborative effort is likely one of the main reasons so many articles are left anonymous or are signed only by "Ed."

In Chapter 9 I'll share my ideas on who wrote what, but it is very difficult in most cases to separate author from editor. William may have had input on some of the anonymous, but the evidence suggests his role consisted primarily of editorial selection. I think he may have contributed to several anonymous articles that appeared after John Taylor assumed the editorship of both the *Wasp* and the *Times and Seasons*. Other authors, including

---

[74] Joseph Smith, Journal, 1832-1834, 22 November 1833, available online at http://josephsmithpapers.org/paperSummary/?target=JSPPJ1_d1e3981

Woodruff, Benjamin Winchester and W.W. Phelps, wrote most of the anonymous and pseudonymous articles that appeared in the *Times and Seasons* between May and October 1842.

A major caveat must be explained. This article assumes 1) that William was not merely the nominal editor, but was actually acting as editor/author at the *Wasp* and the *Times and Seasons*, and 2) that William's own work was being edited. Three candidates for unnamed editors are W.W. Phelps, Gustavus Hills, and by L.O. Littlefield (or all three). If any or all of these were involved in editing, their contributions don't change the main thesis of this article: i.e., that someone other than Joseph Smith was editing both the *Wasp* and the *Times and Seasons*.

One reason for this caveat is William's poor grammar and spelling as late as August 5, 1841—barely eight months before assuming the editorship at the *Wasp*. In a letter he personally wrote to Joseph from Pennsylvania on that date, he used run-on sentences and misspelled common words. William's literacy appears to have been overestimated because until recently, his own writing was not widely accessible. The History of the Church—a widely read and quoted source for historians and lay members—edited his August letter as shown in this comparison:

Comparison of actual letter with how it was reported in the official History of the Church

Original letter[75]	History of the Church 4:391-2
chester, co. Pennsylvania, Aug. 5. 1841	Chester County, Pennsylvania, August 5th, 1841.
Brother Joseph I am at present at the Chester county Branch of the Church in Pennsylvania But I expect to leave here for the Jersey Countrey next week Docter Galland left for Nauvoo last week will arive at your Place Before you Recieve this,— the	Brother Joseph: —I expect to leave here for the Jersey country next week. Doctor Galland left for Nauvoo last week.

---

[75] William Smith, Letter, Chester County, PA, to JS, Nauvoo, IL, 5 Aug. 1841, JS Collection, CHL, available online at http://josephsmithpapers.org/paperSummary/letter-from-william-smith-5-august-1841?p=1&highlight=William%20smith#!/paperSummary/letter-from-william-smith-5-august-1841&p=1

Hogkiss dept Hyram Requested me to do all I could I have ben trying to do so Brother James Ivanz has Recieved orders on you from Docter Galland to the amount of twenty five Hundred Dollars, the Property that he has given these orders for is well worth the money I Expect Mr Hogkiss New Jersey in a fiew days to Recieve this operty the Property is a tavern Stand attacht to six acres of ground with all the apertainances Some of the Jersey People think it worth three thousand Dollars. Now the question is Shall I let Mr Hogkiss have this Property for less than twenty five hundred since that is the price you will have to pay at Nauvoo why I ask this question is I have understood that Hogkiss has said that he would not allow over twenty tow hundred Dols. I got hold of another small piece of land worth five hundred & if Hogkiss will take all at a fare price I shall be anabled to setle the amount of two thousand Dollars soon Pleas write me an answer to the above question—write & tell me how you are a getting along & about all the friends. The caus in— these Easter lands is flourishing & we want more labours fifty doors opned for Preaching where theire is But one labour I wish you would send us help— help. help if you here or See anything of Joshuay & M. Grant tell them to come East amediatly, the Davle is Raging & the Preasts are a howling & Babalon is a falling with her merchandise to Be She cant decieve the People with her fals doctrin where Mormonism takes a hold, I wish you to Reserve that lot for me that was talked of last spring & also one neare the temple the one on the flat across the road from Billries the Tailor I want to sell in order to by me a small farm near Plymouth that neat my family a living while I am traveling to Preach in the wourld, If you will let me have a lot on the hill near the temple & also the one before mentioned & let me sell one of them

In the Hotchkiss business, Hyrum requested me to do all I could.

Brother James Ivins has received orders on you from Doctor Galland to the amount of twenty-five hundred dollars. The property that he has given these orders for, is well worth the money. I expect Mr. Hotchkiss in new Jersey in a few days to receive this property, which is Cook's Mills Tavern stand, attached to six acres of ground with all the appurtenances. Some of the Jersey people think it worth three thousand dollars. Now the question is, shall I let Mr. Hotchkiss have this property for less than twenty-five hundred, since that is the price you will have to pay at Nauvoo. Why I ask this question is—I have understood that Hotchkiss has said that he would not allow over twenty-two hundred dollars. I got hold of another small piece of land, worth five hundred; and if Hotchkiss will take all at a fair price, I shall be enabled to settle the amount of three thousand dollars soon. Please write me an answer to the above question.

The cause in these eastern lands is flourishing, and we want more laborers; fifty doors opened for preaching where there is but one laborer. I wish you would send us help.

I can buy me a small farm in time of need if you cant Reserve two Reserve one the one I spoke to you about if you will let me have two lots you can sell that house & lot of mine in Kirtland to Pay depts if it will do you eny good, some land in Illinois nere my Place will do me more good than Property in Kirtland, I want you should write me amediatly

I want to sell one lot to get some money to by me a piece of land that lies Joining my tavern stand in Plymouth & now is the time to by it before the People rase an the land in that part if you say I may have the Lot write me the Price of the lot when you write so I may know what to ask for it. Plas tell me what number of lots remain unsold nere the temple or not far off Send me the number of two or three or more the distance & course from the temple & price & I will try & sell them for you & get the money for you & Bring to you this I can do from some bretherin that cant leave (the East) for Nauvoo under two or three years that is if the lots are not to high say from three to four hundred Dollars Each state your lowest Price Send the No of some four or five lots state the distance from the temple & the course & &. if you will do this I can Bring you holm some money this fall, My helth at Present is not good from access of labour I have ben trouble with a Pain in my Bresst for som time & what it will amout to I cant tell give my Respects to Emma & mother & finaly all
  Yours in the Bonds of the Covenent
  Wm. Smith

Yours in the bonds of the covenant,
William Smith

While the published editions of the *Wasp* and the *Times and Seasons* do contain occasional typos and spelling different from current usage, they are both generally grammatically correct. The contrast between William's holographic writing and the published material in the *Wasp* indicates some unnamed person was editing the *Wasp*, at least. In the pages of the *Wasp*, the editor often resorts to rough and vulgar attacks on others—but he also quotes (and paraphrases) Shakespeare. He offers Latin phrases and allusions to classical works. The rough language in the *Wasp* appears characteristic of both William's writing style and personality, but the highly literate references do not. Consequently, I think that not only was someone cleaning up William's writing for grammar and spelling, but was also elevating his language.

Challenges of assigning authorship

A good example of the problem of assigning authorship arose as early as September 1832. W.W. Phelps published *The Evening and the Morning Star* in Independence. An unsigned article titled "Writing Letters" appears on page 25 in the September 1832 issue. It could hardly have been written by anyone other than Phelps. Yet the *Latter-Day Saints' Millennial Star*, Volume 12, p. 231, show the author as Joseph Smith.[76] The *Contributor* prefaced its reprint of the article by writing this: "The following interesting article on the above subject was first published in *The Evening and the Morning Star* in 1832. It was incorporated in the history of the Prophet Joseph Smith, and if not written by him, at least had his endorsement and approval."[77] That conclusion undoubtedly arises because the article was reprinted in the *Times and Seasons*—although the publication date was October 15, 1844 (after the martyrdom). But the *Times and Seasons* doesn't print the last paragraph of Phelps' article; instead, it launches into a first-person account of Joseph's without a break.

Potential authors – Joseph Smith

---

[76] "Writing Letters," *The Latter-Day Saints' Millennial Star*, Volume 12, page 231, available online at
https://play.google.com/store/books/details?id=XlooAAAAYAAJ&rdid=book-XlooAAAAYAAJ&rdot=1

[77] "Writing Letters," *The Contributor: A Monthly Magazine*, Junius F. Wells, Ed. (Salt Lake City, June 1881), p. 282, available online at
https://play.google.com/store/books/details?id=ENURAAAAYAAJ&rdid=book-ENURAAAAYAAJ&rdot=1

An inherent aspect of the main thesis of this article is that Joseph Smith could not have written, and therefore did not write, many of the pieces published in 1842 commonly attributed to him. (Evidence that W.W. Phelps acted as a ghostwriter for Joseph Smith beginning in 1843 has been presented by Michael Hicks and Samuel Brown.[78]) Supporting evidence and argument for that proposition will be presented. Essentially this article extends to 1842 the observation made by Michael Hicks:

> During the last two years of his life, Joseph increasingly attached his name to documents written largely by others. As fame, legal battles, and the growing population of the Church threatened to drain all of his time, literary delegation became crucial. The presence of his name on any document from his last years is not an answer but a question.[79]

Hicks offers support for his observation about the last two years of his life, but even in 1842, the evidence suggests other people were writing on behalf of Joseph—even for the material he personally signed. This makes it all the more problematic to ascribe authorship to Joseph for material signed generically as "ED," let alone unsigned material.

In the case of the *Times and Seasons*, there are similar contrasting styles. There are no extant writings of Joseph Smith in his own hand during this period; everything published under his name is available only in print form. The Wentworth letter, for example, is clearly edited from Orson Pratt's work, but only the final product—the version published in the *Times and Seasons*—is available. Consequently, there is no source comparable to William's handwritten letter for assessing Joseph's own writing style in 1842. There are some dictated documents, such as the Book of the Law of the Lord, which offer hints; but because these are all written by someone else, it's impossible to determine if they are verbatim or if the scribe corrected

---

[78] Samuel Brown, "The Translator and the Ghostwriter: Joseph Smith and W. W. Phelps," *Journal of Mormon History* 34:1 (Winter 2008): 26-62 (referred to herein as Ghostwriter).

[79] Michael Hicks, "Joseph Smith, W. W. Phelps, and the Poetic Paraphrase of 'The Vision,'" *Journal of Mormon History* 20:2 (Fall 1994): 70.

grammar. The spelling, of course, would be that of the scribe.

Historians have long taken for granted that John Taylor was involved with the *Times and Seasons* in some capacity, based on statements recorded in March 1842. But Taylor is not mentioned again in connection with the paper until September 1842; the historical record is otherwise silent about his involvement while Joseph was the official Editor. Furthermore, the September reference involves a business matter (moving a press to Keokuk), with no mention of editorial involvement. Even assuming Taylor was continuously involved with the *Times and Seasons* between April and November, when he formally succeeded Joseph as Editor, the scope of his duties are unknown. When he resigned as Editor in November, Joseph said this "commenced Taylor's editorial career," raising an inference that he had not been involved as editor prior to this. Decades later, Benjamin Winchester recalled that he had been "at the paper" until Taylor took over, another implication that Taylor was not editing the *Times and Seasons* before that time.

Editorial duties include seeking content (such as poetry and doctrinal commentary), selecting content (such as from the exchange papers), writing content, and editing everything. For many papers of the time, one person performed all of these functions, but there is evidence both Nauvoo papers had editorial input from more than one person.

Another question is why Joseph had to resign. He could have simply delegated his duties to John Taylor. It appears his main concern was removing his name as the responsible party.

Potential authors – Gustavus Hills

Hills had an on-again, off-again affiliation with the *Times and Seasons*. He worked with Robinson after Don Carlos died. Hills was appointed as one of the Secretaries to the church conference in Nauvoo on Oct 1st 1841[80] and was appointed Alderman on the Nauvoo City Council on October 23,

---

[80] *Times and Seasons*, 15 Oct 1841, 2:576-580, available online at http://josephsmithpapers.org/paperSummary/minutes-1-5-october-1841?p=1&highlight=gustavus%20hills

1841.[81] but on 20 November, 1841, the Quorum of the Twelve held a council at Brigham Young's home "on the subject of the *Times and Seasons*; they not being satisfied with the manner Gustavis [sic] Hills had conducted the editorial department since the death of Robert B. Thompson."[82] No further explanation is given. On January 1, 1842, Joseph Smith's history relates that "Several of the Twelve spent the day at Sylvester B. Stoddard's, and in the City Council, which lasted from 6 P.M. until midnight on the trial of Gustavus Hills."[83] The trial involved claims that he had acted corruptly and erroneously as Alderman, but he was acquitted unanimously.[84]

On 15 January 1842, Robinson announced in the *Times and Seasons* that he had "secured the services of Elder Gustavus Hills as assistant Editor to the *Times and Seasons*." Hills wrote a "salutatory" in which he praised his predecessors and hoped "that the mantle of charity will be thrown over my errors and weaknesses."

Just two weeks later, Joseph announced the revelation that the Twelve should take over the Editorial department of the *Times and Seasons*. Everyone who worked at the paper was fired. However, like Phelps, Hills published poetry in the *Wasp*. He may havé contributed other material and/or performed editing duties.

Hills was charged with adultery, tried in the council, and excommunicated. He agreed to a support settlement with the woman he had impregnated. He subsequently was accepted back into full fellowship and became a clerk to Joseph Smith.

---

[81] John S. Dinger, ed., 23 October 1841, *The Nauvoo City and High Council Minutes* (Signature Books, Salt Lake City, 2011), location 2070 on Kindle version (herein cited as Nauvoo Minutes).

[82] 20 November 1841, History-1838-1856, volume C-1 Addenda, available online at http://josephsmithpapers.org/paperSummary/history-1838-1856-volume-c-1-addenda?p=44&highlight=gustavus%20hills

[83] 1 January 1842, History, 1838-1856, volume C-1, available online at http://josephsmithpapers.org/paperSummary/history-1838-1856-volume-c-1-2-november-1838-31-july-1842?p=442&highlight=gustavus%20hills

[84] *Nauvoo Minutes*, 1 January 1842.

Potential authors – L. O. Littlefield

L. O. Littlefield was an employee at the *Times and Seasons* in 1841 and 1842. He was fired after an incident that will be discussed later in this article, but he may have continued working at the *Wasp*. He wrote a poem titled "My Early Home" that was published in the *Wasp* on June 4, 1842. He had only three signed pieces published in the *Times and Seasons*: a eulogy to Don Carlos Smith (T&S 2:20); an article titled "the Church" that includes rhetoric typical of William Smith's work in the *Wasp* ("Mobocracy-in America-the land of boasted liberty and equal rights-has been allowed to raise its hydra-head, and many of the saints have fallen martyrs at its unhallowed shrine.") (T&S 2:22); and a poem titled "Give Me the Spot" (T&S2:23). In around 1835, Littlefield had been sent by his father to work at the *Missouri Enquirer* to "learn the printing business." He apparently did some writing there, as well.

"My father rented a farm about two miles west of Liberty on the way to the Liberty landing, of a Mr. Hawks. John Corrill was our nearest neighbor, and Bishop Edward Partridge, who had been tarred and feathered at Independence, and W.W. Phelps, lived in the neighborhood, also John Burk and Henry Rollins (now of Minersville) lived near by. Soon after our settlement there my father let me go to the Missouri Enquirer printing office to learn the printing business. The paper was edited by Mr. Robert N. Kelly, who was politically a Democrat and religiously a Methodist preacher. There were one or two boys in the office who were Mormons. Mr. Kelley was friendly toward our people and Mrs. Harriet Williams Kelley, (his wife) was a talented, kind hearted and most estimable lady in whom the writer ever found a friend and sympathizer.[85]

The known samples of Littlefield's writing demonstrate good command of the language, including vocabulary and grammar that reflect the training he received.

Potential authors – W.W. Phelps

---

[85] From Reminiscences of Latter-Day Saints [1888; Logan]

The possibility of Phelps as editor/ghost writer for William arises partly because of his similar role for Joseph Smith, partly because he had a couple of poems published in the *Wasp*, and partly because of a comment Joseph Smith made on May 15, 1843, as recorded by his cousin, George A. Smith, in his own journal.

> Joseph and myself spent this time in conversation on the grass-plot south of the house. Joseph asked my opinion of W. W. Phelps as an editor. I told him that I considered Phelps the sixth part of an editor, and that was the satirist. When it came to the cool direction necessarily intrusted [sic] to an editor in the control of public opinion—the soothing of enmity, he was deficient, and would always make more enemies than friends; but for my part, it I were able, I would be willing to pay Phelps for editing a paper, providing no body else should have the privilege of reading it but myself. Joseph laughed heartily—said I had the thing just right. Said he, "Brother Phelps makes such a severe use of language as to make enemies all the time."[86]

Asking about Phelps as an editor would make little sense if Phelps had not been serving as an editor in some capacity. It's true that Phelps had an early history of editing (he was a newspaper editor for ten years before joining the Church), and he may have provoked some of the Missourians with his editorials as editor of the Latter-day Messenger in Missouri in 1838. It is possible that his involvement in Missouri may have been a reason to keep his name off both papers, despite his contributions to each. Phelps also acted as ghostwriter for Joseph starting in 1843, but there is no direct evidence of his involvement with either newspaper in 1842. While George A. Smith's characterization may have been referring back to the Missouri experience, that seems unlikely given how many years had elapsed by the time of his conversation with Joseph. His description here describes the *Wasp* quite well.

As discussed above, on 16 June 1842, W.W. Phelps wrote to Parley P. Pratt to say "I am now on the largest amount of business that I have ever undertaken, since I have been in the Church: It is to write and compile the history of br. Joseph embracing the e[n]tire history of the church & it will

---

[86] History of the Church 5:390-1.

occupy my time and talents for a long time, should nothing intervene."[87] Between August 1841 and December 1, 1842, Phelps wrote from the end of page 75 through page 130 in the History. However, most of this material consists of copies of revelations (sections 33-36, Moses 7, and sections 37-58:26a), plus a short biography of Edward Partridge, and a copy of a letter by Oliver Cowdery. It is difficult to imagine how copying these revelations could have occupied his "time and talents" for sixteen months, let alone constitute "the largest amount of business" he had ever undertaken since joining the Church.

The entirety of Phelps' signed contributions to the *Times and Seasons* while Joseph was editor consist of a poem titled "The Temple of God at Nauvoo," in the June 15, 1842, edition and another titled "The Spirit of God" in the September 1, 1842 edition. In the *Wasp*, Phelps published a poem "Remember the Poor" on July 2, 1842, a poem titled "The Western World" on August 13, 1842.

Joseph Smith III once wrote a description of Phelps: "He was quite a singular man, spare of flesh, already sufficiently aged to wear spectacles, was methodical and studious in his habits, and not very prepossessing in appearance though of good brain and judgment. He was quite a voluminous writer."[88] The production of four poems, plus copies of revelations, seem a small contribution for sixteen months' work by someone as prolific as W.W. Phelps.

But if Phelps was editing and writing for the *Times and Seasons*, why does his name not appear anywhere except on a couple of poems?

One reason might be the revelation that the paper was to be managed by the Twelve. But another reason became apparent in April 1844. By then, Phelps' involvement as Joseph's ghostwriter was well known. The Warsaw

---

[87] Hicks, 74, citing W. W. Phelps, Letter to Parley P. Pratt, 16 June 1842, Parley Pratt Papers, LDS Church Archives, available online here: https://dcms.lds.org/delivery/DeliveryManagerServlet?dps_pid=IE1738096

[88] Mary Audentia Smith Anderson, ed., *Joseph Smith III and the Restoration* (Independence, Mo. Herald House, 1852), 27, cited in Bruce A. Van Orden, "William W. Phelps's Service in Nauvoo as Joseph Smith's Political Clerk," *BYU Studies* 32, nos. 1, 2 (1992):81-94, p. 85 available at https://byustudies.byu.edu/PDFViewer.aspx?title=6078&linkURL=32.1-2VanOrdenWilliam-ba8643ef-ea02-482a-8025-359ae2c3aacd.pdf

Signal took advantage.

The *Alton Telegraph* had objected to the anti-Mormon rhetoric published in the *Warsaw Signal*. In response, the April 24, 1844, issue of the *Warsaw Signal* published a series of justifications for its anti-Mormon position. One involved Phelps.

> It can be proven that William W. Phelps, who swore that Smith and his clan were guilty, in Missouri, of deeds black as ever were conceived in the brain of Satan himself, is now the bosom friend, and confidential clerk of the Prophet -- thus proving one of two things; either that Smith has a perjured villan [sic] for his most intimate associate, or that he himself has been guilty of acts that would disgrace Nero.[89]

Two weeks earlier, the paper had also complained about Phelps:

> All the articles to which Joe's name has appeared of late, as well as his Statesman-like "Views of the Powers and Policy of the Government of the United States," were written by the Immaculate William W. Phelps, Esq., the City Attorney for the Holy City, and Private Secretary to his Holiness Joe—It will be noticed that this Phelps is the man whom Joe charged with having turned traitor, and sworn false, a few years since in Missouri.
> We do not know whether Joe's charge against Phelps is true or not. This much, however, we do know—that Phelps did swear that Joe was guilty of some of the most diabolical crimes known to our laws. How is it, Joe? Did he swear false? Or are you guilty?[90]

It would be surprising if Joseph and Phelps did not anticipate this line of attack by Joseph's enemies once Phelps' involvement as Joseph's writer became public knowledge. Another line of attack could have focused on the destruction of Phelps' provocative paper in Missouri; i.e., Phelps had antagonized the Missourians once, and there was no need to remind them of

---

[89] "Why Oppose the Mormons?", *The Warsaw Signal*, April 24, 1944, available online at http://www.sidneyrigdon.com/dbroadhu/il/sign1844.htm#0410

[90] *Warsaw Signal*, April 13, 1844, cited in *Mormons in Ohio, Illinois, Missouri, etc.,* News Clippings, 1844, Vol. 2, Brigham Young University Library, Provo, Utah, p. 187, cited in Walter Dean Bowen, "The Versatile W. W. Phelps: Mormon Writer, Educator, and Pioneer," Thesis, BYU, August 1958, p. 114.

that in 1842 when the furor over the attempted assassination of former Governor Boggs had led to sustained efforts to arrest Joseph Smith and extradite him to Missouri.

Phelps responded to the *Warsaw Signal* in the June 12, 1844, *Nauvoo Neighbor*, with the publication of a deposition he had given on May 20, 1844. In this deposition, Phelps essentially claimed that the Missouri statements were a sham "published by Missourians, and swallowed by apostates… a hoax just fit for mean men." Such a characterization of the Missouri charges he had made might have been more persuasive had he made them before the Warsaw Signal's attack, but perhaps he and Joseph did not expect Phelps' role as ghostwriter to become public knowledge.

Phelps during 1842

After December 1st 1842, Phelps indicated in his diary that he did not start writing again until January 1843.[91] After that, his ghostwriting for Joseph Smith has been documented. But what about before?

Example #1: Edits in editorial comments

An editorial comment in the Extra edition of the *Wasp* (July 27th) is a good example of the combination of William Smith's colloquialisms and Phelps' vocabulary and style:

Never, since Cain, with his peck of potatoes, operated against Abel's Lamb, has flesh and blood, with a sacerdotal Tunic on, officiated with such dignified pomposity as the great Mayor of Nauvoo; Major General of the Nauvoo Legion; Master-in-Chancery; Doctor of Medicine; and Elder in Israel, even John C. Bennett. *Auetor purisime impuritatis!* This is the first clue we have that Bennett is a Levite—guess, however, he acted as one of the priests of Baal. Bennett says in the Sangamo:
'Now, remember that if I should be missing, Joe Smith, either by himself or his Danite Band, will be the murderer. Illinoians, then let my blood be avenged:' '
To save beating up for volunteers, as the General may have another *turn of mind,*

---

[91] Ibid, citing W. W. Phelps, Diary, 19 January 1843, holograph, LDS Church Archives.

and elope for Texas, would it not be better to have the Doctor *stereotyped,* ensured, or even embalmed, if it can be done without *duress,* and not injure him, or jeopardise his future usefulness: under Gynesocracy; [sic] and embryo infanticide. Doctor, *murder will out.*
Speaking of Jo Smith, in his insanity, or fogmatically, [sic] in his *Bennettiana,* he says…
[quotation from Bennett]
This is noble; if the Doctor will save enough to pay what he forgot to pay when he acted as bishop of the Campbellite church, and also that he may be wise enough to hold to a sufficient quantity of the needful to save himself the trouble of filling up spurious Diplomas—whereby he quackifies himself as the chief of quackery, he certainly will do some good.
Now Dr. Bennett has tried to terrify some with his affidavit that Rockwell assassinated Gov. Boggs—insinuating that he went to *fulfill* prophecies—But we think the Doctor has now taked [sic] the burden upon himself—and that too, to *fulfill his own prophecies.* (italics in the original)

Much of this passage consists of rambling sentences and grammar typical of William's letter quoted above. It reads more like spoken English than composed written English. However, unusual terms typical of an educated writer also appear. It is likely impossible to tease out each author's specific contribution, but the influence of each is evident here—as it is in the *Times and Seasons.*

This table proposes attribution of phrases from the above passage:

William Smith (colloquial)	W.W. Phelps (educated)
Peck of potatoes*	Sacerdotal tunic
	Comment: see discussion of "sacerdotal" below.
guess, however, he acted as one of the priests of Baal	Auetor purisime impuritatis!
	Comment: Phelps often inserts Latin phrases such as this in his writing
Speaking of Jo Smith, in his insanity	or fogmatically, [sic] in his *Bennettiana,* he says
	Comment: "fogmatically" appears to be a play on words, imparting a connotation of confusion (fog) on "dogmatically," while "Bennettiana" adds the suffice "iana" to Bennet's name. That suffix converts proper

	names into mass nouns, as in Shakespeareana, meaning a collection of items related to Shakespeare.
would it not be better to have the Doctor *stereotyped*, ensured, or even embalmed, if it can be done without *duress*, and not injure him, or jeopardise his future usefulness	under Gynesocracy; [sic] and embryo infanticide. Doctor, *murder will out*.
	Comment: Gynesocracy (gynecocracy) refers to political supremacy of women, while "murder will out" is an expression first used by Chaucer in 1390 in Nun's Priest's Tale.

*A few paragraphs after William's Valedictory in the December 10, 1842, *Wasp*, this paragraph appears:

> *A pech of trouble.*—The St. Louis Gazette, in noticing the intended change of the Wasp to 'The Dove of the West,' measures out a Peck of 'small potatoes,' and says 'the Editor should seek among the creeping things of the earth for a name for his Journal,' rather than among the fowls of the air.'
> Although the Gazette may *creep* unto Bloody Island, *crawl* round a negro burnt alive, and *hop* over Boggs's extermination of the Mormons, still his advise [sic] as to the name of our *intended* paper, is but a *Peck of dirt*, in this boasted land of liberty.—The richest diamonds are found in Toads' heads.

Although this comment appears in the issue in which John Taylor formally takes the Editor's chair, and it is months after William has been dismissed as the actual editor, it is difficult to believe that anyone other than William would have inserted these two paragraphs in the paper. They reflect his annoyance about the name "Dove of the West" and revisit the "peck of potatoes" from the July 27th issue. It's also difficult to identify any trace of W. W. Phelps or John Taylor in these short paragraphs.

Example #2: Sacerdotal

Usage of rare or unusual terms offers clues to authorship. When a particular term appears only in the writings of a particular individual, it serves as a kind of signature. When that same term shows up in an unsigned piece, it raises an inference of attribution.

There are several terms that are used rarely in the Wasp, in the *Times and Seasons*, and in other writings of the possible authors and editors. One example is "sacerdotal." This is a rare term—and rarity offers clues to authorship. The term means "Of or relating to priests or the priesthood; priestly." According to the Oxford English Dictionary, "sacerdotal" is "often used as the epithet of doctrines that assert the existence in the Christian church of an order of priests charged with sacrificial functions and invested with supernatural powers transmitted to them in ordination."

One of his poems, published May 14, 1842, includes the rarely-used term "sacerdotal."

Phelps also uses the term in one of his poems, published in the *Wasp* on May 28 (although it was written in November 1841). The term appears in *Wasp* editorials on June 18 and June 27. It appears only six times in the entire run of the *Times and Seasons*, two of those being editorials signed by Joseph but known to have been written by Phelps. The other four appearances were in unsigned editorials, one of which was *about* William, thereby excluding him as author.

The term also appears in *The Evening and the Morning Star,* March 1834 (Vol II, No. 18). Phelps was the editor of this paper. The context: "see them trample upon the wounded and dying, while they wade through blood, and stain their (sacerdotal) garments with the same." (parenthesis in the original)

Example #3: The Cat's-paw

Determining the authorship of an unsigned article, if it is possible at all, requires analysis of not only the words and style, but the context of the publication, the personalities involved, and any other relevant information. One method involves the appearance of rare words or terms in both the works of known authors and the unsigned works. Such terms can not only trace authorship, but also reveal relationships and dynamics that are otherwise opaque to historians. The term "sacerdotal" is one example, discussed above.

Another good example is "cat's paw," a favorite expression of William Smith's. The term refers to a "person used as a tool by another to accomplish a purpose."[92] It was first used in 1657: "These he useth as the Monkey did the Cats paw, to scrape the nuts out of the fire." By 1837, the term was "common in vulgar speech, but not in writing." One can easily imagine William using the term. It is just as easy to imagine Phelps retaining it to preserve William's "voice" on the page.

Cat's paw in the Wasp

William used the term four times himself in the *Wasp* between April 23 and July 27, 1842. The context gives a sense for William's lively and descriptive prose, which reads as though spoken, but also the insertion of sophisticated vocabulary typical of Phelps.

> April 23 – as for Tom-ass Sharp, he was a turn-coat at one time, a professed Whig at another, and at the same breath a pretended loco, and on the whole, he had been made a **cats-paw** for the Anti Mormon party and was a complete Jackass of an editor and was not a fit subject for either the Whigs, Locos, or Anti Mormons.
>
> May 7 – The editor has become the pliant tool and **cats-paw** of that faction and when their ingenuity fails to propagate a superabundant stock of calumny, he engages all his very *productive* faculties to fill up the vacuum of their defect, and lends all his *puny* and *insignificant* efforts at slander and detraction.
>
> July 27th – Duncan wishes to speculate and make political capital out of the Mormons, and Doctor Bennett is the stock jobber, the singed **cat's paw**. But glory to the virtue and intelligence of the people, so base and degraded a vagabond cannot escape the merited contempt he deserves…. And in regard to the proceedings of the *Sangamo Journal*, we know that the editor of that paper looks upon Bennett as a villian; [sic] his own publications show this; and he has condescended to act the hypocrite, and make a political **cat's-paw** of him, in the present crisis. "Oh shame where is thy blush?"

Cat's paw in the Times and Seasons

The phrase appears five times in the *Times and Seasons*.

---

[92] Oxford English Dictionary, "cat's paw."

1. Vol. 2:23, p. 560 (Oct. 1, 1841) [From the (Philadelphia) Public Ledger. Anti-Mormon Slanders Refuted] His comparing the Minister who had just ceased speaking to a **"pliant cat's paw"** must have produced a ludicrous scene, highly interesting to Mr. Lee's accomplices. [Quotation of Mr. Lee's use of the term.]

2. Vol. 3:5, p. 651 (Jan. 1, 1842) [report on Gubernatorial Convention, considered below]

3. Vol. 3:19, p. 863 (Aug. 1, 1842) [Great Discussion of Mormonism] ... but as the rules were drafted by his committee, gave him about two thirds of the time, they declined being used as **the cats paws** to extract the shilling from the pockets of the people, to line those of West [This is one of the articles signed by "Q" who I propose was Benjamin Winchester.]

4. Vol. 3:19, p. 877 (Aug. 1, 1842) [Reprint of Wasp, July 27]

5. Vol. 4 Chpt. 24:375 [Reply to James Arlington Bennet, signed by Joseph Smith] ...under the sealing power of the Melchesedek priesthood; shall I stoop from the sublime authority of Almighty God, to be handled as a Monkey's cat's paw; and pettify myself into a clown to act the farce of political demagoguery? No, verily no! The whole earth shall bear me witness that I, like the tow... [This letter was written by W.W. Phelps. Joseph Smith had given instructions that Bennet's letter be answered. On Nov. 13, 1843, Phelps read his composition to Joseph, who "made some corrections."[93]

On June 18, William inserted into the *Wasp* the text from the *Times and Seasons*, originally published on January 1, 1842, (#2 above).

June 18 (*Wasp*), January 1 (*T&S* 3:5) – STATE GUBERNATORIAL CONVENTION.
City of Nauvoo, Illinois,
December 20th, A. D. 1841.
To my friends in Illinois:-
The Gubernatorial Convention of the State of Illinois have nominated

---

[93] *Journals*, Vol. 3, May 1843—June 1844, Joseph Smith Papers, (The Church Historian's Press, 2015), p. 128.

COLONEL ADAM W. SNYDER for GOVERNOR, and COLONEL JOHN MOORE for LIEUTENANT-GOVERNOR of the State of Illinois-election to take place in August next. COLONEL MOORE, like JUDGE DOUGLASS, and ESQ. WARREN, was an intimate friend of GENERAL BENNETT long before that gentleman became a member of our community; and General Bennett informs us that no men were more efficient in assisting him to procure our great chartered privileges than were Colonel Snyder, and Colonel Moore.-They are sterling men, and friends of equal rights-opposed to the oppressor's grasp, and the tyrant's rod. With such men at the head of our State Government we have nothing to fear. In the next canvass we shall be influenced by no party consideration-and no Carthagenian [Carthaginian] coalescence or collusion, with our people, will be suffered to affect, or operate against, General Bennett or any other of our tried friends already semi-officially in the field; so the partizans [partisans] in this county who expect to divide the friends of humanity and equal rights will find themselves mistaken-we care not a fig for Whig or Democrat: they are both alike to us; but we shall go for our friends, our TRIED FRIENDS, and the cause of human liberty which is the cause of God. We are aware that "divide and conquer" is the watch-word with many, but with us it cannot be done-we love liberty too well-we have suffered too much to be easily duped-**we have no cat's-paws amongst us**. We voted for GENERAL HARRISON because we loved him-he was a gallant officer and a tried statesman; but this is no reason why we should always be governed by his friends-he is now DEAD, and all of his friends are not ours. We claim the privileges of freemen, and shall act accordingly. DOUGLASS is a Master Spirit, and his friends and our friends-we are willing to cast our banners on the air, and fight by his side in the cause of humanity, and equal rights-the cause of liberty and the law. SNYDER, and MOORE, are his fiends-they are ours. These men are free from the prejudices and superstitions of the age, and such men we love, and such men will ever receive our support, be their political predilections what they may. Snyder, and Moore, are known to be our friends; their friendship is vouched for by those whom we have tried. We will never be justly charged with the sin of ingratitude-they have served us, and we will serve them.
JOSEPH SMITH.
LIEUTENANT-GENERAL OF THE NAUVOO LEGION.

There are several important aspects of this letter. The convention referred to was held on December 17, 1841. There is a gap in Joseph's journal between 13-20 December, so it is reasonable to infer Joseph attended the convention. He writes in first person plural, suggesting others attended with him. Presumably the group included "General Bennett," who was the Mayor of Nauvoo at the time and had personal relationships with the candidates. But what about William Smith?

William ran for the state legislature in the August election referred to in Joseph's letter. Perhaps this convention provided the seed for that endeavor. He ultimately proved to be an articulate (and often acerbic) proponent of the Nauvoo charter (unless he was merely able to read speeches written by Phelps, the way Joseph did when he ran for President).

When he reprinted this letter in the *Wasp*, William introduced it with this statement: "We conclude the mass of testimony, complied for the purpose of establishing beyond a reasonable doubt the positions assumed by us, by quoting a proclamation of Lieutenant General Joseph Smith, which is said by some of his Van Buren friends to have been issued by him in consequence of his nomination for Lieutenant Governor in the Van Buren Convention—it being a principle with that party for every person, when fairly initiated, to use his utmost exertions to sustain its measure... But we give the document from the "Times and Seasons" in which it was published."

What about authorship?

The piece contains the "cat's paw" phrase, and "we care not a fig for Whig or Democrat" is similarly colloquial. But these are juxtaposed with passages such as this: "no Carthagenian coalescence or collusion, with our people, will be suffered to affect, or operate against, General Bennett or any other of our tried friends already semi-officially in the field."

Overall, the combination of disparate styles and thoughts in this letter reflects a pattern that will become typical in both the *Wasp* and the *Times and Seasons*. Both William and Phelps develop a strong interest in politics; a year after this convention, William will deliver a speech to the Illinois Legislature that invoked "equal rights" and other elements of this letter.

Conclusion: William Smith's role as acting editor of the *Times and Seasons* in Nauvoo during 1842 is established by the context of the times, the editorial merging of that paper with the *Wasp*, and William's publication of anonymous and pseudonymous articles written by Phelps and Winchester. Articles signed as "Ed" during this period appear to have been written by a combination of John Taylor, Wilford Woodruff, William Smith, W.W.

Phelps, and perhaps others. These discoveries call for a re-evaluation of the material published in the *Times and Seasons* during Joseph Smith's nominal editorship, material that has long been incorrectly attributed to Joseph Smith himself.

William Smith in *The Prophet*

I discussed William Smith's role at *The Prophet* in *The Lost City of Zarahemla*. I included lots of references there, focusing on William's contentious relationship with Benjamin Winchester. More information on his role is contained in Appendix 6.

There is the intriguing correspondence between William and Phelps in the pages of *The Prophet* and the *Times and Seasons* (T&S 5:24, Jan 1, 1844) that suggests a familiarity between the two. (This is one of my favorites because William refers to Stephens and Catherwood several times.) That letter contains the strange asides and sarcasm that seem typical of William's writing (and many of the editorials in the *Wasp*).

The letter to Phelps appears right after William's classic letter about Winchester, which is reminiscent of the *Wasp's* battles with Thom-ass Sharp. "Who appointed Ben Winchester the Prophet, great dictator and regulator of this church, to direct and dictate to the saints, their faith and doctrine? Did Israel's God do it? If he did, I must confess that men of veracity and truth are getting rather scarce, judging from personal manifestations; but as he is ordained a King, when he is crowned, perhaps, there may be a different manifestation."

This letter concludes with this: "How is it with you Benny? Reflect on thy black deeds. O thou child of hell! Repent before thou die, and art called to judgment with thy sins upon thy head!"

Chapter 6: Convergence between *Wasp* and *Times and Seasons*

-→≫ ≪←-

THE CONVERGENCE BETWEEN THE *WASP* and the *Times and Seasons* is apparent not only in the editorial content and writing style, but even in the typography.

Connections between the Wasp *and the* Times and Seasons

Regardless of the motivation for founding the Wasp, Joseph took occasional interest in the paper, at least in April and May. On 16 April 1842, his History notes:

> I continued busily engaged in making out a list of debtors and an invoice of my property to be passed into the hands of the Assignee until Saturday evening the 16th on which day the first number of "The Wasp" a Miscellaneous weekly newspaper was first published at my Office, William Smith, Editor, devoted to the Arts, Sciences, Literature, Agriculture, Manufcture, [sic] Trade, Commerce and the General news of the day on a small sheet at $1.50 per annum.[94]

The next month, on 28 May 1842, Joseph's journal records that he felt "rather better. Walked to the store with Emma, and did some business in the city. Called at 8 in the eve at the printing office with the night watch. To see the Wasp.—"[95] Apart from these incidents, though, Joseph seems to have little involvement with the *Wasp*. He rarely mentions it or his brother William between May and November of 1842.

---

94   http://josephsmithpapers.org/paperSummary/history-1838-1856-volume-c-1-2-november-1838-31-july-1842?p=498&highlight=the%20wasp
95   http://josephsmithpapers.org/paperSummary/journal-december-1841-december-1842?p=29&highlight=the%20wasp

The *Wasp* and the *Times and Seasons* were published from the same offices on the corner of Water and Bain Streets,[96] using the same printer and supplies. The two papers were even mailed out together,[97] although the *Wasp* was published every Saturday while the *Times and Seasons* was published on the first and the fifteenth of each month. The very first issue of the *Wasp*, published April 16, 1842, contained this editorial comment:

> We take the liberty to send the Wasp to many of the subscribers of the Times and Seasons and if they are pleased with the arrangement they can manifest it by sending us the money by mail or faithful hands, if not they can re-mail them to us again.

The papers also shared content. For example, several articles from the May 2, 1842, *Times and Seasons* were reprinted in the *Wasp* on May 7, 1842. On 12 June 1842, Joseph's journal records that he "Brought some poetry to printing office & got some Newspapers."[98] A note to that entry in the Joseph Smith papers explains, "Poetry, much of it by Eliza R. Snow and William W. Phelps, was a fairly regular feature in both the *Times and Seasons* and *The Wasp*." One Eliza R. Snow poem was published in the *Times and Seasons* on December 15, 1842, and reprinted in the *Wasp* on January 21, 1843.

These accounts indicate the two papers were essentially one operation. This explains how both the *Times and Seasons* and the *Wasp* could be published continuously through the summer and fall of 1842, despite the serious illnesses and absences of Woodruff, Taylor, and Joseph Smith during August and September. In the absence of these putative editors, someone was publishing the *Times and Seasons*; if not William Smith (who was publishing the *Wasp*) then who? Pursuant to the revelation, the Church publications were to be supervised by the Quorum of the Twelve. William Smith satisfied that requirement.

---

[96] Jerry C. Jolley, "The Sting of the Wasp: Early Nauvoo Newspaper—April 1842 to April 1843," BYU Studies 1982.

[97] The 16 July 1842 edition of the *Wasp* includes this comment from the *Quincy Whig*: "The mail yesterday, brought us the Nauvoo papers, the "Times and Seasons," and "The Wasp." of the 1st inst."

[98] http://josephsmithpapers.org/paperSummary/journal-december-1841-december-1842?p=30&highlight=the%20wasp

Later, in November 1842, Joseph Smith resigned because of his inability to "do justice"[99] to the *Times and Seasons*. He did not specify when he became unable to effectively work on the paper, but since he made no reference to editing the *Times and Seasons* after May, it seems plausible that he would have deferred to his younger brother to print and publish the *Times and Seasons* during the summer of 1842, along with the *Wasp*. After all, he had previously relied on his other brother, Don Carlos, for both the *Elders' Journal* and the *Times and Seasons*.

Despite the significant difference in tone and editorial objectives—the *Times and Seasons* was mainly religious, the *Wasp* was mainly secular—the papers naturally touched on similar topics occasionally. In the summer of 1842, however, the editorial content of the papers drew closer, and each paper reprinted material from the other.

There is considerable evidence of a commingling of the two papers that goes beyond their joint production in the same printing shop. In June 1842, the two papers not only shared material but coordinated their publishing schedule. The situation involved John C. Bennett. The one-time Mayor of Nauvoo and close confidant of Joseph Smith had been excommunicated from the Church in May, 1842, for adultery. At first, he confessed his offenses and stated that Joseph had nothing to do with his actions. Bennett left Nauvoo, but then wrote letters to the *Sangamo Journal* accusing Joseph of conspiring to assassinate the former Governor of Missouri, Lilburn Boggs, who had issued the Extermination Order in 1838. Bennett proceeded to accuse the Mormons of multiple offenses and attracted considerable media attention. Note 482 to a letter in the Joseph Smith Papers outlines the sequence:

> John C. Bennett did not begin his anti-Mormon newspaper articles until his notice of disfellowship was published in the *Times and Seasons* on 15 June 1842, followed with full disclosure of his history by JS, with supporting documents, in *The Wasp* on 25 June 1842, which was rerun on 1 July 1842 in the *Times and*

---

[99] Joseph's valedictory statement, announcing his resignation as editor, included this explanation: "The multiplicity of other business that daily devolves upon me, renders it impossible for me to do justice to a paper so widely circulated as the Times and Seasons." *Times and Seasons*, 15 November 1842.

Seasons. Bennett retaliated with a series of articles that began in Springfield's Sangamo Journal on 8 July 1842. This series was widely publicized and became the basis of his 1842 book, The History of the Saints; or, An Exposé of Joe Smith and Mormonism, referred to later in this letter. (JS et al., "Notice," *Times and Seasons* , 15 June 1842, 3:830; JS, "To the Church of Jesus Christ of Latter Day Saints, and to All the Honorable Part of Community," The Wasp, 25 June 1842, [2]–[3]; "To the Church of Jesus Christ of Latter Day Saints, and to All the Honorable Part of Community," *Times and Seasons*, 3:839–843; "Astounding Mormon Disclosures! Letter from Gen. Bennett," Sangamo Journal [Springfield, IL], 8 July 1842, [2].) [100]

The two papers published the identical letter but framed it quite differently. The *Times and Seasons* simply published the disclosure letter without elaboration. The *Wasp* prefaced the letter with an inflammatory editorial and two letters to the editors signed by pseudonyms. The Wasp also published a provocative editorial in the July 8th edition. The editorial language in the *Wasp* reflects William's voice, not Joseph's, but William is speaking for "the General," meaning his brother Joseph. The JSP note doesn't mention the editorial in the *Wasp* on July 8th that used vivid language to dare the *Sangamo Journal* to have Bennett write more in that paper. Maybe the editorial had no effect; after all, Bennett's articles began appearing on the same date. But certainly the *Wasp* did nothing to calm the situation.

The publication sequence went like this:

Wasp	*Times and Seasons*
	June 15, 1842 – NOTICE The subscribers, members of the First Presidency of the church of Jesus Christ of Latter Day Saints, withdraw the hand of fellowship from General John C. Bennett, as a christian, be having been labored with from time to time, to persuade him to amend his conduct, apparently to no good effect.

---

[100] Letter from James Arlington Bennett to Lieut. Gen. Smith, 1 Sep 1842, note 482. http://josephsmithpapers.org/paperSummary/journal-december-1841-december-1842?p=80&highlight=the%20wasp

June 18, 1842 – For the Wasp Letter to the Editor by John C. Bennett, dated June 14, 1842, responding to the Sangamo Journal	
June 25, 1842 - The world is all agog for a shot at 'Jo Smith' —That is, the newspaper world. Sludnge goes a morter; whang sounds a cannon; bang twangs a gun: pop snaps a pistol, and whish hisses a pop gun- It is quite gratifying to the General to be thus noticed. But, oh! you great whales that are writing for glory and living on trust, do be merciful to the small fish around you: when you shoot, spare as many of the little pan gentry us possible; but keep shooting:—kill Boggs: smash the bankrupt law ; and squib away about the General's assets. But for hell's sake. (no, not *hell's*, that's wicked.) hypocrites then, don t shoot at those fellows that tarred and feathered Joseph Smith in Hiram, Ohio, in 1832, with impunity: It will hurt the credit of Ohio: Don't fire at the inhabitants of Jackson county Mo, for tarring and feathering Patridge and Allen: it will disturb their sympathies. Hold up! don't point your pieces over the bleaching bones of men, women and children, *slain for their religion in bloody Missouri!* Oh, no! don't! It will tarnish the honor of the State. While firing your great guns at Gen. Smith, hush about the Court Martial that tried to shoot him without law; keep his prison chains still, but stagger from the grog-shop to the pulpit and swear:—" God dam old Jo Smith!"	
June 25, 1842 - TO THE CHURCH OF JESUS CHRIST OF LATTER DAY SAINTS, AND TO ALL THE HONORABLE PART OF COMMUNITY. It becomes my duty to lay before the	July 1, 1842 - TO THE CHURCH OF JESUS CHRIST OF LATTER DAY SAINTS, AND TO ALL THE HONORABLE PART OF COMMUNITY. It becomes my duty to lay before the

Church of Jesus Christ of Latter Day Saints, and the public generally, some important facts relative to the conduct and character of Dr. JOHN C. BENNETT, who has lately been expelled from the aforesaid church; that the honorable part of community may be aware of his proceedings, and be ready to treat him and regard him as he ought to be regarded, viz: as an imposter [impostor] and base adulterer.... [3,250-word letter and affidavits, signed by Joseph Smith]	Church of Jesus Christ of Latter Day Saints, and the public generally, some important facts relative to the conduct and character of Dr. JOHN C. BENNETT, who has lately been expelled from the aforesaid church; that the honorable part of community may be aware of his proceedings, and be ready to treat him and regard him as he ought to be regarded, viz: as an imposter [impostor] and base adulterer.... [3,250-word letter and affidavits, signed by Joseph Smith]
July 8, 1842 - The Sangamo Journal, that has had a sail out for every breeze, *for* the Mormons and against them, run off with the first morsel against Doctor Bennett, as a dog would with a stolen bone to gnaw. But hark ye! the same Jack at Jobbing, now calls upon Bennett, Rigdon and Robinson to come and make an expose of everything. 0 lordey! what a clever fellow Mr. Bennett is now ! Butter and honey! O, do come and mash Mormonism: Poor fool! do you not see your own ears peer up so J-a-c-k-A-s-s-i-c-a-l-l-y that every body knows how worthless truthless, and contemptible you are, before you *bray!*. Do get Doctor Bennett to write again for you, and you may be Paddyfied to the degree of A. S. S.	

The Wasp – July Extra Edition

In late July, the papers again converged over the John C. Bennett scandal. In response to the *Sangamo* letters, the *Wasp* published a long article denouncing Bennett on July 23. The article, titled "Bennettiana," was reprinted in the Wasp's only "EXTRA" edition on July 27, along with "MORE DISCLOSURES." The EXTRA edition adds a report of a meeting of the citizens of Nauvoo, held at the meeting ground on July 22, 1842. An exact copy of the report was also published in the August 1, 1842, *Times and*

Seasons, albeit with a different introduction. The order of content is arranged a little differently, but the content is essentially identical, with the exception of editorial comments.

Wasp, EXTRA, July 27, 1842	*Times and Seasons*, August 1, 1842
BENNETTIANA	JOHN C. BENNETT (1200-word introductory editorial)
BENNETT AS HE WAS J.C. Bennett is the author of…	At a meeting of the citizens of the city of Nauvoo held in said city at the meeting ground, July 22^d 1842…
BENNETT AS HE IS From the St. Louis Bulletin (the Danites)	AFFIDAVIT OF THE CITY COUNCIL
BENNETT AS HE WAS	BENNETT AS HE WAS
How a man can talk with the 'livery of heaven on to serve the devil in.' Hear him again.	How a man can talk with the 'livery of heaven on to serve the devil in.'
From the *Times and Seasons*, Oct. 1840. 'Fudge! We repeat, Smith and Rigdon should not be given up…	From the *Times and Seasons*, Oct. 1840. 'Fudge! We repeat, Smith and Rigdon should not be given up…
From the *Times and Seasons*, June 1, 1841	From the Sangamo Journal BENNET AS HE IS ST. LOUIS, Mo. July 15th 1842
BENNETT AS HE IS Extract from the Sangamo.	
BENNETT AS HE WAS. From the *Times and Seasons*, Feb. 1, 1842 I stood on Mount Zion…	BENNETT AS HE WAS. From the *Times and Seasons*, Feb. 1, 1842 I stood on Mount Zion…
Doctor Bennett's abolition principles, were …	Dr. Bennett professed then to be a good and a virtuous man; to feel indignant at oppression, and ready to step forward in defence [defense] of the innoecnt [innocent], the injured, and oppressed. How has the scene changed! and how truly he figures in the character of an apostate.
From the *Times and Seasons*, March 15, 1842.	From the *Times and Seasons*, March 15, 1842.
It will be seen by this that Gen. Smith was a great philanthropist as long as Bennett could practice adultery, fornication, and—we were going to say, (Buggery,) without being exposed.	OPINIONS OF THE PRESS It will probably be understood that Dr. Bennett went to St. Louis in order to stir up an excitement, and if possible, to create a mob by publishing his awful disclosures, and lecturing against Mormonism, and if not, he

	expected to make a few shillings by the sale of published detraction and falsehood. The following will shew [show] how far he succeeded in St. Louis:- From the St. Louis Gazette.... (->) The Gazette is entitled to our thanks for his liberality and patriotic course towards Dr. Bennett, and the Mormons. If editors generally would act thus legally and wise, such catch pennies as Bennett, Harris, and about ninety-nine others, would find their common level in their own infamy. BENNETT. The following from the Missouri Reporter, shows Bennett's decline in the western market. It is reported that Greenbush N. Y. has to be smutted with his dust among other unfortunate places.... From the Bostonian. G. W. ROBINSON CERTIFICATE OF HORACE S. ELDRIDGE
At a meeting of the citizens of the city of Nauvoo held in said city at the meeting ground, July 22ᵈ 1842...	
AFFIDAVIT OF THE CITY COUNCIL	

The *Times and Seasons* contained a 1200-word editorial that described the situation in detail. Oddly, it was signed "E.D."

JOHN C. BENNETT.

There has always been, in every age of the church those who have been opposed to the principles of virtue, who have loved the gain of this present world, followed the principles of unrighteousness, and have been the enemies of truth; hence Paul speaks of certain brethren who "coveted the wages of this present world;" John of others whom he says "went out from us because they were not of us." Paul in writing to the Corinthian Church tells them that there is fornications among them, even, "such fornications as is not so much as named among the Gentiles; that one should have his father's wife"-that they defrauded, and that "brother went to law with brother"-that they got drunk when they met to partake of the sacrament; and that many evils existed among them. Peter in prophesying concerning the church says, "But there were false prophets among the people, even as there shall also be false teachers among you, who privily shall bring in damnable heresies, even denying the Lord that bought them, and shall bring upon themselves swift destruction; and many shall follow their pernicious ways, by reason of whom the way of truth shall be evil spokea [spoken] of; and through covetousness shall they with feigned words make merchandise of you; whose judgment of long time lingereth not, and their damnation slumbereth not." Paul in speaking of the difficulties that he had to encounter, says, "I am in perils at home, in perils among false brethren." Such is a brief history of that people; and if we examine the history of this church we shall find it much the same: those who have associated with us and made the greatest professions of friendship, have frequently been our greatest enemies and our most determined foes, if they became unpopular, if their interest or dignity was touched, or if they were detected in their iniquity; they were always the first to raise the hand of persecution, to calumniate and villify [vilify] their brethren, and to seek the downfall and destruction of their friends. In Jackson county Mo. during the first difficulties there were many like those that John speaks of, "they went out from us because they were not of us;" in Kirtland, when persecution raged, Oliver Cowdery, Warren Parrish, Jacob Bumb, and others whose course of conduct had been the most inconsistent were the first to cry out imposture, and delusion; and while some of them had been engaged in extensive frauds in the Bank, and were the principle cause of its not being able to meet its liabilities; they were the first to cry out speculation and fraud, and to try to palm their iniquities upon the unoffending and innocent; they seized hold of the popular prejudice, aided and abetted in obtaining funds for paper, fraudulently obtained by them, instituted vexatious law-suits and made themselves fat at the expense of the innocent; glutted upon the misery, ruin and distress of their brethren-but with what measure they meted it has been measured to them again.

In the State of Missouri we had our Hinkle, our Avard, Marsh, McLellin, and others who were the first to flee in time of danger-the first to tell of things that they never knew, and swear to things that they never before had heard of. They were more violent in their persecutions, more relentless and sanguinary in their proceedings, and sought with greater fury the destruction and overthrow of the Saints of God who had never injured them, but whose virtue made them blush for their crimes. All that were there remember that they were the stoutest and the loudest in proclaiming against oppression; they protested vehemently against mob and misrule, but were the first in robbing, spoiling, and plundering their brethren. Such things we have always expected; we know that the "net will gather

93

together of every kind, good and bad," that "the wheat and tares must grow together until the harvest," and that even at the last there will be five foolish as well as five wise virgins. Daniel, in referring to the last days says, in speaking concerning the "Holy Covenant," that many shall have indignation against it, and shall obtain information from those that forsake the Holy Covenant-and the robbers of thy people shall seek to exalt themselves, but they shall fall. This we have fully proven-we have seen them try to exalt themselves, and we have seen their fall. He goes on further to state, that "many shall cleave unto them by flatteries." Such was Dr. Avard, and John C. Bennett-with the latter we have to do at the present time, and in many ef [of] the foregoing statements and prophecies we shall see his character and conduct exemplified.-He professed the greatest fidelity, and eternal friendship, yet was he an adder in the path, and a viper in the bosom. He professed to be virtuous and chaste, yet did he pierce the heart of the innocent, introduce misery and infamy into families, reveled in voluptuousness and crime, and led the youth that he had influence over to tread in his unhallowed steps;-he professed to fear God, yet did he desecrate his name, and prostitute his authority to the most unhallowed and diabolical purposes; even to the seduction of the virtuous, and the defiling of his neighbor's bed. He professed indignation against Missouri saying, "my hand shall avenge the blood of the innocent;" yet now he calls upon Missouri to come out against the Saints, and he "will lead them on to glory and to victory."

It may be asked why it was that we would countenance him so long after being apprised of his iniquities, and why he was not dealt with long ago. To this we would answer, that he has been dealt with from time to time; when he would acknowledge his iniquity, ask and pray for forgiveness, beg that he might not be exposed, on account of his mother, and other reasons, saying, he should be ruined and undone. He frequently wept like a child, and begged like a culprit for forgiveness, at the same time promising before God and angels to amend his life, if he could be forgiven. He was in this way borne with from time to time, until forbearance was no longer a virtue, and then the first Presidency, the Twelve, and the Bishops withdrew their fellowship from him, as published in the 16th number of this paper. The church afterwards publicly withdrew their fellowship from him, and his character was published in the 17th number of this paper; since that time he has published that the conduct of the Saints was bad-that Joseph Smith and many others were adulterers, murderers, &c.-that there was a secret band of men that would kill people, &c. called Danites-that he was in duress when he gave his affidavit, and testified that Joseph Smith was a virtuous man-that we believed in and practiced polygamy-that we believed in secret murders, and aimed to destroy the government. &c. &c. As he has made his statements very public, and industriously circulated them through the country, we shall content ourselves with answering his base falsehoods and misrepresentations, without giving publicity to them, as the public are generally acquainted with them already. E. D.

The entire "EXTRA" issue of the *Wasp* discusses the J. C. Bennett scandal, using reprints from the *Times and Seasons*, quotations from various newspapers, and William Smith's commentary. He juxtaposes examples of "Bennett as he was" with "Bennett as he is," using examples of Bennett's past writings in the *Times and Seasons* and his *Sangamo* letters.

Here's how the issue begins in the first column on the first page:

BENNETTIANA;
or
THE MICROSCOPE WITH DOUBLE DIAMOND LENSES.

The baser the coward, the bigger the bluster

We have read Doctor Bennett's great sina qua non: Russian ukase: and dictatorial egotism. Desperate cases require desperate doses and so we will give a little of *Bennett as he was, and Bennett as he is.*

BENNETT AS HE WAS.

J. C. Bennett is the author of the communications signed 'Joab General in Israel.' *Wonder* if he was *in duress* when he made the following?

From the *Times and Seasons*, September, 1840.

Burglary! TREASON!! ARSON!!!

MURDER!!!!

Lt. Col. Smith:

I feel disposed to address you a few lines in relation to one of the darkest events…

Yours, Respectfully,

JOAB,

General in Israel.'

After reprinting Bennett's letter in support of the Prophet, William inserts this:

BENNETT AS HE IS

From the St. Louis Bulletin

On the evening of the 29th ultimo, twelve of the Danites, dressed in female apparel, approached my boarding house… in Nauvoo…

Following the quotation from the *St. Louis Bulletin*, William alternates back, inserting this editorial comment before reprinting an excerpt from the *Times and Seasons*:

BENNETT AS HE WAS
How a man can talk with the 'livery of heaven on to serve the devil in.' Hear him again.
From the *Times and Seasons*, Oct. 1840.
'Fudge! We repeat, Smith and Ridgon should not be given up….

BENNETT AS HE IS
Extract from the Sangamo
'If Governor Reynolds, of Missouri, will make another demand for Joe Smith alone… I will deliver him up to justice, or die in the attempt…

William interrupts the *Sangamo Journal* quotations to insert editorial comments such as this: "Gov. Carlin must have had a great desire to please the Doctor, eh!"

The August 1, 1842, *Times and Seasons* duplicates much of the material from the Extra edition of the Wasp. Here is a comparison of the two editorial introductions:

Wasp 27 July 1842	*Times and Seasons*, 1 August 1842
William Smith, Editor	Joseph Smith, editor
We have read Doctor Bennett's great sina qua non: Russian ukase: and dictatorial egotism. Desperate cases require desperate doses and so we will give a little of *Bennett as he was, and Bennett as he is.* BENNETT AS HE WAS.	
J. C. Bennett is the author of the communications signed 'Joab General in Israel.' *Wonder* if he was *in duress* when he made the following?	The readers of the *Times and Seasons* are probably aware that all those articles signed "Joab General in Israel," are from the pen of the Doctor; we will therefore compare some of his last acts with his present proceedings.-

	We wonder whether he was in duress when he made the following.
BENNETT AS HE WAS. How a man can talk with the 'livery of heaven on to serve the devil in.' Hear him again. From the *Times and Seasons*, Oct, 1840. 'Fudge! We repeat, Smith and Rigdon should not be given up….	BENNETT AS HE WAS. How a man can talk with the 'livery of heaven on to serve the devil in.' From the *Times and Seasons*, Oct. 1840. 'Fudge! We repeat, Smith and Rigdon should not be given up….
Doctor Bennett's abolition principles, were quite warm, as the *Times and Seasons* of March 15, 1842, will show by reading the correspondence between himself and Chadre V. Dyer, M.D., of Chicago. From the *Times and Seasons*, March 15, 1842	Dr. Bennett professed then to be a good and a virtuous man; to feel indignant at oppression, and ready to step forward in defence [defense] of the innoecnt [innocent], the injured, and oppressed. How has the scene changed! and how truly he figures in the character of an apostate. From the *Times and Seasons*, March 15, 1842

The *Times and Seasons* follows the same format at the *Wasp*, showing Bennett "AS HE WAS" compared with "AS HE IS." The two papers take different, but congruent, editorial approaches.

Then follows a report on a meeting of the citizens of Nauvoo held at the meeting ground on July 22, 1842. Following that is an AFFIDAVIT OF THE CITY COUNCIL

In the EXTRA edition of the Wasp, the same AFFIDAVIT OF THE CITY COUNCIL is introduced with this:

It is not with a view to excite the passions and prejudices of the people, that the following affidavits, are made public, but to disabuse the community, which can not be less than fomented at the perusal of Dr. Bennett's letters and affidavits which have recently shot forth like meteors. Our space is too small to publish the documents referred to, but as there are no lack of presses and men, to give the Doctor a fair hearing, as well as extensive circulation, we shall presume that every body knows his story about the Mormons at Nauvoo, and proceed to rebut, refute, disprove, or expose, as the nature of the case may require.

The Doctor claims among all his et ceteras a little law, but had he reflected once off lex scripta, where he has ten times to gratify his lustful desires, he would exclaim like the old barrister, "John might swallow a cart load of such stuff without obtaining one particle of truth." His affidavits are mere wind for effect.

Mr. Bennett knows better than to make such foolish quirks. In fact, until the whole City Council of Nauvoo are *impeached,* the Doctor must stand before the public as a perjured man.— There let him stand.

Two things are certainly requisite in witnesses, —knowledge and character: By this rule, as the Doctor fails himself, we think some of his testimony, when properly cross examined will appear a little more than plumb. Who is Mrs. Shindle? A harlot. What next? References to others, whose knowledge of facts and weight of character, will find a brief—*ex necessitali rei.*

The doctor's *duress,* so gravely sworn to, is the climax of his legal sagacity. There is a point at issue in that, which, when the Doctor wakes from his lethargy, will look like a vexed question, with iron eyes, which may refresh his mind with the consolation that sudden and violent moves in public, often bring leisure, repentance in solitude.

As it regards his third letter, concerning fraud, time alone will determine that. Common law, common sense, and common prudence, teach us to try men for crimes that they have committed, not for what they may, commit.

What he says of the proceedings of the Lodge is nothing; he is an expelled mason. Mr. Rigdon's name goes with his certificate, and settles the matter on that point and with his daughter. Elden Marks' name is to the city council's affidavit; and we might add many other things to show the vanity of the man and the enormity of his crimes, but we forbear, though a word or two more may not be amiss. As to the Danite band, which seems like Hamlet's ghost to haunt the Doctor by night and by day, it must be something more than Mormon, for the City Council testifies that they know of no such band. And in justice to the community we ought to say, and strangers who are among us daily bear the same evidence, that nothing of any such league, combination or know of men, is known in Nauvoo.

The certificates of Elders Rigdon, Marks, and Higbee, and Miss Michael, (the Journal's Mitchell) go to show that Doctor Bennett used the names of persons without their consent. These certificates speak for themselves, and lave the doctor before the public as he is, a debaucher, a spoiler of character and virtue, and a living pestilence, walking in darkness to fester in his own infamy.

There is one affidavit out, that Bennett might easily be put out of the way; and in justice to the community, and the aggravation of the crimes which he has committed, (and to substantiate which, the testimony of respectable persons has been properly authenticated, but which is actually too indelicate for publicity,) we say, and every man who has a wife, or a daughter, or a sister, that he wishes uncontaminated with vice of the slyest but most atrocious mien, will say, we will never rest till the law is executed on such a bloody lifed Vampyre.

The *Times and Seasons* takes a less provocative approach, typified by this comment:

> Dr. Bennett professed then to be a good and a virtuous man; to feel indignant at oppression, and ready to step forward in defence [defense] of the innoecnt [innocent], the injured, and oppressed. How has the scene changed! and how truly he figures in the character of an apostate.

Whoever was editing these newspapers were—or was—using the same approach, the same material, and even, in some cases, the same language.

Overlapping editorial content.

Another way to examine editorial content is to compare the material in the three main sources: The *Times and Seasons*, the *Wasp*, and Joseph Smith's journal. A table comparing the three is included in the appendix.

The Editors: Joseph, William and Don Carlos Smith

Chapter 7: Bernhisel Thank-you Note

A LETTER TO JOHN BERNHISEL, DATED NOVEMBER 16, 1841, and signed on behalf of Joseph Smith, is at the core of the long-held assertion that Joseph took a personal interest in Central America. No one knows who originated the letter. The handwriting has been identified as John Taylor's, but there are no indications that Joseph dictated or even reviewed the letter. No contemporary journals mention the letter—with one exception that suggests Joseph *did not* write it, as I'll discuss below.

The letter—essentially a brief thank-you note, combined with information about real estate—expresses appreciation to Dr. Bernhisel for the gift of a two-book set written by Stephens and Catherwood titled *Incidents of Travel in Central America, Chiapas, and Yucatan*, published in 1841. Extracts from the books were published anonymously in the *Times and Seasons* when Joseph was the nominal editor of the newspaper in 1842.

This Bernhisel letter is the sole direct link between Joseph Smith and the Stephens books. For decades, scholars have assumed Joseph dictated the letter,[101] which would mean he had read the Stephens books and therefore believed the ruins in Mesoamerica were evidence of the authenticity of the Book of Mormon. That, in turn, would support the claim that Joseph was the impetus behind the publication of the anonymous articles in the *Times and Seasons*. This is the standard interpretation, reflected this way in the Joseph Smith Papers' Historical Introduction to Orson Pratt's 1840 pamphlet, *A[n] Interesting Account of Several Remarkable Visions*:[102]

---

[101] It is included in the JSP. See http://josephsmithpapers.org/paperSummary/letter-to-john-bernhisel-16-november-1841.

[102] See http://josephsmithpapers.org/paperSummary/appendix-orson-pratt-an-interesting-account-of-several-remarkable-visions-1840. The Historical Introduction, note 6, cites two of the three anonymous articles from the *Times and Seasons* and the 16 November 1841 Bernhisel letter that is the focus of this article. It also cites Terryl L. Givens, *By the Hand of Mormon: The American Scripture That Launched a New World Religion*, (Oxford: Oxford University Press, 2002). The JSP citation does not give the page number, but presumably the

Pratt's association of Book of Mormon peoples with the history of all of North and South America matched common understanding of early Latter-day Saints. Shortly thereafter, when John Lloyd Stephens's *Incidents of Travel in Central America, Chiapas, and Yucatan* became available in Nauvoo in about 1842, JS greeted it enthusiastically and church members used it to map Book of Mormon sites in a Central American setting.[103]

Thanks to the Joseph Smith Papers project, new information has been brought to light that suggests a different reality. The historical fact remains that, even including the note to Bernhisel, not a single reference to the Stephens books—or Central America—has been found with Joseph's signature or explicit approval.

In this article, I offer evidence that 1) the thank-you note originated with Wilford Woodruff, 2) Joseph never read the Stephens books, and 3) Joseph had nothing to do with the anonymous articles in the *Times and Seasons*.

To understand the 16 November letter in context, it is important to review the relationship between John Bernhisel and Joseph Smith. Dr. Bernhisel (1799-1881) was a physician in New York City who was baptized into the LDS church by November 1840 when he was ordained an elder.[104] He moved to Nauvoo by 1843 and then on to Utah, where he became a prominent political figure, serving as Utah's non-voting delegate to Congress for many years in Washington D.C. He is also known for his important copy of the inspired version manuscript of Joseph's translation of the Bible.[105]

---

reference is to pp. 101-102, in which Givens writes, "Joseph was quick to see how the Book of Mormon had arrived on the scene of this mystery [Stephens' question about the origin of the Mayans] with impeccable timing. Responding immediately to the Stephens account, Joseph wrote back to Bernhisel."

[103] A 2013 article published by the Neal A. Maxwell Institute uses similar language: "Latter-day Saints also **greeted** these discoveries **with enthusiasm**" (emphasis added), Roper, Fields and Nepal, "Joseph Smith, the Times and Seasons, and Central American Ruins," *Journal of the Book of Mormon and Other Restoration Scripture* 22/2 (2013): 84-97.

[104] John Milton Bernhisel Biography, Joseph Smith Papers, available online here: http://josephsmithpapers.org/person/john-milton-bernhisel?p=1

105 Robert J. Matthews, "The Bernhisel Manuscript Copy of Joseph Smith's Inspired

While living in New York, Bernhisel desired to purchase real estate in Nauvoo and had been corresponding with Joseph Smith on that subject since at least March 6, 1841. Seven letters between the two men have been found and are included in the Joseph Smith Papers. The exchange gives us insight into the practical realities of Joseph's life during this period in Nauvoo; although Bernhisel asked Joseph to purchase property for him and sent him the money in July 1841, Joseph didn't actually purchase the property until January 1842.

The following summary of the letters shows how the relationship between the two men developed. The full text of the letters is included as an appendix to this article.

13 April 1841 – letter to John Bernhisel (handwriting of Robert B. Thompson, two pages)[106]

> This letter refers to "Yours of the 6th ultimo" meaning March 6th. Bernhisel had inquired about purchasing land in Nauvoo. Joseph told him there were "plenty of opportunities" in Nauvoo and that if Bernhisel would send money, he would make a "suitable purchase" for him.

12 July 1841 – letter from John Bernhisel (handwriting of John Bernhisel, 3 pages)[107]

> Bernhisel encloses a certificate of deposit for $425 and asks Joseph to purchase "as large a tract of good land, with a sufficient quantity of timber, in a healthful location, and within a convenient distance, say one two or three miles of Nauvoo" for $500, with the balance of $75 to be paid by July 1 1842.

3 August 1841 – letter to John Bernhisel (handwriting of Robert B. Thompson, 1 page)[108]

Version of the Bible," BYU Studies 11:3 (1971), online at https://byustudies.byu.edu/content/bernhisel-manuscript-copy-joseph-smiths-inspired-version-bible.

[106] http://josephsmithpapers.org/paperSummary/letter-to-john-bernhisel-13-april-1841

[107] http://josephsmithpapers.org/paperSummary/letter-from-john-bernhisel-12-july-1841

[108] http://josephsmithpapers.org/paperSummary/letter-to-john-bernhisel-3-august-1841

Joseph acknowledges the receipt of the $500 deposit but explains that "If a purchase could have been made early in the spring it could have been done to much better advantage than at present."

18 August 1841 – letter from John Bernhisel (handwriting of John Bernhisel, 2 pages)[109]

Not having heard from Joseph, and having heard that land prices were rising, Bernhisel asks Joseph to purchase a parcel within ten miles of the city, but defers to Joseph's judgment because "a small piece of ground near the city may be better than a larger one at a greater distance."

8 September 1841 – letter from John Bernhisel (handwriting of John Bernhisel, 1 page)[110]

Bernhisel gives this letter to Wilford Woodruff, along with the Stephens books, to deliver to Joseph Smith. Bernhisel acknowledges receipt of the 3 August letter and reminds Joseph he was going to purchase property on his behalf.

16 November 1841 – letter to John Bernhisel (handwriting of John Taylor, 1 page)[111]

This is the letter thanking Bernhisel for the Stephens books that is the focus of this article. Joseph still has not purchased land and hopes Bernhisel will visit Nauvoo to select property for himself.

4 January 1842 – letter to John Bernhisel (handwriting of Willard Richards, who copied the original letter into JS Letterbook 2)[112]

This letter acknowledges a letter from Bernhisel dated 11 December which is not extant. Presumably that letter urged Joseph to buy the land because Bernhisel could not come to Nauvoo for a while longer. Joseph informs

---

[109] http://josephsmithpapers.org/paperSummary/letter-from-john-bernhisel-18-august-1841

[110] http://josephsmithpapers.org/paperSummary/letter-from-john-bernhisel-8-september-1841

[111] http://josephsmithpapers.org/paperSummary/letter-to-john-bernhisel-16-november-1841

[112] http://josephsmithpapers.org/paperSummary/letter-to-john-bernhisel-4-january-1842

Bernhisel that he purchased "this day" 60 acres of land "about 2 miles east by south of the Temple" that "was the best chance which presented itself to me at present." At the end, Richards wrote that he "omitted all but the business Part."

Bernhisel moved to Nauvoo in 1843 and lived in Joseph Smith's Mansion House. He became a trusted companion of Joseph's, attending meetings and acting as physician. He wrote the letter to Governor Ford of Illinois, dated June 14, 1844, that vouches for Joseph Smith's character: "He is a man of calm judgment, enlarged views, and is eminently distinguished by his love of justice… his heart is felt to be keenly alive to the kindest and softest emotions of which human nature is susceptible."[113] He signed the affidavit of 20 June 1844 that described threats against the Latter-day Saints in Nauvoo and delivered it to Governor Ford with John Taylor.[114] After the martyrdom, Bernhisel prepared the bodies of Joseph and Hyrum for burial. Almost five months later, he delivered David Hyrum Smith, the last child of Joseph and Emma Smith.[115]

There is no question that Bernhisel had a close relationship with Joseph Smith, yet apart from his note accompanying the gift and Wilford Woodruff's journal, I have found no reference in Bernhisel's papers to the Stephens books. I wouldn't be surprised if such references exist, however.

Wilford Woodruff and other members of the Twelve returned from their mission to England in 1841, arriving in New York City on May 20th. Woodruff spent a few days visiting and touring the city with Dr. Bernhisel, who was then the Bishop of the Church in New York. Woodruff left to visit

---

[113] Letter, John Bernhisel to Thomas Ford, quoted in *History of the Church of Jesus Christ of Latter-day Saints*, B.H. Roberts, ed., (Deseret Book 1957), 6:467-8, online at https://byustudies.byu.edu/content/volume-6-chapter-22.

[114] See Affidavit, http://josephsmithpapers.org/paperSummary/affidavit-from-john-p-greene-and-john-bernhisel-20-june-1844.

[115] Lynn M. and Hope A. Hilton, "Bernhisel, John Milton," Utah History Encyclopedia, online at http://www.uen.org/utah_history_encyclopedia/b/BERNHISEL_JOHN.html.

Boston and other places and spent 41 days with his father and other relatives in the East before returning to New York City in August. (The other members of the Twelve had gone ahead to Nauvoo.) Woodruff met with Bernhisel on August 24th. He left New York on September 1st to preach on Long Island and returned to the city on the 6th. On September 9th, he met with Bernhisel again. He recorded, "I recieved $40 dollars of Dr John M Bernhisel for President Joseph Smith also Stephens travels in central America in 2 volums also one letter."

The letter Bernhisel gave Woodruff explains the gift and the money:

> New York September 8th. 1841.
>
> Dear Brother
>
> You will herewith receive a copy of Stephen's Incidents of Travel in Central America, Chiapas, and Yucatan, which I hope you will do me the favor to accept, as a small testimony of my gratitude to you for the valuable services you are rendering me, and as a token of my regard for you as a Prophet of the Lord.
>
> > With sentiments of the highest consideration, I am yours in the bonds of the New and Everlasting Covenant.
> >
> > J. M. Bernhisel
>
> P.S. I have had the pleasure to receive your favor of the 5th ultimo, acknowledging the receipt of the certificate of deposite for four hundred and twenty five dollars, and kindly saying that you would expend it to the best advantage. In addition to the above Elder Wilford Woodruff will hand you forty dollars, and the balance I will endeavor to remit you soon after you inform me that you have made the purchase, but certainly before the first of May next. On the genuineness of the bills you may place the most implicit reliance, for one of them I obtained at the bank from which it was issued, and the other at the Greenwich bank. I sincerely condole with you on the death of your brother Don Carlos Smith.

A few hours after meeting with Bernhisel, Woodruff, his wife Phebe and four others boarded a boat at 6 p.m. and "departed for Albany on our road for Nauvoo."

Neither Bernhisel nor Woodruff explain what accounted for Bernhisel's interest in the books or why they were considered a suitable gift for Joseph Smith. Presumably Bernhisel had read or heard about the books, inasmuch as they were bestsellers at the time. The June 15, 1841, *Times and Seasons* contains an editorial introduction to the Stephens books, along with an extract from the *New York Weekly Herald* about lectures given by Stephens and his illustrator Catherwood. Bernhisel would naturally conclude that Joseph Smith would be interested in the Stephens books.[116] His reference to "valuable services" shows he intended the gift as a way to prompt Joseph to finally purchase the property as he'd requested in the July 12 letter.

Bernhisel does not indicate when he purchased the books, but Woodruff does not mention them in connection with his visit on August 24th. This suggests Bernhisel purchased the books after August 24th. Perhaps another factor was the late August visit of Benjamin Winchester to New York on his way from Philadelphia to Salem, Massachusetts, where he had been assigned to serve as a missionary with Erastus Snow. Winchester, a well-known

---

[116] The source of the extract from the *Weekly Herald* is unknown. To a considerable extent, the *Times and Seasons* relied on submissions. I suspect the extract was sent from Philadelphia because of a short, out-of-context note that immediately follows the extract. This reads, "On Friday last eleven wagons passed through this place with families for the City of Nauvoo, Illinois, the Mormon city. More, we learned from one of them are to follow soon. They are all from Chester co. Pa.-Journal." Chester co. is adjacent to Philadelphia. This raises two possibilities; either the editors extracted the material from two separate papers, or the *Pa.-Journal* included both the extract from the *Weekly Herald* and the brief mention of the Mormon wagons. Original editions of either paper that contain these articles would likely answer the question, but I have not been able to locate any. However, the June 15 issue of the *Times and Seasons* contains other items from Pennsylvania: a letter from William Smith, who was writing from Pennsylvania, and a notice from John Bills, Tailor, who "has just received the latest fashions direct from Philadelphia (through the politeness of President Hyrum Smith)." Because William Smith was a traveling agent of the *Times and Seasons* at the time, he could have sent the articles from the *Pa.-Journal*. The next issue of the *Times and Seasons*, July 1st, recognizes the receipt of the *Gospel Reflector* from Philadelphia and reprints an article from that publication.

There are no news items from New York in the *Times and Seasons*, a point Bernhisel raised in his 12 July 1841 letter. He had been sending the *New York Evangelist* to the editors and asked Joseph to inquire whether the editors found it of any service so he could cancel it if they weren't going to use it. His mention of this and no other paper implies that he was not sending other papers.

Mormon who had visited New York previously, would probably call upon Dr. Bernhisel, the presiding authority in New York. A few months previously, Winchester had published an article in the March 15, 1841, *Gospel Reflector* that linked the Book of Mormon to popular books about ancient American archaeology. This was before the Stephens book was published in June or July 1841, but it seems likely Winchester knew of these books by the time he reached New York.

On September 9, 1841, Bernhisel gave a copy of the Stephens' books, *Incidents of Travel*, to Woodruff to deliver to Joseph. Woodruff read them during the journey and was highly impressed with what he learned. He made two journal entries (emphasis mine, spelling and punctuation original):[117]

> Sept. 13, 1841 – "I spent the day in reading the 1ˢᵗ vol. of INCIDENTS OF TRAVELS IN Central America Chiapas and Yucatan BY JOHN L STEPHEN'S... I felt **truly interested** in this work for **it brought to light a flood of testimony in proof of the book of Mormon** in the discovery & survey of the city Copan in Central America A correct drawing of the monuments pyramids, portraits, & Hieroglyphics as executed by Mr. Catherwood is now presented before the publick & is truly a wonder to the world. Their whole travels **were truly interesting**."
>
> Sept. 16, 1841 – "I perused the 2d Vol of **Stephens** travels In Central America Chiapas of Yucatan & the ruins of Palenque & Copan. It is truly **one of the most interesting histories I have ever read**."

Woodruff arrived in Nauvoo on October 6, 1841, after more than two years' absence. He stayed with Brigham Young that night. The next night he stayed at Heber C. Kimball's house and remained there until October 11ᵗʰ when he moved to a house he bought. He spent the rest of the month mowing hay and gathering his family's effects that had been stored in Iowa.

The first time he mentioned seeing Joseph Smith was on October 31ˢᵗ, at the council in which Joseph "severely reproved Benjamin Winchester."

---

[117] All references to Woodruff's journal are to the typeset version published by Signature books, Scott Kenney, editor. http://signaturebooks.com/wilford-woodruffs-journal-1833-1898-typescript/ . Portions of the journal are available online here: http://www.ristow.us/foswiki/pub/Genealogy/WilfordWoodruffsJournalKrautsPioneerPress/ Woodruff_Wilfords_Journal_-_Krauts_Pioneer_Press.pdf.

(Winchester had traveled to Nauvoo seeking work in the printing business.) While it's likely Woodruff saw Joseph before this, there are no records of such a meeting. Therefore October 31st is the first known opportunity for Woodruff to transfer the Stephens books to Joseph.

From November 1-4, Woodruff records that he was sick, but getting better. On November 5th he records only one activity for the day: "I wrote a letter to Dr Bernhisel & also one to Father & Mother Carter."

Neither of those letters has been found. Instead, we have the letter from Joseph to Bernhisel, dated Nauvoo November 16, 1841, written in John Taylor's handwriting and mailed on the 23d.[118]

> Dear Sir
>
> I received your kind present by the hand of Er. [sic] Woodruff & feel myself under many obligations for this mark of your esteem & friendship which to me is **the more interesting** as it **unfolds** & developes [sic] many things that are of great importance to this generation & corresponds with & supports the testimony of The Book of Mormon; I have read the **volumnes** [sic] with the greatest interest & pleasure & must say that **of all histories that have been written** pertaining to the antiquities of this country it is the most correct luminous & comprehensive.—
>
> In regard to the land referred to by you I would simply state that I have land both in and out of the City some of which I hold deeds for and others bonds for deeds when you come which I hope will be as soon as convenient you can make such a selection from among those as shall best meet with your veiws [sic] & feelings. In gratefull [sic] remembrance of your kindness I remain your affectionate Brother in the bonds of the
>
> Everlasting Covenant
Joseph Smith

---

[118] Although the envelope has no postmark, it bears the notation, "Nauvoo Nov 23d" suggesting this is the day it was mailed or sent by courier. The numeral looks more like 25, but the "d" suggests 23. The letter is available in the Joseph Smith Papers here: http://josephsmithpapers.org/paperSummary/letter-to-john-bernhisel-16-november-1841?p=1&highlight=bernhisel

Figure 8 - Bernhisel letter 16 Nov. 1841

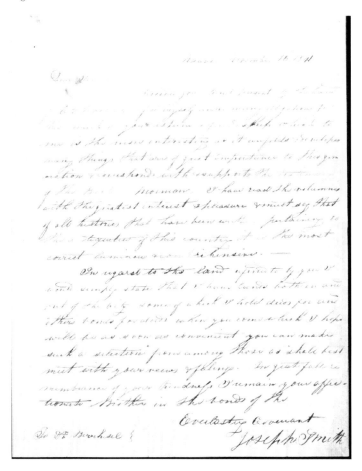

Apart from the letter itself, there is no entry in any known journal or any other document that corroborates any connection between Joseph and the note or its origins.

Certainly it's possible that Joseph dictated the note to John Taylor.

It is also possible he directed Taylor to write it without giving specifics. Or he may have directed someone else to write it and for Taylor to copy it. Joseph could have directed Taylor to add the part about the land transaction to the thank-you note Woodruff wrote on November 5th. In any of these cases, Joseph may or may not have reviewed the letter before it was sent.

Based on the evidence, we need to decide which the most likely scenario under the circumstances.

The note claims Joseph "read the volumnes [sic] with the greatest interest & pleasure." Because there are no sources that describe Joseph doing so, and because he never personally mentioned the books, we must consider extrinsic evidence and probabilities.[119]

First, it is somewhat surprising that Woodruff does not record that he gave the books to Joseph. Because of Woodruff's personal interest in them and his deep respect for the Prophet, one would expect Woodruff to note the Prophet's reaction, but his journal is silent on the matter. Neither he nor anyone else mentions that Joseph read them or discussed them with anyone—let alone that Joseph greeted them enthusiastically.

In fact, Woodruff's own enthusiasm about the books contrasts with his silence about Joseph's reaction—assuming Joseph *had* a reaction.

It would have been an extraordinary accomplishment for Joseph to read the Stephens books at all. Vol. I is 424 pages, plus illustrations, and Vol. II is 486 pages, plus illustrations and index. On top of that, the letter compares these books to "all histories that have been written pertaining to the antiquities of this country," a comparison that, if honest, would have required considerable additional reading beyond the Stephens books themselves.

---

[119] One author, citing no evidence other than the letter itself, concludes "Based upon current information it appears that Smith either dictated the letter to a scribe, or that he directed him to write to Bernhisel on his behalf using the words he deemed proper. In either case, it would be unlikely for Taylor or any other of his scribes to knowingly attribute to Smith views and opinions that were not his own or that were inconsistent with revelatory teachings of the Prophet. As with several other letters of this kind, it is reasonable to see the content of the letter to Bernhisel as an accurate representation of Joseph Smith's intent, if not his own words. Joseph Smith's comments are notable in that they constitute a very brief but informative book review expressing the Prophet's personal evaluation of what he had read." Matthew Roper, "John Bernhisel's Gift to a Prophet: Incidents of Travel in Central America and the Book of Mormon," *Interpreter: A Journal of Mormon Scripture* 16 (2015): 207-253. Of course, that argument simply assumes the conclusion that the letter originated with Joseph, a begging the question logical fallacy. In addition, the wording of the thank-you note is ambiguous enough to fit a variety of interpretations.

Joseph hardly lived a life of leisurely study. In December 1841, Joseph began re-reading the Book of Mormon, a project that took him several months. The Book of Mormon is shorter than Stephens' Vol. 1. And, apart from his own history, Joseph's journal mentions him reading not a single book other than the Book of Mormon during 1841-1842. Nor did any of his associates mentioned him reading any other books.

The exchange of letters between Joseph and Bernhisel offer insight into the time pressures Joseph faced during this period. He noted in the 13 April letter that "Yours of the 6th. ultimo is received, **which should have been answered before, had not I been so much engaged in the business of the conference.**" He added this postscript: "The Brethren in New York wrote to me sometime ago on the subject of Babtizm [baptism] for the dead please to inform them **I well attend to it as soon as I possibly can.** J. S."

On July 12, Bernhisel requested that Joseph purchase land and deposited $425 toward the $500 purchase price. Joseph replied on August 3, promising to buy a property "**the first opportunity I have.**" Joseph didn't purchase the land until January 4, 1842. This delay of five months, particularly when Joseph had already warned Bernhisel that land prices were rising rapidly, is consistent with other external evidence of the many demands on Joseph's time and attention.

Consider the note itself. Would Joseph Smith take the time to read these two lengthy books when he didn't have time to write, or even sign, a simple thank-you note?

Apart from the thank-you note, the sole evidence that Joseph ever saw these books is a receipt from the Nauvoo Library in 1844,[120] showing that Joseph donated a copy of the Stephens books along with many others. Here is the list of books he donated:

Review of Edwards on the Will
Life of Tecumseh
Whepleys Compend
Scotts Poetical Works in 5 vols

---

[120] http://mormonhistoricsites.org/wp-content/uploads/2013/04/The-Complete-Record-of-the-Nauvoo-Library-and-Literary-Institute.pdf

Gillmores Lectures

Merrills Harmony

Epicureo

Krumanachers Works

Catholic Piety

Home Physician

Apochryphal Testament

Bruns' Travels

Rebel & other Travels

Browns' Appeal. gram

Browns English Syntascope

Studies in Poetry & Prose

Old World & the New – Vol 1st

Voyage & Travels of Ross Perry & others

Bennetts Book Keeping 2 Copies

Incidents of Travel in Yucatan by Stephens

Stephens Travels in Central America

Mosheims Church History 1 Vol

Times & Seasons 1 2 & 3 Vol also Vol 1 & 2

Dick's Philosophy

Millenium & other Poems

Beaumonts Experiments

Dictionary of the Holy Bible

Parkers Lectures on Universalism

Sanders Discourse

Metropolitan

Goodrich's History of the United States

Doddridges Sermons

Catholic Manuel

Whelpleys Compend

Herveys Meditations

Historia de Charles

Rollin 2 Vol

Book of Mormon

This would be a formidable reading list for anyone, but in the context of 1840s Nauvoo, where Joseph functioned in multiple demanding capacities and often commented on how pressed he was, claims that Joseph read any of these books would require specific and unambiguous evidence that does not exist. As mentioned, his journals show him reading only two books: The Book of Mormon and his own history.

The assertion that Joseph read the Stephens books is consistent with similar assertions by critics of Joseph Smith who have suggested he was so well-read that he drew from multiple sources to compose the Book of Mormon and develop his unique theology.[121] In both cases, the assertions suffer from a lack of factual support.

Historical interpretation requires a weighing of evidence and probabilities in context; i.e., in light of all the known circumstances, personalities, and practical realities of life in the time and place under consideration. In this case, we have the bare fact of the 16 November letter. Juxtaposed with the totality of the circumstances of Joseph Smith's life in 1841 Nauvoo, the probability that Joseph read the Stephens books—not to mention all the other histories with which they compared—is *de minimus*.

The implausibility of Joseph Smith actually reading the Stephens books leads us to consider alternative explanations. Who else might have written the thank-you note?

The evidence points to Wilford Woodruff.

As previously mentioned, Woodruff read the books on his journey to Nauvoo from New York and wrote a letter to Bernhisel on November 5, 1841. Could this be the letter that was eventually dated November 16, 1841?

I think it is, for several reasons.

Although later letters from Woodruff to Bernhisel have been found,[122] no

---

[121] E.g., compare D. Michael Quinn, *Early Mormonism and the Magic World View* (Signature Books, 1987), and Grant Palmer, *An Insider's View of Mormon Origins* (Signature Books, 2002) with Roper, Fields, Nepal, cited previously.

[122] I discuss these later in this article.

letter dated November 5, 1841, is extant.[123] There is no record of prior correspondence between the two men. It is possible that Woodruff wrote his own thank-you letter to Bernhisel, but what is the likelihood that he would thank Bernhisel personally for a gift made to Joseph Smith? Quite low, it seems to me.

Nevertheless, Woodruff's enthusiasm for the books—an enthusiasm that would persist for years as we will see—would motivate him to thank Bernhisel somehow.

Recall that Woodruff wrote the letter after several days of illness that immediately followed his first mention of seeing Joseph Smith on October 31st—his first opportunity to give the Stephens books to Joseph. (More likely, given the Winchester proceeding on that date, he merely showed them—or mentioned them—to Joseph).

Assuming Woodruff gave the books to Joseph, there are two possible outcomes. Either Joseph read the books and dictated the 16 November letter, or he didn't read them and asked someone to write a thank-you note. We've seen that, apart from the letter itself, there is no evidence that Joseph ever read the books. On the other hand, we've seen that, at his earliest opportunity after meeting with Joseph, Woodruff wrote a letter to Bernhisel. A closer look at the letter suggests it was Woodruff's interpretation of what Joseph would want him to write.

The letter has two paragraphs. The first is the expression of appreciation for the Stephens book that reflects Woodruff's own reaction to the Stephens books as he read them. The second paragraph relates to the ongoing land transactions between Bernhisel and Joseph that were the topic of previous correspondence between the men. However, the note marks a distinct difference in the relationship.

In the previous correspondence, Joseph had agreed to purchase land on behalf of Bernhisel. In response, Bernhisel sent him the $425, followed by the $40 and the Stephens books. Now, instead of purchasing property for

---

[123] The discovery of such a letter would clarify what happened among Woodruff, Joseph, and Bernhisel.

Bernhisel, Joseph is telling him to come to Nauvoo soon and select a property himself.

Here's how I envision the scene. Woodruff comes to the Winchester disciplinary council on October 31ˢᵗ, the Stephens books in hand. He shows them to Joseph, along with Bernhisel's letter. Joseph asks Woodruff to read the letter. The dialogue goes something like this:

Joseph: "Brother Bernhisel wants me to buy property for him, but I don't have time. He has to live on it; he should pick it himself. Would you tell him to come to Nauvoo and select the property he wants?"

Woodruff: "Should I mention the books?"

Joseph: "Did you read them? What did you think?"

Woodruff: "They're most interesting."

Joseph: "Then thank him for them on my behalf."

Joseph then proceeds with the Winchester council and doesn't think about the Stephens books again.

The next day, Woodruff is sick. He doesn't feel good enough to even write a letter until November 5ᵗʰ, when he writes to Bernhisel and the Carters.

I realize this is conjecture, but it is a hypothesis based on the evidence that makes sense under the totality of the circumstances. I think it's the most complete explanation for the available evidence.

One obvious objection to Woodruff being the source of the 16 November letter: it is not in Woodruff's handwriting. He did not write that letter. The handwriting is John Taylor's.

A second obvious objection is that Woodruff wrote to Bernhisel on November 5ᵗʰ, but the letter attributed to Joseph was dated November 16ᵗʰ and mailed on the 23.

These two facts actually help explain what happened. I propose that Woodruff drafted the thank-you note part of the letter, but John Taylor added the part about the land transaction and copied Woodruff's note to make it one letter.

Before addressing that point, it's important to take a close look at the letter itself.

The wording of the thank-you note is brief and not exceptional; terms such as *generation, antiquities, luminous* and *comprehensive* are common in the *Times and Seasons* and other contemporary sources, including the writings of Woodruff, Taylor, and Joseph Smith.

The phrase "kind present" appears unique—I couldn't find another example in my database—but it may offer a useful clue because Woodruff used the terms in his journal with the same connotations.

For example, he wrote of people who "had been vary *kind* to me." He describes a sister who "possesses good and *kind* feeling." One brother "was made comfortable by the *kind* treatment" of a sister. He wrote that his "feelings have been often hurt since my arrival in Liverpool by the *unkind* feelings and speeches made towards me by" some of the Elders. He wrote of *kindness* and described people as *kindly*.

Joseph also used the terms *kind, kindly,* and *kindness*. This term, by itself, is so ubiquitous it has little if any probative value.

Present, though, may be a useful clue. Woodruff used the term *present* 144 times in his 1841-1845 journal. Many of these uses were in the sense of a gift. On Jan. 1, 1841, Woodruff wrote that one of his converts "made both of us a *present* of a nice silk handkerchief." Later that month he made another note about this: "She made me a *present* of 2 silk." In February, he recorded another "*present* of a nice silk hankerchief [sic]," "a *present* of a nice guilt frame,", and "a *present* of a large Hare." He relates, "I made him a *present* of the Book of Mormon." In March he received "a *present* of 3 shillings." In April, "I also received a *present* of a dress pattern… I had a *present* of a nice silk work bag." Before leaving England for America, Woodruff notes that he made "in all a *present* of Books of mormon to friends 42." He mentions several additional presents, including a case involving a friend of his who visited Nauvoo. "I made him a *present* of the above works," Woodruff wrote on April 12, 1842.

Unlike the term *kind,* I could not find a single use of the term *present* in the connotation of a gift in the writings of Joseph Smith or John Taylor. Joseph frequently used the term *gift,* of course, referring to gifts of God. Woodruff and Taylor also used the term *gift* in this spiritual context, but never in connection with a personal exchange.

This leads me to conclude that the phrase "kind present" would be expected from Woodruff but not from either Joseph or Taylor. This type of analysis is not determinative, but it corroborates one interpretation of the facts and contradicts the others.

The phrase "under many obligations" appears unique in my database, but "under obligation" appears in Woodruff's journals several times, while never in Joseph's or Taylor's writings.

Additional anomalies in the 16 November note offer more clues.

First, the thank-you note is addressed "Dear Sir." The three other letters from Joseph to Bernhisel, dated April 13, 1841, August 3, 1841, and January 4, 1842, are all addressed "Dear Brother," as are the letters from Bernhisel to Joseph dated July 12, 1841, August 18, 1841, and September 8, 1841.[124]

Of the seven extant letters between Joseph and Bernhisel, only the 16 November letter is addressed "Dear Sir," as if the author was not aware of the pattern of correspondence. It seems unlikely that Joseph would have dictated "Dear Sir" when the pattern he and Bernhisel otherwise followed was "Dear Brother."

A series of Woodruff's letters from the 1840s all start with "Dear Sir" or "Sir."[125] A letter dated May 8, 1849, starts "Elder Saml Dam Sir I have just…" A letter dated Nov. 27, 1849, starts "Hon A W. Babbit Dear Sir The deep…" I have looked at several examples of Woodruff's correspondence with Bernhisel and *in every case*, the letters start with "Dear Sir."

Here are two letters sent on consecutive days.

---

[124] http://josephsmithpapers.org/paperSummary/letter-from-john-bernhisel-8-september-1841?p=1&highlight=bernhisel#!/paperSummary/letter-from-john-bernhisel-8-september-1841&p=1

[125] The letters are found in MS 1352: Wilford Woodruff journals and papers 1828-1898, Wilford Woodruff letters, 1849, online at
https://dcms.lds.org/delivery/DeliveryManagerServlet?dps_pid=IE6378228

Figure 9 - Woodruff letter to Bernhisel 4 Dec. 1849

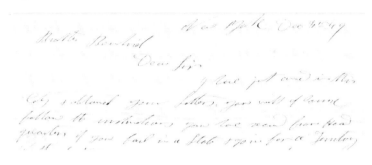

Figure 10 - Woodruff letter to Bernhisel 5 Dec. 1849

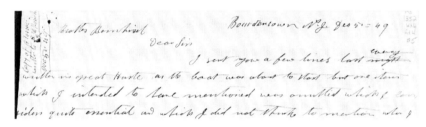

A letter dated March 26, 1850, starts the same way. A letter dated July 20 from the 1856 folder, shows "Dear Brother" replaced with "Dear Sir."[126]

---

[126] Wilford Woodruff journals and papers: Wilford Woodruff Outgoing Correspondence (retained copies), 1831-1861, Wilford Woodruff letters, 1856. Church History Library, The Church of Jesus Christ of Latter-day Saints, Salt Lake City, Utah, MS 1352, box 6, folder 6, item 17. https://dcms.lds.org/delivery/DeliveryManagerServlet?dps_pid=IE6361996

Figure 11 - Woodruff letter to Bernhisel 26 Mar. 1850

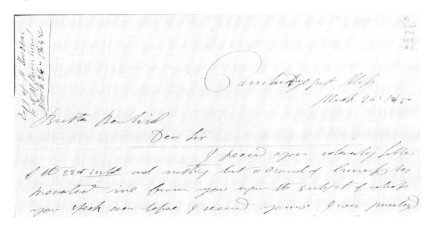

Figure 12 - Woodruff letter to Bernhisel 1856

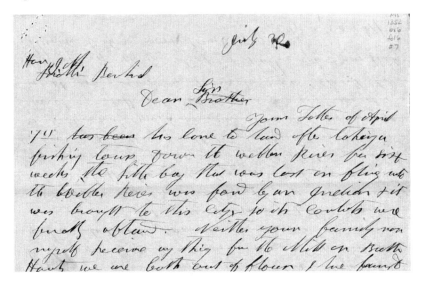

Because this July letter is in the folder of retained copies, presumably this is a draft of a letter, prepared by Woodruff for someone else to write out formally—without the editing changes—and then send. It's anyone's guess why the first draft read "Brother Bernhisel" and "Dear Brother," compared with the final version "Hon. J. M. Bernhisel" and "Dear Sir," but I suggest this change reflects Woodruff's sign of respect to Dr. Bernhisel.

Other letters in this folder show similar signs of editing. Of course, it's a normal practice to draft letters and make changes before finalizing them. This practice, combined with the Woodruff's pattern of using "Dear Sir" as the salutation generally and with Bernhisel specifically, matches the 16 November 1841 letter to Bernhisel and therefore corroborates the theory that Woodruff drafted the thank-you note and John Taylor added the land transaction paragraph before sending it.

A second anomaly is the spelling in the letter, which includes some unusual features. "Comprihensive" is a unique misspelling. Close examination suggests the writer may have dotted an original "e" for some reason. I haven't found any other examples of this spelling. However, the spelling of "volumnes" may be significant. While it's true that spelling was not uniform in 1842, this spelling with the "n" is not a recognized variant in the 1828 Webster's dictionary. It appeared in Early Modern English but is not found in the Bible. It appears to be unique to Woodruff, with only a single exception noted below. Woodruff uses variant spellings in his journal from 1841 through 1884. Here are the variant spellings Woodruff used in 1841 (Vol. 2, 1841-1845):

April 3rd – p. 80: Moved by Elder Young seconded by Elder Richards that Elder Parley P. P. Pratt Conduct the Publication of the Millennial Star as Editor and Sole proprietor of the same after the Close of this present **volumn.**

April 14th – p. 88: I spent the day counting out the Millennial Stars. I obtained for my share 76 whole **volums.**

April 16th – p. 90: Baptized more than 5,000 souls Printed 5,000 Books of mormon 3000 Hymn Books 2,500 **Volumes** of the Millennial Star & about 50,000 tracts, & gatherd to the land of Joseph 1,000 Souls

June 4th – p. 105: 4th I wrote a letter to D.C. Smith. Sent for the second **volumn** of times & Seasons to be sent to Aphek Woodruff from Commencment to Ezra Carter from 13th No.

September 7 – p. 124: I recieved $40 dollars of Dr John M Bernhisel for President Joseph Smith also Stephens travels in central America in 2 **volums** also one letter.

In 1845, Woodruff made these entries:

July "28th Monday In company with Elder Hedlock I counted all of John Taylors Times & Seasons IV & Vth **volumns** & found the following to be the exact number now remaining:"

September "23d   I wrote three letters to friends. I recieved by Amos Fielding 7 letters from Nauvoo from Kimball Webster Ells & Br Young And the remainder of the Times & Seasons from Br John Taylor to finish out the whole of the Vth **volumn**."

November 2nd, "This Publication has continued from that time untill the present month Just five years being now on the VI volumn... The Nauvoo Neighbor was published commencing on the 1st of May 1843 & has continued untill the present time. Is now in its third **volumn**."

Woodruff continued this spelling throughout his journal. Notice how often he refers to his interest in history, which is also reflected in the Bernhisel thank-you note.

July 10, 1848 (Vol. 3) – p. 357 "I bought the six **volumns** of the Times & seasons of Babbit for $7."

October 21, 1865 (Vol. 6) – p. 254 "My Journal is Continued in 2d **volumn** red Covered Book."

June 2, 1866 (Vol. 6) – p. 287 "I signed with Parley Pratt for the History of the Rebelion in two **volums** for the H.O. for $5."

Sept. 16, 1881 (Vol. 8) – p. 51 "O Pratt was appointed Historian May 9, 1874, making his labor as Historian for 7 years up to May 7, 1881. During this time He has got up a history documentary [p.52] for 22 years, Making 34 **volumes** of 41,259 Pages, averaging 1,213 1/2 pages each vol, at a cost of $12,377.70. There was 54 pages of indexing for Each vol as title page, making $400 per **volumn** including Binding, paper, ruling pens and ink and indexing. Total $13,600. But none of this work has been Compared with its Copy."

Sept 22, 1884 (Vol. 8) – p. 277 "I spent my last day with Mr H. H. Bancroft the great Historian of the last days. He is writing up the western Country in 32 **volums** and devotes one vol to Utah and the Mormons and he has been spending some 3 weeks in our office searching our histories and looking to us for information that he may make a Correct record as a true historian."

This spelling is significant because the word is never spelled this way in the *Journal of Discourses* or in a database of John Taylor, Parley P. Pratt, Benjamin Winchester, Oliver Cowdery, Orson Pratt, William Smith, and Joseph Smith.

It is spelled this way in three places in the *Times and Seasons*:

Vol. 1:9, p. 137 (July 1840) ... I shall not attempt to fathom the depths of our persecution, though **volumns** be written on the subject which would tell a tale that would make the savage of the wilderness blush, or the barbarian hide his head for shame.

This is an undated letter written by A [Alanson] Ripley, Bishop, to the saints. It is the only example of this spelling I could find outside of Woodruff's writings.

By coincidence, Brother Ripley is connected to an unrelated example of how Joseph Smith directed others to write in his name. On 26 March 1841, William Clayton recorded in his diary, "Friday. I went over the river to see Brother Ripley and ask his council. I called at the store and made Joseph acquainted with the circumstance who ordered Brother Thompson to write a few lines to Bishop Ripley in his name requesting him to take the matter into his own hands and appear with me before the justice. I saw Brother Ripley who said I need trouble myself no further he would see to it."[127]

Another example of Joseph's pattern occurred two years later, on 9 November 1843, when he received a letter from James Arlington Bennet. His journal records that he "gave instruction to have it answered." The following Monday, 13 November, the journal entry says "called at the office A M. with Hyrum and heard Judge [William W.] Phelps read letter to Jas A Bennet & made some corrections."[128]

In the first case, there is no record that Joseph reviewed the letter, but in the second case, he did. The difference is the importance of the letter. Bennet's letter announced he intended to run for Governor of Illinois.

---

[127] William Clayton diary, available online at http://www.boap.org/LDS/Early-Saints/clayton-diaries

[128] *Journals*, Vol. 3, May 1843—June 1844, Joseph Smith Papers, (The Church Historian's Press, 2015), p. 128.

Joseph refused to assist him. Both letters were published in the *Times and Seasons*. Obviously, Joseph would take care to get the wording just right under these circumstances. It took Phelps four days to draft the letter for Joseph's review.

Here is the second unusual spelling of *volume* in the *Times and Seasons*:

Vol. 3:12, p. 761 (April 15, 1842): NOTICE. On looking over our subscription list we find many who have paid but one dollar, on the present **volumne**, which pays for six months; and as that time expires with this number, all who wish the paper continued to the end of the **volumne** would do well to forward the money immediately.

Woodruff was in charge of the business aspects of the printing shop so this notice would naturally come from him. The third and final misspelling is another example of a business-related notice of the type Woodruff would be responsible for.

Vol. 5:9, p. 519 (May 1, 1844) TO OUR SUBSCRIBERS. We take this opportunity of informing our subscribers that the present number of the Times and Seasons (No. 9.) closes the year with a considerable portion of our readers, we therefore acquaint all those who have honored us with their patronage, that we have adoped [sic] one uniform plan, without respect of persons. viz.-That the Times and Seasons will be discontinued, in every case (where the time has expired) should the subscriptions not be renewed before our next publication. Our friends will therefore see the necessity of making arrangements without delay. Should any of our readers be in want of any of the back numbers they can be supplied by calling at the office. Also the first, second, third, and fourth **volumns** may be obtained.

It is also noteworthy that the boilerplate at the end of the issue reads thus: "JOHN TAYLOR, EDITOR AND PROPRIETOR. Terms.-Two Dollars per annum, payable in all cases in advance. Any person procuring five new subscribers, and forwarding us Ten Dollars current money, shall receive one **volume** gratis. All letters must be addressed to John Taylor, editor, POST PAID, or they will not receive attention."

John Taylor used the term *volume* three times in his *Mediation and Atonement,* all spelled v-o-l-u-m-e. I have found other uses in his correspondence from 1840 to 1850 and in his 1844-5 Nauvoo diary, all of which spell the term v-o-l-u-m-e. I can find no example of him spelling the term any other way. Nor could I find the term "volumn" in any writings of early Church authors, apart from Woodruff. Even my search for "volumn" in the Joseph Smith Papers produced zero results.

The question remains, why would Taylor misspell the word in the Bernhisel letter but nowhere else?

Upon reflection, the answer is simple. Taylor was copying Woodruff's thank-you note as the first part of the Bernhisel letter and retained the original spelling, whether intentionally or because of the copying process.

It's also interesting that in the second paragraph, the spelling of the term *veius* appears only in John Taylor's writings, again corroborating the theory that he wrote the last paragraph but copied the first one.

While there is no evidence that Joseph ever read or cared about the Stephens books, Woodruff took great interest in them. Here are his journal entries that mention Stephens.

Sept. 13, 1841 – "I spent the day in reading the 1ˢᵗ vol. of INCIDENTS OF TRAVELS IN Central America Chiapas and Yucatan BY JOHN L STEPHEN'S... I felt truly interested in this work for it brought to light a flood of testimony in proof of the book of Mormon in the discovery & survey of the city Copan in Central America A correct drawing of the monuments pyramids, portraits, & Hieroglyphics as executed by Mr. Catherwood is now presented before the publick & is truly a wonder to the world. Their whole travels were truly interesting." (emphasis mine, spelling and punctuation original)

Sept. 16, 1841 – "I perused the 2d Vol of **Stephens** travels In Central America Chiapas of Yucatan & the ruins of Palenque & Copan. It is truly one of the most interesting histories I have ever read."

August 17, 1843 [in New York] – "Elder O. Pratt addressed the people concerning the Book of Mormon. He spoke in an edifying manner concerning the Book of Mormon its history what it was &c. That it was a History of nearly one half of the globe & the people that inhabited it, that it gave a history of all those cities that have been of late discoverd by Cartherwood & **Stephens**, that it named those cities That it spoke of the esstablishing of our goverment & what is more highly interesting it reveals its final fate & destiny, so that by reading the Book of mormon you can clearly see what will befal this nation, and what will be its final end."

October 2, 1843 [in New York] – "I Bought all of **Stephens** works for J Taylor. Paid cash. $8.00"

October 17, 1843 – A cold day among the mountains. We had a slight squal of hall or snow. I have been for the last two days reading **Stephens** works & travels in Yucatan his second work. I red his first work on my Journey to Nauvoo with family in 1841. I found them highly interesting & also the present work. It is a great proof of the truth of the Book of Mormon. I read them with the highest degree of interest.

18th We continued to Clime the mountains by locks. It is more mild than it was yesterday. I spent the day reading **Stephens** works. We came to the end of the canal east of the Allegany mountain in the evening. The road during the day was vary mountaineous. Was 47 locks in 30 miles. A good deal of the way was in the Juneatta river.

22d Sunday Left Beaver & rode to wheeling & spent the night. I finished reading **Stephens** travels & found them highly interesting.

January 18, 1844 – It was A rainy day. I visited & administered to several sick but I spent most of the day in reading the first vol of **Stephens** travels in Egypt, Arabia, Petrea and the Holy Land, and I was highly edified with it.

19th I parted with Elder Wm. Smith in the morning who went to Lowell. I spent the day with Br Little. I read during the day the second vol of **Stephens** travels in Egypt Arabia & the Holy Land &c. And I was exeedingly interested in the same Thinking that perhaps I might follow his footsteps over some of the same ground in some of my travels in the earth. It was interesting to trace him in his travels through Edom among the Palaces Cut out of the Solid rock and through the Holy land, visiting the Holy sepulcher and all places spoken of in the scripture.

A few years later, in February 1846, Woodruff was crossing the Atlantic on his way home from England when he recorded more evidence of his fascination with history.

February 18, 1846 – I have spent most of the last two days reading the travels of Edward Daniel Clark, L.L.D. through Russia Tartary and Turkey which I found to be highly interesting. His style of writing is quite similar to that to **Stephen**[s]. He draws however a Horrid picture of the whole Russin [sic] Nation.

These excerpts from Woodruff's journal show that he had a long-lasting and extensive interest in history. An overview of Woodruff's later contributions as Church Historian includes this observation:

> Woodruff began to love history as he came of age. Biographer Matthias Cowley wrote that though Woodruff hated to read as a child, he soon came to describe the act of reading as "most exaltant" and "most delightsome." Before joining the church, he had already read "histories of the United States, England, Scotland, Greece, and Rome," as well as the works of Josephus, which were popular during the period.[6] Thus, he came into the church with the importance of historical work already planted in his mind.[129]

For example, One September 12, 1840, Woodruff wrote "a lengthy historical letter" to Heber C. Kimball, the first letter he wrote to Kimball.[130] In it, he describes visits to the Tower of London, St. Paul's Cathedral, etc. He recorded in his journal that August 21, 1840: "This was the most interesting day of my life as far as viewing the splendid works of man was concerned."

On March 6, 1841, Woodruff was at a member's home in England where he spent the day "reading the history of Rome" by Edward Coxe. He wrote four pages of notes in his journal.

On May 14, 1841, while crossing the Atlantic, he records "I commenced reading the History of England by the Rev John Adams."

Woodruff's extensive reading of history is consistent with the comment in the 16 November 1841 thank-you note: "of all histories that have been written pertaining to the antiquities of this country it is the most correct luminous & comprehensive." It was Wilford Woodruff, not Joseph Smith,

---

[129] Benjamin E. Park, "Developing a Historical Conscience: Wilford Woodruff and the Preservation of Church History," chapter 5 in *Preserving the History of the Latter-day Saints*, Richard E. Turley Jr. and Steven C. Harper, editors (Religious Studies Center, BYU, Provo, Utah, and Deseret Book Company, Salt Lake City, Utah, 2010), available online here: https://rsc.byu.edu/archived/preserving-history-latter-day-saints/front-matter-0 Fn 6 in the original is to Matthias F. Cowley, *Wilford Woodruff* (Salt Lake City: Deseret News, 1909), 25.

[130] Scott H. Faulring, "Wilford Woodruff's Historical 'Address,'" *Mormon Historical Studies* (Fall 2000), p. 111, online at http://mormonhistoricsites.org/wp-content/uploads/2013/05/mhs1.2FaulringFall2000.pdf

who was familiar with "all histories that have been written."

Under the totality of these circumstances, it seems unlikely that a busy Joseph Smith would read the Stephens books in the first place, and far more likely that he would ask Woodruff to send a thank-you note to Bernhisel—or that Woodruff would have suggested such a note. Woodruff had personally accepted the gift from Bernhisel and had read the volumes with pleasure. His enthusiasm led him to purchase copies for John Taylor—which is another interesting point.

Woodruff purchased the copies for Taylor in October 1843. Joseph donated copies to the Nauvoo Library only a few months later, sometime between January and April 1844 (along with numerous other books). Woodruff doesn't explain why he needed to buy copies for Taylor if Joseph already had them. If Joseph was going to donate them to the library anyway, surely he would have loaned them to Taylor upon request.

Maybe Woodruff wanted copies—particularly of the latest set of Stephens' travels in Yucatan, published in 1843—to read on the way home from New York. It's also interesting that on August 27, 1843, at a conference in New York attended by some of the Quorum of the Twelve, John Page and Orson Pratt discussed the Book of Mormon. Woodruff records that Pratt

> spoke in an edifying manner concerning the Book of Mormon its history what it was &c. That it was a History of nearly one half of the globe & the people that inhabited it, that it gave a history of all those cities that have been of late discoverd by Cartherwood & Stephens, that it named those cities That it spoke of the esstablishing of our goverment & what is more highly interesting it reveals its final fate & destiny, so that by reading the Book of mormon you can clearly see what will befal this nation, and what will be its final end. In that Book you will find recorded the pure principles of the gospel of Jesus Christ as taught by himself on the continant of America so plain that no two persons could disagree as to the points of doctrin set forth.

Did Orson Pratt read the Bernhisel copies, or did he own his own?

Pratt's claim that the Book of Mormon "named those cities" is quite interesting. Perhaps he had been making similar claims earlier that led to the Zarahemla article in the *Times and Seasons*. Woodruff's comments seem deferential to Pratt's expertise; Woodruff never made a similar claim of his own, even though he, too, had read the Stephens books.

I've tried to track down the actual books donated to the Nauvoo Library, so far to no avail.

So far, the evidence shows these facts connected to the 16 November 1841 letter:

1. It is the only one in the series between Joseph and Bernhisel that begins with "Dear Sir" instead of "Dear Brother."
2. All known correspondence between Woodruff and Bernhisel begins with "Dear Sir."
3. There are other examples of draft letters in Woodruff's files, including a draft letter to Bernhisel that changes "Dear Brother" to "Dear Sir."
4. The spelling of "volumnes" in the letter is unique, except for in the other writings of Woodruff.
5. Woodruff had a great interest in history generally.
6. Woodruff had a special interest in the work of John Lloyd Stephens.
7. There are other examples of Joseph Smith directing people to write letters on his behalf.
8. In October and November 1841, Joseph was busy with numerous responsibilities.
9. Apart from the letter itself, there are no contemporary accounts of Joseph reading or even acknowledging the Stephens books. Not even Woodruff mentions giving the books to Joseph, Joseph's reaction to them, etc.

As previously mentioned, Woodruff did not write the 16 November letter because it is not in his handwriting. Plus, he wrote a letter to Bernhisel on 5 November. If Woodruff wrote the original draft for the letter on 5 November, what accounts for the discrepancy in dates?

Here is the sequence of events in November 1841 that Woodruff recorded in his journal. The detail helps put the evidence in context:

5 November: "I wrote a letter to Dr. Bernhisel & also one to Father and Mother Carter."
6 November: "I attended the city counsel [sic] for the first time.

7 November: "Sunday. I first called upon Br. Joseph with some of the Twelve."

8-13 November: [He worked on his house.]

14 November: "Sunday. I met in counsel with the Twelve… Joseph preached to a large congregation at the Temple."

15 November: "I laid a floor in my bedroom."

16 November: "I run 12 bushels of lime for plastering & rode in company with J. H. Hale 2 ½ miles on the prairie to Br Zerah Pulsiphers. I bought for acres of land of him in section 32 for $44 dollars. I paid him $20 dollars in silver & am to pay him the other $24 dollars in a year. The ground is ploughed. I met in the evening with the company owning the land. They appointed me to sell some of the land to raise the money to pay Brother Daniel S. Miles Part on the land."

17 November: "I sold 5 acres of Daniel S. Miles land in section 32 for $10 per acre to Sister Mary Pitt for which she paid me $50 dollars in gold which money I delivered to Zerah Pulsipher as one of the committee of the company. He gave his recept [sic] for the Same."

18th I spent the day in lathing.

19th I assisted Daniel S Miles in Selling 16 acres of land in Section 32 for $10 dollars per acre. I also bought of Daniel S Miles 5 acres of land in Section 32 at $10 dollars per acre. Am to give my notes when I get a bond for a deed.

20th I spent the day making lime morter &c. I attended the city council at night.

21 st Sunday I met in Council with the Twelve at Elder B. Youngs. Then attended the general Assembly near the Temple. Heard a discours by Elder Taylor followed by President Hyram Smith. I then met the Twelve at B. Youngs untill 4 o-clock at which time we repaired to the Baptismal Font in the Temple for the purpose of Baptizing for the dead, for the remision of Sins & for healing. It was truly an interesting seene. It was the first FONT erected for this glorious purpose in this last dispensation. It was dedicated By President Joseph Smith & The Twelve for Baptizing for the Dead &c & this was the first time the font had been prepared for the reception of candidates. On the sabbath a large Congregation assembled. Elders B. Young H C Kimball & J Taylor went forward & Baptized about 40 persons. Elders W Richards, G. A. Smith & myself assisted in confirming them. I then Spent the evening with the Twelve at Br Kimball.

Nov 22d I got my Bedroom plastered by J. Hodson.

23d I spent the day to work at home.

24th I Commenced taking charge of the provision store for the committee of the Nauvoo House. I also cut & drew two loads of wood to my door.

25th I spent a part of the day at the store. We have a severe snow storm. About 200 Saints have just landed at warsaw from England. It is bad for them in this snow storm.

26th A Cold morning. I spent the day at home. **I mailed a letter to father Carters family.**

This record shows that two days after writing to Bernhisel on the 5th, Woodruff met with Joseph Smith. It's possible he discussed the letter, or even gave it to Joseph to review, but there is no evidence one way or another on that point. He could have simply told Joseph he'd written the thank-you note. Maybe the topic never arose again between the two men.

Obviously, a discovery of Woodruff's letters to the Carters from November 1841 would clarify the sequence of events. Currently, the Wilford Woodruff collection of correspondence at the Church History Library has a gap between May 24, 1841, and March 12, 1846.[131] The collection of retained copies of outgoing correspondence has a gap between September 12, 1840 and May 1845.[132] We are left to interpret the evidence in light of all the circumstances.

Woodruff spent the next week working on his house. His journal doesn't mention Bernhisel or the letter again, as might be expected whether he had mailed the letter or had drafted the thank-you note and given it to Joseph or Taylor to send. Again, the evidence is equivocal.

However, a detail from Woodruff's journal may help explain the time delays. When he wrote a letter to Bernhisel on November 5th, he also wrote a letter to "Father and Mother Carter," (the parents of his wife Phebe). Then, in the 26th, Woodruff records "I mailed a letter to father Carters family." It's odd that he doesn't mention *mailing* the 5 November letter or *writing* the 26 November letter. Woodruff rarely mentions mailing letters; in Volume 2 of his journal (1841-1845), he only recorded mailing letters twelve times, despite having written hundreds of letters. When he does refer to mailing letters, he usually wrote about writing them first. For example, on January 13 and 14, 1841, he wrote a letter to Phebe that he mailed on the 18th. On

---

[131] Wilford Woodruff collection: Correspondence. Church History Library, Salt Lake City, Utah, MS 19509.

[132] Wilford Woodruff journals and papers: Wilford Woodruff Outgoing Correspondence (retained copies), 1831-1861, Wilford Woodruff letters, 1845-1846. Church History Library, Salt Lake City, Utah, MS 1352.

February 19, 1841, Woodruff wrote "I mailed the two letters to Phebe & Father Woodruff" that he described writing the day before. Later, in August 1844, he recorded that he wrote a letter to Azmon Woodruff on the 20th but didn't mail it until the 24th, when the boat he was on arrived in port. On April 1, 1845, he wrote "one large sheet" to Brigham Young, which he mailed on the 3rd.

Woodruff recorded writing only the two November 5th letters for the entire month of November. He was conscientious about keeping track of his activities; at the end of each year, he listed the number of miles traveled, the number of meetings he held, the number of people he baptizes, etc. At the end of 1841, Woodruff recorded "Wrote 100 Letters & Received 67 Letters." (In his journal for 1841, Woodruff mentioned writing 93 letters, but some of these references could have meant multiple letters, such as this one: "I wrote a letter to Br Azmon & Thompson W."). It would be uncharacteristic of Woodruff to write a second letter to the Carters in November without noting that fact.

His prolific letter writing argues against the idea that Woodruff would have someone else copy a letter he drafted, but there is good reason to think the letter to Dr. Bernhisel would be an exception. Most of the letters Woodruff wrote were to family and friends. The 5 November 1841 letters were the first letters he records writing after he returned to Nauvoo, and the only letters he wrote that month. Because we don't have the 5 November letter, we don't know what Woodruff's handwriting looked like on that day, after he'd been sick for several days, but based on the documents we do have, including other letters and his journal, we would expect there to be some corrections on his first draft of this letter. Although Woodruff wrote often, his penmanship was not good. His journal is written in cramped printed characters, [133] while his correspondence is mostly written in cursive that is often difficult to decipher.

Taylor used straight lines and consistent style.

A letter to Dr. Bernhisel would be different from other letters he wrote. Woodruff was explicitly enthusiastic about and impressed by the Stephens

---

[133] Two pages of Woodruff's journal are visible here:
https://history.lds.org/exhibit/foundations-of-faith?lang=eng#mv28.

books. He would want to make a good impression on the New York doctor, particularly because he was writing on behalf of Joseph Smith. This would require no line outs or corrections on the letter itself, as well as clear, legible writing. Perhaps he would have thought it inappropriate to send a letter written in his own hand when he was referring to himself in the third person, again on behalf of Joseph.

What would account for the delay between writing the Carter letter on the 5th and mailing it on the 26th? Maybe he had someone copy that one as well, although that seems unlikely given the long history of correspondence between Woodruff and the Carters. It's possible he wrote the letter to the Carters and set it aside, forgetting about it until Taylor returned the Bernhisel letter to him for approval and mailing. The Bernhisel letter wasn't sent until the 23rd, so whatever caused the delays for that letter may have caused the delay for the Carter letter.

On November 16th, Woodruff rode out to the home of Zera Pulsipher, the man who baptized Woodruff near Richland, NY, on December 31, 1833. Woodruff purchased property on that occasion. There does not appear to be any connection between Woodruff's land transactions and the land purchased for Bernhisel as indicated in the letter to Bernhisel dated January 4, 1842, but presumably Taylor was involved with the real estate business in Nauvoo and it makes sense that he would add the second paragraph.

Unless and until additional evidence surfaces, the evidence points to Wilford Woodruff as the original author of the first paragraph (the thank-you note), with John Taylor copying Woodruff's note and adding the second paragraph about the land transaction.

One objection to consider is whether Wilford Woodruff would have represented to Dr. Bernhisel that Joseph had read the Stephens books, when in fact it was Woodruff and not Joseph who read them. In the context of a private thank-you note that Joseph didn't even sign, this objection is overly technical. In the first place, the letter is vague.[134] It refers to the "kind present" that "unfolds & developes many things that are of great importance

---

[134] I discuss the contents of the letter in more detail in *The Lost City of Zarahemla*.

to this generation & corresponds with & supports the testimony of the Book of Mormon." That can be taken in any number of ways, including the idea that the descendants of the surviving Lamanites migrated southward to Central America (an interpretation that would actually correspond to the dating of the ruins Stephens describes, which are not from the Book of Mormon era). In the second place, it is not only the claim that Joseph read the Stephens books that is problematic, but worse is the assertion that he had compared the Stephens books to "all histories that have been written pertaining to the antiquities of this country." Only Woodruff could—or would—make such a claim..

Finally, the question often arises about whether, even given its lack of specificity, the letter accurately reflects Joseph's views on the underlying question of Book of Mormon geography and historicity. There is a pervasive, long-held assumption that Joseph's close associates, including Wilford Woodruff and John Taylor, knew what he thought about every topic.

But Woodruff himself dismissed that assumption.

On Nov. 1, 1844, just months after the martyrdom, Woodruff wrote:

I also had another dream. Was in the Presence of Br Joseph Smith. Was conversing about his death. Told him I felt bad about it & If I had known he would have been taken away so soon I should have conversed more with him & asked him more questions. Said it was not his fault that I did not.

In 1892, Woodruff was asked about what Joseph thought on an important topic. He said, ""I have heard representations that the doctrine [on marriage] as put into the book of doctrine and covenants . . . by Oliver Cowdery . . . was represented as being contrary to the wishes of Joseph smith, but I couldn't swear that that was the fact."[135] The assumption Joseph's closest associates knew what he thought about every topic is more wishful thinking than a historically verified, or even supported, reality.

---

[135] Brian C. Hales, "'Guilty of Such Folly'? Accusations of Adultery or Polygamy against Oliver Cowdery," in *Days Never to Be Forgotten: Oliver Cowdery*, Religious Studies Center, BYU, available online at https://rsc.byu.edu/archived/days-never-be-forgotten-oliver-cowdery/10-guilty-such-folly-accusations-adultery-or#_edn34, citing Wilford Woodruff, testimony given at the Temple Lot Case, Part 3, Question 769, 70 (complete transcript).

Chapter 8: The Wentworth Letter

THE 1 MARCH 1842 EDITION OF THE *TIMES AND SEASONS* CONTAINS one of the significant contributions by Joseph Smith to appear in 1842. Like the Book of Abraham and the letters he would write in September, the Wentworth letter would, in part, be canonized. The Articles of Faith in the Pearl of Great Price are taken from this letter.

Elder Bruce R. McConkie of the Quorum of the Twelve Apostles spoke at an August 1984 symposium on the New Testament at BYU. He wrote:

> Also by way of having all things in perspective, we should be aware that there are approved and inspired writings that are not in the standard works. These writings also are true and should be used along with the scriptures themselves in learning and teaching the gospel. Next to the standard works five of the greatest documents in our literature are—

> 1. The "Wentworth Letter." (See History of the Church, 4:535-41.) Written by the Prophet Joseph Smith, it contains an account of the coming forth of the Book of Mormon, of the ancient inhabitants of the Americas, of the organization of the Church in this dispensation, and of the persecutions suffered by the early Latter-day Saints. The thirteen Articles of Faith are part of this letter.[136]

The Church published a lesson manual in 2011 titled *Teachings of the Presidents of the Church—Joseph Smith*. The manual contains an entire chapter on the Wentworth letter.[137] However, a key portion of the letter was deleted, as I explain below.

---

[136] Excerpt from *The Bible, a Sealed Book*, available online at http://emp.byui.edu/SATTERFIELDB/Talks/BibleSealedBook.html

[137] The chapter is available here. https://www.lds.org/manual/teachings-joseph-smith/chapter-38?lang=eng&query=Wentworth+letter

The Wentworth letter had its origins in a pamphlet written by Orson Pratt titled *An Interesting Account of Several Remarkable Visions, and of the Late Discovery of Ancient American Records.* Joseph used Pratt's pamphlet as a source, adopting some of it word for word. However, he made some detailed and significant doctrinal changes to Pratt's material.

One of the most significant changes involved Book of Mormon geography. Pratt described in some detail a hemispheric model for Book of Mormon setting.

Joseph Smith edited it out.

He replaced it with a simple statement that the remnant of the Book of Mormon people are the Indians that live in this country.

That statement was part of the passage that was inexplicably omitted from the 2011 Church manual.

Joseph used the Wentworth letter as the basis for an essay published as "Latter Day Saints"[138] in September 1843, thereby reaffirming the points he made in the Wentworth letter. W. W. Phelps made some additions to that letter. There is some speculation that Phelps may have contributed to—or even composed—the Wentworth letter itself. I find that unlikely because Phelps was not known for concise writing. The edits made to Pratt's work focus on simplifying, clarifying, and correcting doctrinal errors. Those are the type of edits Joseph would be expected to make.

Because we have only the printed version, however, it is possible that Phelps edited Orson Pratt's pamphlet, or took extracts from it, as a working document for Joseph Smith to edit personally. This is all speculation, however; so far as I know, there is no historical evidence one way or the other as to the relative contributions to the Wentworth letter made by

---

[138] The essay was a response to a request from Clyde, Williams & Co. of Harrisburg, Pennsylvania, for an account of the Church. It was eventually published in April 1844. For more information, see
http://josephsmithpapers.org/paperSummary/?target=x4786#!/paperSummary/latter-day-saints-1844&p=7

Phelps, Joseph, or anyone else.

All we know is Joseph's name appears in print as a signature after the letter, and it is written in first person.

In *Zarahemla* I included an abbreviated table that shows a few of the changes Joseph made. This table includes the entire letter (except for the Missouri portion). The left column is Orson Pratt's pamphlet; the right column is Joseph Smith's letter. Joseph's edits are shown in the left column with strike-throughs for deletions and ***bold italics*** for additions.

Some passages in the right column are bolded for emphasis.

AN INTERESTING ACCOUNT OF SEVERAL REMARKABLE VISIONS, AND OF THE LATE DISCOVERY OF ANCIENT AMERICAN RECORDS WHICH RESPECT THE HISTORY OF THAT CONTINENT FROM THE EARLIEST AGES AFTER THE FLOOD, TO THE BEGINNING OF THE FIFTH CENTURY OF THE CHRISTIAN ERA. WITH A SKETCH OF THE RISE, FAITH, AND DOCTRINE OF THE CHURCH OF JESUS CHRIST OF LATTER DAY SAINTS. Orson Pratt 1840	"CHURCH HISTORY" T&S 3:9, 1 Mar. 1842, pp. 706-710 (known as the Wentworth Letter) Joseph Smith
	At the request of Mr. John Wentworth, Editor, and Proprietor of the "Chicago Democrat," I have written the following sketch of the rise, progress, persecution, and faith of the Latter-Day Saints, of which I have the honor, under God, of being the founder. Mr. Wentworth says, that he wishes

<table>
<tr>
<td></td>
<td>to furnish Mr. Bastow, a friend of his, who is writing the history of New Hampshire, with this document. As Mr. Bastow has taken the proper steps to obtain correct information **all that I shall ask at his hands, is, that he publish the account entire, ungarnished, and without misrepresentation.** (emphasis mine)</td>
</tr>
</table>

Comment: Joseph made this request because a previous letter he had written had been edited. In 2011, the Church published a manual titled "Teachings of the Presidents of the Church: Joseph Smith." Chapter 38 is on the Wentworth letter. However, the Church Curriculum Department *deleted a key portion of the letter*, which I'll point out below. Joseph was concerned that Mr. Bastow would not publish the entire letter as Joseph requested, but it was the Church Curriculum Committee that actually omitted key portions of the letter.

Fortunately, the entire letter is available from many sources, including the July 2002 Ensign.[139]

<table>
<tr>
<td>~~Mr Joseph Smith, jun., who made the following important discovery,~~ *I* was born in the town of Sharon, Windsor county, Vermont, on the 23d of December, a.d. 1805. When ten years old, ~~his~~ *my* parents, ~~with their family,~~ *re*moved to Palmyra, New York; ~~in the vicinity of which he~~ *where we* resided for about ~~eleven~~ *four* years, ~~the latter part in~~ *and from thence we removed to* the town of Manchester.</td>
<td>I was born in the town of Sharon, Windsor County, Vermont, on the 23rd of December, A.D. 1805. When ten years old, my parents removed to Palmyra, New York, where we resided about four years, and from thence we removed to the town of Manchester.</td>
</tr>
</table>

Comment: Joseph shortens the text and corrects a detail, but doesn't correct the grammar (his parents didn't move to Palmyra when *they* were ten years old), possibly because this passage was taken from Joseph's original 1832 history, complete with the same grammatical error, albeit in different words.[140] ("at the age of about ten years my Father Joseph Smith Seignior moved to Palmyra Ontario County in the State of New York.")

---

[139] The July 2002 *Ensign* is available online here: https://www.lds.org/ensign/2002/07/the-wentworth-letter?lang=eng

[140] Joseph Smith History circa summer 1832, in *JS Letterbook*, JS Collection, CHL. Available online at http://josephsmithpapers.org/paperSummary/?target=x6547#!/paperSummary/history-circa-summer-1832&p=1

~~Cultivating the earth for a livelihood was his occupation, in which he employed the most of his time. His advantages, for acquiring literary knowledge, were exceedingly small; hence, his education was limited to a slight acquaintance with two or three of the common branches of learning. He could read without much difficulty, and write a very imperfect hand; and had a very limited understanding of the ground rules of arithmetic. These were his highest and only attainments; while the rest of those branches, so universally taught in the common schools throughout the United States, were entirely unknown to him.~~	My father was a farmer and taught me the art of husbandry.

Comment: Joseph may deem Pratt's characterization irrelevant or incorrect, it's not clear which, but he rejects all of Pratt's text here.

When ~~somewhere~~ about fourteen ~~or fifteen~~ years *of age* ~~old~~, ~~he~~ *I* began ~~seriously~~ to reflect upon the ~~necessity~~ *importance* of being prepared for a future state ~~of existence: but how, or in what way, to prepare himself, was a question, as yet, undetermined in his own mind: he perceived that it was a question of infinite importance, and that the~~*, and upon inquiring the plan of* salvation ~~of his soul depended upon a correct understanding of the same. He saw, that if he understood not the way, it would be impossible to walk in it, except by chance; and the thought of resting his hopes of eternal life upon chance, or uncertainties, was more than he could endure.~~ *I found that there was a great clash in religious sentiment;*	When about fourteen years of age, I began to reflect upon the importance of being prepared for a future state, and upon inquiring the plan of salvation, I found that there was a great clash in religious sentiment;

Comment: Again, Joseph corrects a detail and deletes what appears to be Pratt's speculation about Joseph's thinking.

If ~~he~~ *I* went to ~~the religious~~	if I went to one society they referred me

~~denominations to seek for information, each one pointed to its particular tenets, saying~~ ~~"This is the way, walk ye in it;"~~ ~~while, at the same time, the doctrines of each were, in many respects, in direct opposition to one~~ another. ~~It, also, occurred to his mind, that~~ God ~~was~~ **could** not ~~*be*~~ the author of ~~but one doctrine, and therefore could not acknowledge but one denomination as his church; and that such denomination must be a people, who believe, and teach, that one doctrine, (whatever it may be,) and build upon the same. He then reflected upon the immense number of doctrines, now, in the world, which had given rise to many hundreds of different denominations. The great question to be decided in his mind, was if any one of these denominations be the Church of Christ, which one is it? Until he could become satisfied, in relation to this question, he could not rest contented. To trust to the decisions of fallible man, and build his hopes upon the same, without any certainty, and knowledge, of his own, would not satisfy the anxious desires that pervaded his breast. To decide, without any positive and definite evidence, on which he could rely, upon a subject involving the future welfare of his soul, was revolting to his feelings.~~	to one plan, and another to another; each one pointing to his own particular creed as the summum bonum of perfection: considering that all could not be right, and that God could not be the author of so much confusion I determined to investigate the subject more fully, believing that if God had a church it would not be split up into factions, and that if he taught one society to worship one way, and administer in one set of ordinances, he would not teach another principles which were diametrically opposed.

Comment: Joseph shortens and simplifies the language and edits out Pratt's comments about Joseph's thinking.

~~The only alternative, that seemed to be left him, was to read the Scriptures, and endeavour to follow their directions. He, accordingly,~~	Believing the word of God I had confidence in the declaration of James; "If any man lack wisdom let him ask of God who giveth to all men liberally and

~~commenced perusing the sacred pages~~ ~~of the Bible, with sincerity, believing~~ ~~the things that he read. His mind soon~~ ~~caught hold of the following passage:~~ "If any of you lack wisdom, let him ask of God, that giveth to all men liberally, and upbraideth not; and it shall be given him."--James i.5. ~~From~~ ~~this promise he learned, that it was the~~ ~~privilege of all men to ask God for~~ ~~wisdom, with the sure and certain~~ ~~expectation of receiving, liberally;~~ ~~without being upbraided for so doing.~~ ~~This was cheering information to him:~~ ~~tidings that gave him great joy. It was~~ ~~like a light shining forth in a dark~~ ~~place, to guide him to the path in~~ ~~which he should walk. He, now, saw~~ ~~that if he inquired of God, there was,~~ ~~not only, a possibility, but a~~ ~~probability; yea, more, a certainty,~~ ~~that he should obtain a knowledge,~~ ~~which, of all the doctrines, was the~~ ~~doctrine of Christ; and, which, of all~~ ~~the churches, was the church of~~ ~~Christ.~~	upbraideth not and it shall be given him,"
~~He, therefore,~~ *I* retired to a secret place, in a grove, ~~but a short distance~~ ~~from his father's house, and knelt~~ ~~down,~~ and began to call upon the Lord. ~~At first, he was severely tempted~~ ~~by the powers of darkness, which~~ ~~endeavoured to overcome him; but he~~ ~~continued to seek for deliverance,~~ ~~until darkness gave way from his~~ ~~mind; and he was enabled to pray, in~~ ~~fervency of the spirit, and in faith.~~ ~~And, while thus pouring out his soul,~~ ~~anxiously desiring an answer from~~ ~~God, he, at length, saw a very bright~~ ~~and glorious light in the heavens~~ ~~above; which, at first, seemed to be at~~ ~~a considerable distance. He continued~~	I retired to a secret place in a grove and began to call upon the Lord,

~~praying, while the light appeared to be~~ ~~gradually descending towards him;~~ ~~and, as it drew nearer, it increased in~~ ~~brightness, and magnitude, so that, by~~ ~~the time that it reached the tops of the~~ ~~trees, the whole wilderness, for some~~ ~~distance around, was illuminated in a~~ ~~most glorious and brilliant manner.~~ ~~He expected to have seen the leaves~~ ~~and boughs of the trees consumed, as~~ ~~soon as the light came in contact with~~ ~~them; but, perceiving that it did not~~ ~~produce that effect, he was encouraged~~ ~~with the hopes of being able to endure~~ ~~its presence. It continued descending,~~ ~~slowly, until it rested upon the earth,~~ ~~and he was enveloped in the midst of~~ ~~it. When it first came upon him, it~~ ~~produced a peculiar sensation~~ ~~throughout his whole system; and,~~ ~~immediately his~~ *while fervently engaged in supplication my* mind was ~~caught~~ *taken* away, from the ~~natural~~ objects with which ~~he~~ *I* was surrounded; and ~~he~~ *I* was enwrapped in a heavenly vision, and saw two glorious personages, who exactly resembled each other in their features ~~or~~ *and* likeness, *surrounded with a brilliant light which eclipsed the sun at noon-day.* ~~He was informed, that his sins were forgiven.~~	while fervently engaged in supplication my mind was taken away from the objects with which I was surrounded, and I was enwrapped in a heavenly vision and saw two glorious personages who exactly resembled each other in features, and likeness, surrounded with a brilliant light which eclipsed the sun at noon-day.
~~He was also informed upon the~~ ~~subjects, which had for some time~~ ~~previously agitated his mind, viz.~~ *They told me* that all the religious denominations were believing in incorrect doctrines; and, ~~consequently,~~ that none of them was acknowledged of God, as his church and kingdom. And *I* ~~he~~ was expressly commanded, to go not after them; ~~and he received~~ *at the same time receiving* a promise	They told me that all religious denominations were believing in incorrect doctrines, and that none of them was acknowledged of God as his church and kingdom. And I was expressly commanded to "go not after them," at the same time receiving a promise that the fulness of the gospel should at some future time be made

that the ~~true doctrine~~ the fulness of the gospel, should, at some future time, be made known to *me* ~~him; after which, the vision withdrew, leaving his mind in a state of calmness and peace, indescribable. Some time after having received this glorious manifestation, being young, he was again entangled in the vanities of the world, of which he afterwards sincerely and truly repented.~~	known unto me.
~~And it pleased God,~~ on the evening of the 21st of September, A.D. 1823, ~~to again hear his prayers. For he had retired to rest, as usual, only that his mind was drawn out, in fervent prayer, and his soul was filled with the most ernest desire, "to commune with some kind of messenger, who could communicate to him the desired information of his acceptance with God," and also unfold the principles of the doctrine of Christ, according to the promise which he had received in the former vision.~~ While *I was praying unto God, and* ~~he thus continued to pour out his desires before the Father of all good;~~ endeavouring to exercise faith in ~~his~~ *the* precious promises *of scripture*; "on a sudden, a light like that of day, only of a purer and far more glorious appearance and brightness, burst into the room. Indeed, the first site was as though the house was filled with consuming fire.	On the evening of the 21st of September, A. D. 1823, while I was praying unto God, and endeavoring to exercise faith in the precious promises of scripture on a sudden a light like that of day, only of a far purer and more glorious appearance, and brightness burst into the room, indeed the first sight was as though the house was filled with consuming fire;

Comment: the quotation marks in the original denote a quotation from Oliver Cowdery's letter IV to W. W. Phelps, published in the *Latter Day Saints' Messenger and Advocate*, Feb. 1835. This letter was republished in the *Times and Seasons* and in the *Gospel Reflector*, as well as in a pamphlet published in England in 1844. Joseph may have deleted this section because it had been published so many times, or because it was unnecessarily wordy.

~~This sudden~~ **the** appearance ~~of a~~	the appearance produced a shock that

~~light so bright, as must naturally be expected, occasioned~~ *produced* a shock *that affected* ~~or sensation visible to the extremities of~~ the *whole* body. ~~It was, however, followed with a calmness and serenity of mind, and an overwhelming rapture of joy, that surpassed understanding, and,~~ in a moment, a personage stood before *me* ~~him.~~"	affected the whole body; in a moment a personage stood before me
~~Notwithstanding the brightness of the light which previously illuminated the room,~~ "~~yet there seemed to be an additional~~ *surrounded with a* glory ~~surrounding or accompanying this personage, which shone with an increased degree of brilliancy, of which he was in the midst; and though his countenance was as lightning, yet, it was of a pleasing, innocent, and glorious appearance; so much so, that every fear was banished from the heart, and nothing but calmness pervaded the soul."~~ *yet greater than that with which I was already surrounded.* "~~The stature of this personage was a little above the common size of men of this age; his garment was perfectly white, and had the appearance of being without seam."~~	surrounded with a glory yet greater than that with which I was already surrounded.

Comment: Joseph simplifies the story but doesn't change the meaning.

This *messenger proclaimed* ~~glorious being declared~~ himself to be an Angel of God, sent ~~forth, by commandment, to communicate to him that his sins were forgiven, and that his prayers were heard; and also,~~ to bring the joyful tidings, that the covenant which God made with ancient Israel, ~~concerning their posterity,~~ was at hand to be fulfilled; that the ~~great~~ preparatory work for the second	This messenger proclaimed himself to be an angel of God sent to bring the joyful tidings, that the covenant which God made with ancient Israel was at hand to be fulfilled, that the preparatory work for the second coming of the Messiah was speedily to commence; that the time was at hand for the gospel, in all its fulness [fullness] to be preached in power, unto all nations that a people might be prepared for the millennial reign.

coming of the Messiah, was speedily to commence; that the time was at hand for the gospel, in *all* its fulness, to be preached in power unto all nations; that a people might be prepared with faith and righteousness, for the Millennial reign ~~of universal peace and joy.~~	
~~He~~ *I* was informed, that *I* ~~he~~ was ~~called and~~ chosen to be an instrument in the hands of God, to bring about some of his ~~marvellous~~ purposes in this glorious dispensation.	I was informed that I was chosen to be an instrument in the hands of God to bring about some of his purposes in this glorious dispensation.
~~It was also made manifest to him, that the "American Indians" were a remnant of Israel; that when they first emigrated to America, they were an enlightened people, possessing a knowledge of the true God, enjoying his favour, and peculiar blessing from his hand; that the prophets, and inspired writers among them, were required to keep a sacred history of the most important events transpiring among them: which history was handed down for many generations, till at length they fell into great wickedness: the most part of them were destroyed, and the records, (by commandment of God, to one if the last prophets among them,) were safely~~ deposited, ~~to preserve them from the hands of the wicked, who sought to destroy them.~~ ~~He~~ I was *also* informed, ~~that these records contained many sacred revelations pertaining to the gospel of the kingdom, as well as prophecies relating to the great events of the last days; and that to fulfill his promises to the ancients, who wrote the records, and to accomplish his purposes, in the restitution of their children, &c., they were to come forth~~	I was also informed concerning the aboriginal inhabitants **of this country**, and shown who they were, and from whence they came; a brief sketch of their origin, progress, civilization, laws, governments, of their righteousness and iniquity, and the blessings of God being finally withdrawn from them as a people was made known unto me: I was also told where there was deposited some plates on which were engraven an abridgement of the records of the ancient prophets that had existed on this continent. The angel appeared to me three times the same night and unfolded the same things.

to the knowledge of the people. If faithful, he was to be the instrument, who should be thus highly favoured in bringing these sacred things to light: at the same time, being expressly informed, that it must be done with an eye single to the glory of God, that no one could be entrusted with those sacred writings, who should endeavour to aggrandize himself, by converting sacred things to unrighteous and speculative purposes. After giving him many instructions concerning things past and to come, which would be foreign to our purpose to mention here, he disappeared, and the light and glory of God withdrew, leaving his mind in perfect peace, while a calmness and serenity indescribable pervaded the soul. But, before morning, the vision was twice renewed, instructing him further, and still further, concerning the great work of God, about to be performed on the earth. In the morning, he went out to his labour as usual; but soon the vision was renewed the Angel again appeared; and having been informed by the previous visions of the night, concerning the place where those records were deposited, he was instructed to go immediately and view them.

Comment: Joseph here uses fewer words but expands on the topics about which the angel instructed him.

Accordingly, he repaired to the place, a brief description of which shall be given, in the words of a gentleman, by the name of Oliver Cowdery, who has visited the spot.

[Pratt includes a lengthy extract from Cowdery's Letter VII to W.W. Phelps.]

~~We here remark, that the above quotation is an extract from a letter written by Elder Oliver Cowdery, which was published in one of the numbers of the "Latter Day Saints' Messenger and Advocate."~~

Comment: Joseph omits this entire excerpt from Oliver Cowdery's letter VII to W.W. Phelps from the July 1835 *M&A*, but he does not correct or change the concepts Cowdery expressed. The first obvious reason is to save space. Another likely reason is that Joseph knew Cowdery's letter had been republished twice just a year earlier (after Pratt published his pamphlet), both times at his personal direction. The first republication was in the 15 Mar. 1841 *Gospel Reflector*, and the second was in the 15 Apr. 1841 *Times and Seasons*. Cowdery's letter would be published yet again in 1844 in Liverpool. Joseph also had his scribes copy Cowdery's letters into his personal journal in 1835. Cowdery's description of the hill Cumorah and the final battles that took place there were well known among the early Saints. That Joseph saw no need to correct the information, even when he was correcting other doctrinal errors in Pratt's piece, is further evidence that he approved of Cowdery's description. He had previously given Winchester express permission to publish the Cowdery letters and presumably gave his brother Don Carlos similar permission to publish them in the *Times and Seasons*. I discuss the letter at length in *Letter VII: Oliver Cowdery's Message to the World about the Hill Cumorah.*

~~Although many more instructions were given by the mouth of the angel to Mr Smith, which we do not write in this book, yet the most important items are contained in the foregoing relation. During the period of the four following years, he frequently received instruction from the mouth of the heavenly messenger. And~~ on the morning of the 22d of September, A.D. 1827, the angel of the Lord delivered the records into ~~his~~ *my* hands.	After having received many visits from the angels of God unfolding the majesty, and glory of the events that should transpire in the last days, on the morning of the 22d of September A. D. 1827, the angel of the Lord delivered the records into my hands.

Comment: One correction Joseph makes here is that he received visits from angels, plural, not just the angel.

These records were ~~engraved~~ *engraven* on plates, which had the appearance of gold. Each plate was *six inches wide and* ~~not far from seven by~~ eight inches **long and** ~~in width and length, being~~ not quite as thick as	These records were engraven on plates which had the appearance of gold, each plate was six inches wide and eight inches long and not quite so thick as common tin. They were filled with engravings, in Egyptian characters and bound together in a volume,

common tin. They were filled ~~on both sides~~ with engravings, in Egyptian characters, and bound together in a volume, as the leaves of a book, ~~and fastened at one edge~~ with three rings running through the whole. This volume was something near six inches in thickness, a part of which was sealed. The characters ~~or letters upon~~ *on* the unsealed part were small, and beautifully engraved. The whole book exhibited many marks of antiquity in its construction, ~~as well as~~ *and* much skill in the art of engraving. With the records was found "a curious instrument, ~~called by~~ *which* the ancients *called* ~~the~~ Urim and Thummim, which consisted of two transparent stones, ~~clear as crystal,~~ set in the *rim* ~~two rims~~ of a bow *fastened to a breastplate*. ~~This was in use, in ancient times, by persons called seers. It was an instrument, by the use which, they received revelation of things distant, or of things past or future."~~

[NOTE: After this follows a long description of efforts to steal the plates from Joseph, which I moved below to correspond with Joseph's comments on that point.]

~~Having provided himself with a home, he commenced translating the record, by the gift and power of God,~~ through the ~~means~~ *medium* of the Urim and Thummim *I translated the record by the gift, and power of God.*~~; and being a poor writer he was under the necessity of employing a scribe, to write the translation as it came from his mouth.~~

[NOTE: After this follows a description of Martin Harris' visit to

as the leaves of a book with three rings running through the whole. The volume was something near six inches in thickness, a part of which was sealed. The characters on the unsealed part were small, and beautifully engraved. The whole book exhibited many marks of antiquity in its construction and much skill in the art of engraving. With the records was found a curious instrument which the ancients called "Urim and Thummim," which consisted of two transparent stones set in the rim of a bow fastened to a breastplate.

Through the medium of the Urim and Thummim I translated the record by the gift, and power of God.

Anthon which I omitted here because Joseph never mentioned it in the letter.] ~~But to return. Mr Smith continued the work of translation, as his pecuniary circumstances would permit, until he finished the unsealed part of the records. The part translated is entitled the "Book of Mormon," which contains nearly as much reading as the Old Testament.~~	

Comment: Joseph simplifies this history but doesn't make any doctrinal or substantive changes to what Pratt wrote. Perhaps he didn't want to repeat Pratt's characterization of him as a "poor writer," which presumably referred to Joseph's penmanship and not his creativity, since Joseph was translating, not writing in the creative sense.

In this important and ~~most~~ interesting book, ~~we can read~~ the history of ancient America *is unfolded*, from its ~~early~~ *first* settlement by a colony ~~who~~ *that* came from the tower of Babel, at the confusion of languages, to the beginning of the fifth century of the Christian era.	In this important and interesting book the history of ancient America is unfolded, from its first settlement by a colony that came from the tower of Babel, at the confusion of languages to the beginning of the fifth century of the Christian era.

Comment: Here Joseph shifts to passive voice, which appears to be a change in style, not substance.

~~By these Records~~ we are informed *by these records*, that America, in ancient times, has been inhabited by two distinct races of people. The first *were called Jaredites and* ~~or more ancient race,~~ came directly from the ~~great~~ tower of Babel~~, being called Jaredites.~~	We are informed by these records that America in ancient times has been inhabited by two distinct races of people. The first were called Jaredites and came directly from the tower of Babel.

Comment: Joseph retains Pratt's first person plural and moves some phrases around with no substantive change.

The second race came directly from the city of Jerusalem, about six-hundred years before Christ~~, being Israelites, principally the descendants of Joseph.~~ *They were principally Israelites, of the descendants of Joseph.*	The second race came directly from the city of Jerusalem, about six hundred years before Christ. They were principally Israelites, of the descendants of Joseph.

149

Comment: In this passage Joseph makes an important doctrinal clarification. Instead of Lehi's group "being Israelites, principally the descendants of Joseph," they "were principally Israelites, of the descendants of Joseph." The correction specifies that not everyone in Lehi's party was an Israelite.

The ~~first nation, or~~ Jaredites, were destroyed about the time that the Israelites came from Jerusalem, who succeeded them in the inheritance of the country.	The Jaredites were destroyed about the time that the Israelites came from Jerusalem, who succeeded them in the inheritance of the country.

Comment: This minor change shows Joseph read the sentence and affirmed the timing of the destruction of the Jaredites. The statement contradicts a common line of argument among some modern scholars who claim the Jaredites survived until around 200 B.C.

The principal nation of the second race, fell in battle towards the close of the fourth century.	The principal nation of the second race fell in battle towards the close of the fourth century.
The ~~remaining~~ remnant, ~~having dwindled into an uncivilized state, still continue to inhabit the land, although divided into a "multitude of nations,"~~ and are ~~called by Europeans the "American Indians."~~ *the Indians that now inhabit this country.*	The remnant are the Indians that now inhabit this country.

Comment: Here and in Pratt's ensuing paragraphs, Joseph deletes 2,700 words of Pratt's speculation about Lehi's descendants inhabiting all of North and South America and simply declares that the "remnant are the Indians that now inhabit this country." Pratt claims the Jaredites came "to the shores of North America" (which he later associates with Baja), that they occupied "principally North America," that Lehi and his group "were safely brought across the great Pacific ocean, and landed upon the western coast of South America," that the Mulekites "landed in North America; soon after which they emigrated into the northern parts of South America, at which place they were discovered by the remnant of Joseph, something like four hundred years after," that the "persecuted nation emigrated towards the northern parts of South America, leaving the wicked nation in possession of the middle and southern parts of the same," that "in the process of time, the Nephites began to build ships near the Isthmus of Darien, and launch them forth into the western ocean, in which great numbers sailed a great distance to the northward, and began to colonize North America. Other colonies emigrated by land, and in a few centuries the whole continent became peopled. North America, at that time, was almost entirely destitute of timber," and so forth. All of this Joseph deleted to state simply that the "remnant are the Indians that now inhabit this country." The importance of that sentence will be discussed later in this chapter.

Few if any commentators now accept a hemispheric model such as the one advocated by Orson Pratt. A practical interpretation of the text limits the setting to a smaller area; the focus now is on determining *what* limited setting the text describes. While some of his contemporaries promoted Pratt's ideas or similar hemispheric theories, there are no documents signed by Joseph Smith or directly attributable to him that endorse a hemispheric model.

[**Note**: William Smith referred to the "remnants of Joseph" as "a multitude of nations" in M&A, Jan. 1837.]

[**Note**: the following material was in Pratt's pamphlet but not in the Wentworth letter. I merged the columns to save space.]

We learn from this very ancient history, that at the confusion of languages, when the Lord scattered the people upon all the face of the earth, the Jaredites, being a righteous people, obtained favour in the sight of the Lord, and were not confounded. And because of their righteousness, the Lord miraculously led them from the tower to the great ocean, where they were commanded to build vessels, in which they were marvellously brought across the great deep to the shores of North America.

And the Lord God promised to give them America, which was a very choice land in his sight, for an inheritance. And He swore unto them in his wrath, that whoso should possess this land of promise, from that time henceforth and forever, should serve him, the true and only God, or they should be swept off when the fulness of his wrath should come upon them, and they were fully ripened in iniquity. Moreover, he promised to make them a great and powerful nation, so that there should be no greater nation upon all the face of the earth.

Accordingly, in process of time, they became a very numerous and powerful people, occupying principally North America; building large cities in all quarters of the land; being a civilized and enlightened nation. Agriculture and machinery were carried on to a great extent. Commercial and manufacturing business flourished on every hand; yet, in consequence of wickedness, they were often visited with terrible judgments. Many prophets were raised up among them from generation to generation, who testified against the wickedness of the people, and prophesied of judgments and calamities which awaited them, if they did not repent, &c. Sometimes they were visited by pestilence and plagues, and sometimes by famine and war, until at length (having occupied the land some fifteen or sixteen hundred years) their wickedness became so great, that the Lord threatened, by the mouth of his prophets, to utterly destroy them from the face of the land. But they gave no heed to these warnings; therefore the word of the Lord was fulfilled; and they were entirely destroyed; leaving their houses, their cities, and their land desolate; and their sacred records also, which were kept on gold plates, were left by one of their last prophets whose name was Ether, in such a situation, that they were discovered by the remnant of Joseph, who soon afterwards

151

were brought from Jerusalem to inherit the land.

This remnant of Joseph were also led in a miraculous manner from Jerusalem, in the first year of the reign of Zedekiah, king of Judah. They were first led to the eastern borders of the Red Sea; then they journeyed for some time along the borders thereof, nearly in a south-east direction; after which, they altered their course nearly eastward, until they came to the great waters, where, by the commandment of God, they built a vessel, in which they were safely brought across the great Pacific ocean, and landed upon the western coast of South America.

In the eleventh year of the reign of Zedekiah, at the time the Jews were carried away captive into Babylon, another remnant were brought out of Jerusalem; some of whom were descendants of Judah. They landed in North America; soon after which they emigrated into the northern parts of South America, at which place they were discovered by the remnant of Joseph, something like four hundred years after.

From these ancient records, we learn, that this remnant of Joseph, soon after they landed, separated themselves into two distinct nations. This division was caused by a certain portion of them being greatly persecuted, because of their righteousness, by the remainder. The persecuted nation emigrated towards the northern parts of South America, leaving the wicked nation in possession of the middle and southern parts of the same. The former were called Nephites, being led by a prophet whose name was Nephi. The latter were called Lamanites, being led by a very wicked man whose name was Laman. The Nephites had in their possession a copy of the Holy Scriptures, viz. the five books of Moses, and the prophecies of the holy prophets, down to Jeremiah, in whose days they left Jerusalem. These Scriptures were engraved on plates of brass, in the Egyptian language. They themselves also made plates, soon after their landing, on which they began to engrave their own history, prophecies, visions, and revelations. All these sacred records were kept by holy and righteous men, who were inspired by the Holy Ghost; and were carefully preserved and handed down from generation to generation.

And the Lord gave unto them the whole continent, for a land of promise, and he promised, that they, and their children after them, should inherit it, on condition of their obedience to his commandments; but if they were disobedient, they should be cut off from his presence. And the Nephites began to prosper in the land, according to their righteousness, and they multiplied and spread forth to the east, and west, and north; building large villages, and cities, and synagogues, and temples, together with forts, and towers, and fortifications, to defend themselves against their enemies. And they cultivated the earth, and raised various kinds of grain in abundance. They also raised numerous flocks of domestic animals, and became a very wealthy people; having in abundance gold, silver, copper, tin, iron, &c. Arts and sciences flourished to a great extent. Various kinds of machinery were in use. Cloths, of various kinds, were manufactured. Swords, cimeters, axes, and various implements of war were made, together with head-shields, arm-shields, and breastplates, to defend themselves in battle with their enemies. And in the days of their righteousness, they were a civilized, enlightened, and happy people.

But, on the other hand, the Lamanites, because of the hardness of their hearts, brought down many judgments upon their own heads; nevertheless, they were not destroyed as a nation; but the Lord God sent forth a curse upon them, and they became a dark, loathsome, and filthy people. Before their rebellion, they were white and exceedingly fair, like the Nephites; but the Lord God cursed them in their complexions, and they were changed to a dark colour; and they became a wild, savage, and ferocious people; being great enemies to the Nephites, whom they sought, by every means, to destroy, and many times came against them with their numerous hosts to battle, but were repulsed by the Nephites, and driven back to their own possessions, not, however, generally speaking, without great loss on both sides; for tens of thousands were frequently slain, after which they were piled together in great heaps upon the face of the ground, and covered with a shallow covering of earth, which will satisfactorily account for those ancient mounds, filled with human bones, so numerous at the present day, both in North and South America.

The second colony, which left Jerusalem eleven years after the remnant of Joseph left that city, landed in North America, and emigrated from thence, to the northern parts of South America; and about four hundred years after, they were discovered by the Nephites, as we stated in the foregoing.

They were called the people of Zarahemla. They had been perplexed with many wars among themselves; and having brought no records with them, their language had become corrupted, and they denied the being of God; and at the time they were discovered by the Nephites they were very numerous, and only in a partial state of civilization; but the Nephites united with them, and taught them the Holy Scriptures, and they were restored to civilization, and became one nation with them. And in the process of time, the Nephites began to build ships near the Isthmus of Darien, and launch them forth into the western ocean, in which great numbers sailed a great distance to the northward, and began to colonize North America. Other colonies emigrated by land, and in a few centuries the whole continent became peopled. North America, at that time, was almost entirely destitute of timber, it having been cut off by the more ancient race, who came from the great tower, at the confusion of languages; but the Nephites became very skilful in building houses of cement; also, much timber was carried by way of shipping from South the North America. They also planted groves and began to raise timber, that in time their wants might be supplied. Large cities were built in various parts of the continent, both among the Lamanites and Nephites. The law of Moses was observed by the latter. Numerous prophets were raised up from time to time throughout their generations.

Many records, both historical and prophetical, which were of great size, were kept among them; some on plates of gold and other metals, and some on other materials. The sacred records, also, of the more ancient race who had been destroyed, were found by them. These were engraved on plates of gold. They translated them into their own language by the gift and power of God, through the means of the Urim and Thummim. They contained an historical account from the creation down to the Tower of Babel, and from that time down until they were destroyed, comprising a period of about thirty-four hundred, or thirty-five hundred years. They also contained many prophecies, great and marvellous, reaching forward to the final end and consummation of all things, and the creation of the new heaven and new earth.

The prophets also among the Nephites prophesied of great things. They opened the secrets of futurity, and saw the coming of Messiah in the flesh, and prophesied of the blessings to come upon their descendants in the latter times, and made known the history of unborn generations, and unfolded the grand events of ages to come, and viewed the power, and glory, and majesty of Messiah's second advent, and beheld the establishment of the kingdom of peace, and gazed upon the glories of the day of righteousness, and saw creation redeemed from the curse, and all the righteous filled with songs of everlasting joy.

The Nephites knew of the birth and crucifixion of Christ, by certain celestial and terrestrial phenomena, which, at those times, were shown forth in fulfilment of the predictions of many of their prophets. Notwithstanding the many blessings with which they had been blessed, they had fallen into great wickedness, and had cast out the saints and the prophets, and stoned and killed them. Therefore, at the time of the crucifixion of Christ, they were visited in great judgment. Thick darkness covered the whole continent. The earth was terribly convulsed. The rocks were rent into broken fragments, and afterwards found in seams and cracks upon all the face of the land. Mountains were sunk into valleys, and valleys raised into mountains. The highways and level roads were broken up and spoiled. Many cities were laid in ruins. Others were buried up in the depths of the earth, and mountains occupied their place. While others were sunk, and waters came up in their stead, and others still were burned by fire from heaven.

Thus, the predictions of their prophets were fulfilled upon their heads. Thus, the more wicked part, both of the Nephites and Lamanites, were destroyed. Thus, the Almighty executed vengeance and fury upon them, that the blood of the saints and the prophets might no longer cry from the ground against them.

Comment: Joseph's deletion of the above passage could be attributed to space requirements, except, as previously noted, he completely changed the meaning by confining the remnant to the "Indians that now inhabit this country." In my view, Joseph rejected Pratt's hemispheric model. Unlike Cowdery's Letter VII, Pratt's hemispheric ideas were never published in a Church newspaper and Joseph did not include them in his journal.

~~Those who survived these terrible judgments, were favoured with the personal ministry of Christ. For after He arose from the dead, and finished his ministry at Jerusalem, and ascended to heaven, he descended in the presence of the Nephites,~~ **who were assembled round about their temple in the northern parts of South America.** ~~He exhibited to them his wounded hands, and side, and feet; and commanded the law of Moses to be abolished; and introduced and established the Gospel in its stead; and chose twelve disciples from among them to administer the same; and instituted the sacrament; and prayed for and blessed their little children; and healed their sick, and blind, and lame, and deaf, and those who were afflicted in any way, and raised a man from the dead, and showed forth his power in their midst; and expounded the Scriptures, which had been given from the beginning down to that time; and made known unto them all things which should take place down until He should come in his glory, and from that time down to the end, when all people, nations, and languages should stand before God to be judged, and the heaven and the earth should pass away, and there should be a new heaven and new earth. These teachings of Jesus were engraved upon plates, some of which are contained in the book of Mormon; but the more part are not revealed in that book, and are hereafter to be made manifest to the saints.~~

This book also tells us that our Saviour made his appearance **upon this continent** after his resurrection, that he planted the gospel here in all its fulness, and richness, and power, and blessing; that they had apostles, prophets, pastors, teachers and evangelists; the same order, the same priesthood, the same ordinances, gifts, powers, and blessing, as was enjoyed on the eastern continent, that the people were cut off in consequence of their transgressions, that the last of their prophets who existed among them was commanded to write an abridgement of their prophesies, history &c., and to hide it up in the earth, and that it should come forth and be united with the bible for the accomplishment of the purposes of God in the last days.

For a more particular account I would refer to the Book of Mormon, which can be purchased at Nauvoo, or from any of our travelling elders.

~~After Jesus had finished ministering unto them, he ascended into heaven; and the twelve disciples, whom he had chosen, went forth upon all the face of the land, preaching the gospel; baptizing those who repented for the remission of sins, after which they laid their hands upon them, that they might receive the Holy Spirit. Mighty miracles were wrought by them, and also by many of the church.~~

Comment. Here Joseph clarifies that the Savior appeared "on this continent" and not "in the northern parts of South America" as Pratt claimed. He refers readers to the text instead of adopting Pratt's hemispheric geography. Recall that Joseph is writing to a fellow Illinois resident, Mr. Wentworth in Chicago, who would have understood "this continent" to mean the one on which they were both residing; i.e., North America. The juxtaposition with "the Eastern continent" could be interpreted as a sort of parallel, suggesting Joseph was referring to the "Western continent" as encompassing all of the western hemisphere. On the other hand, passages in the *Times and Seasons* refer to the "Continent of Europe," the "Oriental Continent," and the "Continent of America." The last reference is in an epistle of the Twelve "to the brethren scattered abroad on the Continent of America," all of whom were east of the Mississippi. For whatever reason, Joseph left the terms vague here. They are susceptible to multiple interpretations.

[The following material is more of Pratt's hemispheric model, which Joseph completely deleted.]

The Nephites and Lamanites were all converted unto the Lord, both in South and North America: and they dwelt in righteousness above three hundred years; but towards the close of the fourth century of the Christian era, they had so far apostatized from God, that he suffered great judgments to fall upon them. The Lamanites, at that time, dwelt in South America, and the Nephites in North America.

A great and terrible war commenced between them, which lasted for many years, and resulted in the complete overthrow and destruction of the Nephites. This war commenced at the Isthmus of Darien, and was very destructive to both nations for many years. At length, the Nephites were driven before their enemies, a great distance to the north, and north-east; and having gathered their whole nation together, both men, women, and children, they encamped on, and round about the hill Cumorah, where the records were found, which is in the State of New York, about two hundred miles west of the city of Albany. Here they were met by the numerous hosts of the Lamanites, and were slain, and hewn down, and slaughtered, both male and female -- the aged, middle aged, and children. Hundreds of thousands were slain on both sides; and the nation of the Nephites were destroyed, excepting a few who had deserted over to the Lamanites, and a few who escaped into the south country, and a few who fell wounded, and were left by the Lamanites on the field of battle for dead, among whom were Mormon and his son Moroni, who were righteous men.

Mormon had made an abridgement, from the records of his forefathers, upon plates, which abridgement he entitled the "Book of Mormon;" and, (being commanded of God,) he hid up in the hill Cumorah, all the sacred records of his forefathers which were in his possession, except the abridgement called the "Book of Mormon," which he gave to his son Moroni to finish. Moroni survived his nation a few years, and continued the writings, in which he informs us, that the Lamanites hunted those few Nephites who escaped the great and tremendous battle of Cumorah, until they were all destroyed, excepting those who were mingled with the Lamanites, and that he was left alone, and kept himself hid, for they sought to destroy every Nephite who would not deny the Christ. He furthermore states, that the Lamanites were at war one with another, and that the whole face of the land was one continual scene of murdering, robbing, and plundering. He continued the history until the four hundred and twentieth year of the Christian era, when, (by the commandment of God,) he hid up the records in the hill Cumorah, where they remained concealed, until by the ministry of an angel they were discovered to Mr Smith, who, by the gift and power of God, translated them into the English language, by the means of the Urim and Thummim, as stated in the foregoing.

After the book was translated, the Lord raised up witnesses to bear testimony to the nations of its truth, who, at the close of the volume, send forth their testimony, which reads as follows:-- [then follows the testimonies of the 3 Witnesses and the 8 Witnesses]

[NOTE: This following is the section I moved from above so it matches up with the way Joseph changed it in his letter.]

In the mean time, the inhabitants of that vicinity, having been informed that Mr Smith had seen heavenly visions, and that he had discovered sacred records, began to ridicule and mock at those things. And after having obtained those sacred things, while proceeding home through the wilderness and fields, he was waylaid by two ruffians, who had secreted themselves for the purpose of robbing him of the records. One of them struck him with a club before he perceived them; but being a strong man, and large in stature, with great exertion he cleared himself from them, and ran towards home, being closely pursued until he came near his father's house, when his pursuers, for fear of being detected, turned and fled the other way.

~~Soon~~ *As soon as* the news of *this discovery was made known* ~~his discoveries spread abroad throughout all those parts.~~ False reports, misrepresentations, and *slander* ~~base slanders,~~ flew as *on the* ~~if upon~~ wings of the wind in every direction. The house was frequently beset by mobs and evil designing persons. Several times ~~he~~ *I* was shot at, and very narrowly escaped~~.~~ *and* Every device was used to get the plates away from *me* ~~him~~. *but the power and blessing of God attended me, and several began to believe my testimony.* ~~And being continually in danger of his life, from a gang of abandoned wretches, he at length concluded to leave the place, and go to Pennsylvania; and, accordingly, packed up his goods, putting the plates into a barrel of beans, and proceeded upon his journey. He had not gone far, before he was overtaken by an officer with a search warrant, who flattered himself with the idea, that he should surely obtain the plates; after searching very diligently, he was sadly disappointed at not finding them. Mr Smith then drove on; but before he got to his journey's end, he was again overtaken by an officer on the same business, and after ransacking the waggon very carefully, he went his way, as much~~

As soon as the news of this discovery was made known, false reports, misrepresentation and slander flew as on the wings of the wind in every direction, the house was frequently beset by mobs, and evil designing persons, several times I was shot at, and very narrowly escaped, and every device was made use of to get the plates away from me, but the power and blessing of God attended me, and several began to believe my testimony.

chagrined as the first, at not being able to discover the object of his research. Without any further molestation, he pursued his journey until he came to the northern part of Pennsylvania, near the Susquehannah river, in which part his father in law resided.	
Also, in the year 1829, Mr Smith and Mr Cowdery, having learned the correct mode of baptism, from the teachings of the Saviour to the ancient Nephites, as recorded in the "Book of Mormon," had a desire to be baptized; but knowing that no one had authority to administer that sacred ordinance in any denomination, they were at a loss to know how the authority was to be restored, and while calling upon the Lord with a desire to be informed on the subject, a holy angel appeared and stood before them, and laid his hands upon their heads, and ordained them, and commanded them to baptize each other, which they accordingly did. In the year 1830, a large edition of the "Book of Mormon" first appeared in print. And as some began to peruse its sacred pages, the spirit of the Lord bore record to them that it was true; and they were obedient to its requirements, by coming forth, humbly repenting before the Lord, and being immersed in water, for the remission of sins, after which, by the commandment of God, hands were laid upon them in the name of the Lord, for the gift of the Holy Spirit.	
And on the sixth of April, in the year of our Lord one thousand eight hundred and thirty, *On the 6th of April, 1830* the "Church of Jesus	On the 6th of April, 1830, the "Church of Jesus Christ of Latter-Day Saints," was first organized in the town of Manchester, Ontario co., state of New York. Some few

Christ of Latter Day Saints" was *first* organized, in the town of Manchester, Ontario County, State of New York, ~~North America~~. Some few were called and ordained by the spirit of revelation and prophecy, and began to preach ~~and bear testimony,~~ as the spirit gave them utterance; and ~~although~~ ~~they were the~~ weak ~~things of the earth~~, yet they were strengthened by the *power of God and* ~~Holy Ghost, and gave forth their testimony in great power, by which means~~ many were brought to repentance, ~~and came forward with broken hearts and contrite spirits, and were immersed in water confessing their sins,~~ and were filled with the Holy Ghost by the laying on of hands; ~~and~~ *They* saw visions and prophesied. Devils were cast out, and the sick ~~were~~ healed by the ~~prayer of faith, and~~ laying on of hands. ~~Thus was the word confirmed unto the faithful by signs following. Thus the Lord raise up witnesses, to bear testimony of his name, and lay the foundations of his kingdom in the last days. And thus the hearts of the saints were comforted, and filled with great joy. In the foregoing, we have related the most important facts concerning the visions and the ministry of the angel to Mr Smith; the discovery of the records; their translation into the English language, and the witnesses raised up to bear testimony of the same.~~

~~We have also stated when, and by whom they were written; that they contain the history of nearly one half of the globe, from the earliest ages after the flood, until the beginning of~~

were called and ordained by the spirit of revelation, and prophesy, and began to preach as the spirit gave them utterance, and though weak, yet were they strengthened by the power of God, and many were brought to repentance, were immersed in the water, and were filled with the Holy Ghost by the laying on of hands. They saw visions and prophesied, devils were cast out and the sick healed by the laying on of hands.

~~the fifth century of the Christian era;
that this history is interspersed with
many important prophecies, which
unfold the great events of the last days,
and that in it also is recorded the
gospel in its fulness and plainness, as it
was revealed by the personal ministry
of Christ to the ancient Nephites. We
have also given an account of the
restoration of the authority in these
days, to administer in the ordinances
of the gospel; and the time of the
organization of the church; and of the
blessings poured out upon he same
while yet in its infancy.~~

[**Note**: the following sections are from the Wentworth letter, with no corresponding material in Pratt's pamphlet. I merged the cells in the interest of space.]

From that time the work rolled forth with astonishing rapidity, and churches were soon formed in the states of New York, Pennsylvania, Ohio, Indiana, Illinois and Missouri; in the last named state a considerable settlement was formed in Jackson co.; numbers joined the church and we were increasing rapidly; we made large purchases of land, our farms teemed with plenty, and peace and happiness was enjoyed in our domestic circle and throughout our neighborhood; but as we could not associate with our neighbors who were many of them of the basest of men and had fled from the face of civilized society, to the frontier country to escape the hand of justice, in their midnight revels, their sabbath breaking, horseracing, and gambling, they commenced at first ridicule, then to persecute, and finally an organized mob assembled and burned our houses, tarred, and feathered, and whipped many of our brethren and finally drove them from their habitations; who houseless, and homeless, contrary to law, justice and humanity, had to wander on the bleak prairies till the children left the tracks of their blood on the prairie, this took place in the month of November, and they had no other covering but the canopy of heaven, in this inclement season of the year; this proceeding was winked at by the government and although we had warrantee deeds for our land, and had violated no law we could obtain no redress.

There were many sick, who were thus inhumanly [inhumanely] driven from their houses, and had to endure all this abuse and to seek homes where they could be found. The result was, that a great many of them being deprived of the comforts of life, and the necessary attendances, died; many children were left orphans; wives, widows; and husbands widowers.-Our farms were taken possession of by the mob, many thousands of cattle, sheep, horses, and hogs, were taken and our household goods, store goods, and printing press, and type were broken, taken, or otherwise destroyed.

Many of our brethren removed to Clay where they continued until 1836, three years; there was no violence offered but there were threatenings of violence. But in the summer of 1836, these threatenings began to assume a more serious form; from threats, public meetings were called, resolutions were passed, vengeance and destruction were threatened, and affairs again assumed a fearful attitude, Jackson county was a sufficient precedent, and as the authorities in that county did not interfere, they boasted that they would not in this, which on application to the authorities we found to be too true, and after much violence, privation and loss of property we were again driven from our homes.

We next settled in Caldwell, and Davies counties, where we made large and extensive settlements, thinking to free ourselves from the power of oppression, by settling in new counties, with very few inhabitants in them; but here we were not allowed to live in peace, but in 1838 we were again attacked by mobs an exterminating order was issued by Gov. Boggs, and under the sanction of law an organized banditti ranged through the country, robbed us of our cattle, sheep, horses, hogs &c., many of our people were murdered in cold blood, the chastity of our women was violated, and we were forced to sign away our property at the point of the sword, and after enduring every indignity that could be heaped upon us by an inhuman, ungodly band of maurauders [marauders], from twelve to fifteen thousand souls men, women, and children were driven from their own fire sides, and from lands that they had warrantee deeds of, houseless, friendless, and homeless (in the depth of winter,) to wander as exiles on the earth or to seek an asylum in a more genial clime, and among a less barbarous people.

Many sickened and died, in consequence of the cold, and hardships they had to endure; many wives were left widows, and children orphans, and destitute. It would take more time than is allotted me here to describe the injustice, the wrongs, the murders, the bloodshed, the theft, misery and woe that has been caused by the barbarous, inhuman, and lawless, proceedings of the state of Missouri.

Comment. Joseph likely added all this detail about Missouri hoping that other newspapers would publish it and help around public sentiment in favor of the Mormon position.

[**Note:** the following sections are from the Wentworth letter, with no corresponding material in Pratt's pamphlet. I merged the cells in the interest of space.]

In the situation before alluded to we arrived in the state of Illinois in 1839, where we found a hospitable people and a friendly home; a people who were willing to be governed by the principles of law and humanity. We have commenced to build a city called "Nauvoo" in Hancock co., we number from six to eight thousand here besides vast numbers in the county of the state. We have a city charter granted us and a charter for a legion the troops of which now number 1500. We have also a charter for a university, for an agricultural and manufacturing society, have our own laws and administrators, and posses all the privileges that other free and enlightened citizens enjoy.

Persecution has not stopped the progress of truth, but has only added fuel to the flame, it has spread with increasing rapidity, proud of the cause which they have espoused and conscious of their innocence and of the truth of their system amidst calumny and reproach have the elders of this church gone forth, and planted the gospel in almost every state in the Union; it has penetrated our cities, it has spread over our villages, and has caused thousands of our intelligent, nobel, and patriotic citizens to obey its divine mandates, and be governed by its sacred truths. It has also spread into England, Ireland, Scotland and Wales: in the year of 1839 where a few of our missionaries were sent over five thousand and joined the standard of truth, there are numbers now joining in every land.

Our missionaries are going forth to different nations, and in Germany, Palestine, New Holland, the East Indies, and other places, the standard of truth has been erected: no unhallowed hand can stop the work from progressing, persecutions may rage, mobs may combine, armies may assemble, calumny may defame, but the truth of God will go forth boldly, nobly, and independent till it has penetrated every continent, visited every clime, swept every country, and sounded in every ear, till the purposes of God shall be accomplished and the great Jehovah shall say the work is done.

Comment: the following material shows how the Articles of Faith were adapted in part from Pratt's pamphlet.

~~We now proceed to give a sketch of the faith and doctrine of this Church.~~ ~~First,~~ We believe in God the Eternal Father, and in his Son Jesus Christ, and in the Holy Ghost~~, who bears record of them, the same throughout all ages and for ever~~.	We believe in God, the Eternal Father, and in His Son, Jesus Christ, and in the Holy Ghost.
We believe that ~~all mankind, by the transgression of their first parents, and not by~~ ***men will be punished for*** their own sins, ***and not for Adam's transgression.*** ~~were brought under the curse and penalty of that transgression, which consigned them to an eternal banishment from the presence of God, and their bodies to an endless sleep in the dust, never more to rise, and their spirits to endless misery under the power of Satan; and that, in this awful condition, they were utterly lost and fallen, and had no power of their own to extricate themselves therefrom.~~	We believe that men will be punished for their own sins, and not for Adam's transgression.

Comment: The Articles of Faith, canonized in the Pearl of Great Price, were largely adapted from Orson Pratt's text. Joseph's edits not only simplified the language, but

both clarified and corrected the doctrine.	
[Note: to save space, I've put all of Pratt's material into one column below.]	We believe that through the atonement of Christ all mankind may be saved by obedience to the laws and ordinances of the Gospel.

We believe, that through the ~~sufferings, death, and~~ atonement of ~~Jesus~~ Christ, all mankind **may be saved by obedience to the laws and ordinances of the Gospel.** ; ~~without one exception, are to be completely, and fully redeemed, both body and spirit, from the endless banishment and curse, to which they were consigned, by Adam's transgression; and that this universal salvation and redemption of the whole human family from the endless penalty of the original sin, is effected, without any conditions whatsoever on their part; that is, that they are not required to believe, or repent, or be baptized, or do any thing else, in order to be redeemed from that penalty; for whether they believe or disbelieve, whether they repent or remain inpenitent, whether they be baptized or unbaptized, whether they keep the commandments or break them, whether they are righteous or unrighteous, it will make no difference in relation to their redemption, both soul and body, from the penalty of Adam's transgression. The most righteous man that ever lived on the earth, and the most wicked wretch of the whole human family, were both placed under the same curse, without any transgression or agency of their own, and they both, alike, will be redeemed from that curse, without any agency or conditions on their part. Paul says, Rom. v. 18. "Therefore, as by the offence of one, judgment came upon ALL men to condemnation; even so, by the righteousness of one, the free gift came upon ALL men unto the justification of life." This is the reason, why ALL men are redeemed from the grave. This is the reason, that the spirits of ALL men are restored to their bodies. This is the reason that ALL men are redeemed from their first banishment, and restored into the presence of God, and this is~~ the reason that the Saviour said, John xii. 32, "If I ~~be lifted up from the earth I will draw ALL men unto me." After this full, complete, and universal redemption, restoration, and salvation of the whole of Adam's race, through the atonement of Jesus Christ, without faith, repentance, baptism, or any other works, then, all and every one of them, will enjoy eternal life and happiness, never more to be banished from the presence of God, IF they themselves have committed no sin: for the penalty of the original sin can have no more power over them at all, for Jesus hath destroyed its power, and broken the bands of the first death, and obtained the victory over the grave, and delivered all its captives, and restored them from their first banishment into the presence of his Father; hence eternal life will then be theirs, IF they themselves are not found transgressors of some law.~~ [Then follows more doctrinal exposition.]

[Note: to save space, I've put all of Pratt's material into one column below.]	We believe that these ordinances are 1st, Faith in the Lord Jesus Christ; 2d, Repentance; 3d, Baptism by immersion for the remission of sins; 4th, Laying on of hands for the gift of the Holy Ghost.

We believe that these ordinances are 1st, Faith in the Lord Jesus Christ; the first condition to be complied with on the part of sinners is, to believe in God, and in the sufferings and death of his Son Jesus Christ, to atone for the sins of the whole world, and in his resurrection and ascension on high, to appear in the presence of his Father, to make intercessions for the children of men, and in the Holy Ghost, which is given to all who obey the gospel.

2d, Repentance; That the second condition is, to repent, that is, all who believe, according to the first condition, are required to come humbly before God, and confess their sins with a broken heart and contrite spirit, and to turn away from them, and cease from all their evil deeds, and make restitution to all they have in any way injured, as far as it is in their power.

3d, Baptism by immersion for the remission of sins; That the third condition is, to be baptized by immersion in water, in the name of the Father, Son, and Holy Ghost, for remission of sins; and that this ordinance is to administered by one who is called and authorized of Jesus Christ to baptize, otherwise it is illegal, and of no advantage, and not accepted by him; and that it is to be administered only to those persons, who believe and repent, according to the two preceding conditions.

4th, And that the fourth condition is, to receive the laying on of hands, in the name of Jesus Christ, for the gift of the Holy Ghost; and that this ordinance is to be administered by the apostles or elders, whom the Lord Jesus hath called and authorized to lay on hands, otherwise it is of no advantage, being illegal in the sight of God; and that it is to be administered only to those persons, who believe, repent, and are baptized into this church, according to the three preceding conditions. These are the first conditions of the gospel. All who comply with them receive forgiveness of sins, and are made partakers of the Holy Ghost. Through these conditions, they become the adopted sons and daughters of God. Through this process, they are born again, first of water, and then of the spirit, and become children of the kingdom — heirs of God — saints of the most High — the church of the first-born—the elect people, and heirs to a celestial inheritance, eternal in the presence of God. After complying with these principles, their names are enrolled in the book of the names of the righteous.

They are then required to be humble, to be meek and lowly in heart, to watch and pray, to deal justly; and inasmuch as they have the riches of this world, to feed the hungry and clothe the naked, according to the dictates of wisdom and prudence; to comfort the afflicted, to bind up the broken-hearted, and to do all the good that is in their power: and besides all these things, they are required to meet together as often as circumstances will admit, and partake of bread and wine, in remembrance of the broken body, and shed blood of the Lord Jesus; and, in short, to continue faithful to the end, in all the duties enjoined upon them by the word and spirit of Christ.

[Note: to save space, I've put all of Pratt's material into one column below.]	We believe that a man must be called of God by "prophesy, and by laying on of hands" by those who are in authority to preach the gospel and administer in the ordinances thereof.

We believe ~~that there has been a general and awful apostasy from the religion of the New Testament, so that all the known world have been left for centuries without the Church of Christ among them; without a priesthood authorized of God to administer ordinances; that every one of the churches has perverted the gospel; some in one way, and some in another. For instance, almost every church has done away "immersion for remission of sins." Those few who have practised it for remission of sins, have done away with the ordinance of the~~ "laying on of hands" ~~upon baptized believers for the gift of the Holy Ghost. Again, the few who have practised this last ordinance, have perverted the first, or have done away the ancient gifts, and powers, and blessings, which flow from the Holy Spirit, or have said to inspired apostles and prophets, we have no need of you in the body in these days. Those few, again, who have believed in, and contended for the miraculous gifts and powers of the Holy Spirit, have perverted the ordinances, or done them away. Thus all the churches preach false doctrines, and pervert the gospel, and instead of~~ having authority ~~from God~~ to administer its ordinances, ~~they are under the curse of God for perverting it. Paul says, Gal. i. 8, "Though we, or an angel from heaven, preach any other gospel unto you than that which we have preached unto you, let him be accursed."~~
~~We believe that there are a few, sincere, honest, and humble persons, who are striving to do according to the best of their understanding; but, in many respects, they err in doctrine, because of false teachers and the precepts of men, and that they will receive the fulness of the gospel with gladness, as soon as they hear it.~~ [Note: this paragraph follows the next one in Pratt's work. I rearranged it for easier comparison.]
Comment. Rather than delve into the apostasy, Joseph explains simply that one must have divine authority to administer the gospel; by implication, no one can have such authority except through the Church of Jesus Christ of Latter-day Saints.

We believe *in the same organization that existed in the primitive church, viz:* ~~that inspired~~ apostles ~~and~~ prophets, *pastors, teachers, evangelists &c.* ~~together with all the officers as mentioned in the New Testament, are necessary to be in the Church in these days.~~ [Note: this paragraph comes after the next paragraph in Pratt's work.]	We believe in the same organization that existed in the primitive church, viz: apostles, prophets, pastors, teachers, evangelists &c.
~~"It is the duty and privilege of the saints thus organized upon the~~	We believe in the gift of tongues, prophesy, revelation, visions, healing,

~~everlasting gospel, to believe in and enjoy all the gifts, powers, and blessings which flow from the Holy Spirit. Such, for instance, as~~ *We believe in* the gifts of *tongues, prophecy,* revelation, ~~prophecy,~~ visions, ~~the ministry of angels,~~ healing, *interpretation of tongues &c.* ~~the sick by the laying on of hands in the name of Jesus, the working of miracles, and, in short, all the gifts as mentioned in Scripture, or as enjoyed by the ancient saints."~~ [Note: Elder Adams copied this in an article he sent to the *Boston Bee*, published in T&S 4:9, 15 Mar. 1843, p. 141.]	interpretation of tongues &c.
~~The gospel in the "Book of Mormon," is the same as that in the New Testament, and is revealed in great plainness, so that no one that reads it can misunderstand its principles. It has been revealed by the angel, to be preached as a witness to all nations, first to the Gentiles, and then to the Jews, then cometh the downfall of Babylon. Thus fulfilling the vision of John, which he beheld on the Isle of Patmos, Rev. xiv. 6, 7, 8,~~ [followed by the entire quotation.]	We believe the bible to be the word of God as far as it is translated correctly; we also believe the Book of Mormon to be the word of God.
[Note: to save space, I've put all of Pratt's material into one column below.]	We believe all that God has revealed, all that he does now reveal, and we believe that he will yet reveal many great and important things pertaining to the kingdom of God.

~~Many revelations and prophecies have been given to this church since its rise, which have been printed and sent forth to the world. These also contain the gospel in great plainness, and instructions of infinite importance to the saints. They also unfold the great events that await this generation; the terrible judgments to be poured forth upon the wicked, and the blessings and glories to be given to the righteous.~~ We believe *all* that God *has revealed, all that he does now reveal, and we believe that he will yet reveal many great and important things pertaining to the kingdom of God.* ~~will continue to give revelations by visions, by the ministry of angels, and by the inspiration of the Holy Ghost, until the saints are guided unto all truth, that is, until~~

they come in possession of all the truth there is in existence, and are made perfect in knowledge. So long, therefore, as they are ignorant of any thing past, present, or to come, so long, we believe, they will enjoy the gift of revelation. And when in their immortal and perfect state—when they enjoy "the measure of the stature of the fulness of Christ"—when they are made perfect in one, and become like their Saviour, then they will be in possession of all knowledge, wisdom, and intelligence: then all things will be theirs, whether incipalities or powers, thrones or dominions; and, in short, then they will be filled will all the fulness of God. And what more can they learn? What more can they know? What more can they enjoy? Then they will no longer need revelation.

We believe that wherever the people enjoy the religion of the New Testament, there they enjoy visions, revelations, the ministry of angels, &c. And that wherever these blessings cease to be enjoyed, there they also cease to enjoy the religion of the New Testament.

We believe that God has raised up this church, in order to prepare a people for his second coming in the clouds of heaven, in power, and great glory; and that then the saints who are asleep in their graves will be raised, and reign with him on earth a thousand years.	We believe in the literal gathering of Israel and in the restoration of the Ten Tribes. That Zion will be built upon this continent. That Christ will reign personally upon the earth, and that the earth will be renewed and receive its paradasaic glory.
	We claim the privilege of worshipping Almighty God according to the dictates of our conscience, and allow all men the same privilege let them worship how, where, or what they may.
	We believe in being subject to kings, presidents, rulers, and magistrates, in obeying, honoring and sustaining the law.
	We believe in being honest, true, chaste, benevolent, virtuous, and in doing good to all men; indeed we may say that we follow the admonition of Paul "we believe all things we hope all things," we have endured many things and hope to be able to endure all things. If there is any thing virtuous, lovely, or of good report or praise worthy we seek after these things.
	Respectfully &c., JOSEPH SMITH.

And now we bear testimony to all, both small and great, that the Lord of Hosts hath

> ~~sent us with a message of glad tidings—the everlasting gospel, to cry repentance to the nations, and prepare the way of his second coming. Therefore repent, O ye nations, both Gentiles and Jews, and cease from all your evil deeds, and come forth with broken hearts and contrite spirits, and be baptized in water, in the name of the Father, Son, and Holy Ghost, for remission of sins, and ye shall receive the gift of the Holy Spirit, by the laying on of the hands of the Apostles or Elders of this church; and signs shall follow them that believe, and if they continue faithful to the end, they shall be saved. But woe unto them, who hearken not to the message which God has now sent, for the day of vengeance and burning is at hand, and they shall not escape. Therefore, REMEMBER, O reader, and perish not!~~

The Wentworth letter relates to the authorship of the 900 words because it is a crucial piece of evidence regarding Joseph Smith's thinking at a critical time. Recall that the thank-you note to John Bernhisel was written and mailed in November, 1841. This is the note that supposedly endorsed a Mesoamerican setting for the Book of Mormon. If Joseph had anything to do with the Bernhisel note (which I don't think he did), than one would expect him to be consistent in March 1842. Instead of explicitly rejecting Orson Pratt's hemispheric model, Joseph would have embraced it, or at least limited it to Central America. He could have condensed it and still kept Pratt's original concept.

But he didn't.

Instead, he replaced it with the clarification that the "remnant" of the Book of Mormon people are "the Indians who now inhabit this country."

Because this point is so crucial, some promoters of the Mesoamerican theory have insisted that when Joseph wrote to Mr. Wentworth and referred to "this country," he actually meant all of North and South America. That debate is beyond the scope of this book, but there are plenty of online references for anyone interested in following it.

For my purposes here, it seems unlikely that Joseph was thinking about how someone trying to promote a Mesoamerican setting in the twenty-first century might interpret the phrase. He was writing to a fellow resident of Illinois, knowing the article was intended for publication in the United States. Certainly Mr. Wentworth would understand the phrase to refer to the country in which he and Joseph both lived. If Joseph wanted to convey a hemispheric idea to Wentworth, he would have written "the Indians who live in North and South America" or similar words.

Another important edit Joseph made regards the visitation of Christ. Pratt wrote that Christ visited the temple in South America. Joseph changed that to an appearance on "this continent." Again, what would Wentworth have understood by that term? Like Joseph, Wentworth was familiar with the Continental Army led by George Washington, the Continental Congress that drafted the Constitution, and other terms that referred to the original colonies as a unit instead of separately. It's difficult to conceive how Joseph would have meant, or how Wentworth would have understood, an appearance in Mesoamerica from the term "this continent."

Apart from its doctrinal significance, the Wentworth letter is important as one of only eleven documents signed by Joseph Smith and published in the *Times and Seasons* while he is listed as Editor in 1842 (not counting various affidavits, official statements related to his civic offices, and official orders to the Nauvoo Legion that he signed as Lieutenant General).

Some of these eleven documents are as short as a sentence or two, and some are in combination with others (the First Presidency and Quorum of the Twelve). In all eleven of them, Joseph asserts his authority in an official capacity or biographical sense; i.e., these are pieces no one else could have taken credit for.

In addition, there are two unsigned sets of documents that later became canonized as scripture—the Book of Abraham and the History of Joseph Smith, both in the Pearl of Great Price. These share the attribute of the signed documents; i.e., Joseph communicates with authority and clarity as Prophet and President of the Church. Still, he relied on scribes to help with his history. It is not clear how much, if any, of this history was originally written by Joseph himself; the manuscript source for the *Times and Seasons* history is in the handwriting of James Mulholland. Consequently, "the relationship of author and scribe was conflated, making it difficult to distinguish between Joseph Smith's contribution and that of his scribes."[141]

When evaluating the pieces Joseph signed (or published above his printed signature), it is important to realize that his signature alone did not mean he actually wrote the piece. Wilford Woodruff wrote a letter to Parley P. Pratt on June 12, 1842, in which he mentioned how busy Joseph was:

> I had your letter read you sent Joseph it was a good one I don't know whether it was answered or not, I have never seen Joseph as full of business as of late he hardly gets time to sign his name.[142]

If Joseph hardly gets time to sign his name, how could he have time to write the material he signed? And how would he have time to write material he didn't even sign?

In the days of the Kirtland Safety Society Bank, it appears that Joseph Smith had W.W. Phelps sign notes for him. Such secretarial signatures were frequently used on these notes.[143]

It should not be surprising that Joseph had others write for him; letters published over Joseph's signature in the *Times and Seasons* in 1843 and 1844 were actually written by W. W. Phelps,[144] and this may be true even in 1842. One historian observed, "Because of his lack of formal education, Joseph Smith depended on others to do most of the actual writing of both the sources and the completed history. More than two dozen scribes and writers are known to have assisted him."[145]

The possible involvement of Phelps deserves further mention.

---

[141] *Histories*, Volume 1, *Joseph Smith Histories, 1832-1844*, p. 202.

[142] Wilford Woodruff, *letter to Parley P. Pratt*, June 12, 1842, from Nauvoo, CHL, available online at https://dcms.lds.org/delivery/DeliveryManagerServlet?dps_pid=IE1738096 (Woodruff letter to Pratt).

[143] Comment by Rick Grunder, online at http://www.rickgrunder.com/kbn5.htm .

[144] Brown, "Ghostwriter," p. 44-51.

[145] Howard C. Searle, "History of the Church (History of Joseph Smith)," *Encyclopedia of Mormonism* (Brigham Young University, Provo, Utah 2007), available online at http://eom.byu.edu/index.php/History_of_the_Church_%28History_of_Joseph_Smith%29

Immediately preceding the Wentworth letter in March 1, 1842, *Times and Seasons,* is the first installment of the Book of Abraham. I think it is likely that Phelps (or John Taylor) wrote the introduction to the Book of Abraham, which reads:

> A TRANSLATION
> Of some ancient Records that have fallen into our hands, from the Catecombs [Catacombs] of Egypt, purporting to be the writings of Abraham, while he was in Egypt, called the BOOK OF ABRAHAM, written by his own hand, upon papyrus.

This passage, like so much other unsigned material in the paper, has long been attributed to Joseph Smith directly. Yet this introduction has an odd mixture of concepts. First it claims to be a translation of ancient records, but then it says these records are merely "purporting" to be the writings of Abraham. Would Joseph have written "our hands" if he was claiming responsibility for the translation of the papyrus? Or would it make more sense that someone else—and editor, say—would use this term collectively?

This happens to be the first time the term "purporting" is used in the *Times and Seasons.* (except for a quotation from the Quincy Whig in January 1840). Phelps used the phrase "purporting to be" a couple of times in the *Evening and the Morning Star.* It's not a common phrase, but it's not unique enough, on its own, to be an identifier.

It seems possible to me that Joseph Smith gave the manuscript of the Book of Abraham to Phelps (or John Taylor) for publication. Phelps (or Taylor) could have been responsible to write the introduction, which Joseph may or may not have even seen or noticed until after it was printed. This would be consistent with Joseph's pattern.

It's also interesting that my database of John Taylor's work, including his books, shows only a single instance of the term "purporting." It's in his 1840 "Answer to Some False Statements by the Rev. Robert Heys."

Further study and analysis of this introduction to the Book of Abraham may shed more light on the provenance of this challenging passage. For example, the recently released draft of an unpublished introduction to the Book of Abraham, in the handwriting of Willard Richards and found in

Appendix 7, includes this phrase: "as penend by the hand. of Father Abraham."

We can't tell whether this was dictated by Joseph to Willard Richards or whether Richards composed it as an early draft. That it was never published suggests Joseph did not approve of the phrase; in fact, it seems likely to me that the actual introduction, which says the papyrus was merely "purporting" to be written by Abraham, rejects the Richards draft which claims it was actually "penned" by the hand of Abraham.

Richards also wrote a draft of the Introduction to the Book of Abraham[146] and a journal entry on April 17, 1843, both using the term "purporting."[147] My database of Joseph Smith's holographic writing does not include the term "purporting." The term "purporting" shows up in Winchester (1840, involving signatures and translations), Charles Thompson (1841, quoting the *Quincy Whig*), and Parley P. Pratt (1838 and 1845). In my database, Phelps used the term more than anyone else, apart from Willard Richards.

In my view, Joseph most likely left the editorial comments to others, as I think he did throughout his tenure as the nominal editor of the paper.

---

[146] http://www.josephsmithpapers.org/paper-summary/willard-richards-copy-of-abraham-manuscript-early-1842-a-abraham-11-218/1?highlight=purporting#facts

[147] http://www.josephsmithpapers.org/paper-summary/journal-december-1842-june-1844-book-2-10-march-1843-14-july-1843/161?highlight=purporting#historical-intro

Chapter 9: Nauvoo Editorials from the *Wasp* and the *Times and Seasons*—1 October 1842

--->>> <<<---

BECAUSE OCTOBER 1, 1842, WAS A SATURDAY, *The Wasp* and the *Times and Seasons* were published on the same date. The correlation between the two papers had been evident for several months, but these editions displayed a closer-than-usual connection: mutual editorials about the progress of Nauvoo. Much more information about the integration of the two newspapers is contained in *Brought to Light*.

From the *Wasp*:

BY INDUSTRY WE THRIVE

The great change on the face of the earth in Nauvoo has been wrought by the industry of the saints. The wilderness has been made to blossom as the rose; and where hazle-brush grew and muskitoes [sic] cousined [sic], gardens decorate, and the saints rest. We say 'rest,' because it is a luxury for them to be let alone two or three years. But to our purpose, the country for several miles around, is already risen into the great mass of a city, built by the only people on the earth, that while they labor incessantly to make this earth like the garden of the Lord, labor also, without purse or script, to make men fit subjects for his kingdom and coming.

The city, we think, may now contain from one to two thousand houses, with a population of 14 or 15000: and no matter what the enemy of true religion may say, nor how many may choose to return to the beggarly elements of the world, as in every age when Christ had a church upon the earth, and as, in every place where the saints have been located for the time being, whatsoever they have to do, in righteousness they have done with their might.

If this world would drop the scales from their eyes but once, and see what is designed for the benefit and salvation of mankind, by the course the saints are pursuing, we think that persecution would find less advocates, and honest men more friends. Instead of falsehood, foolish reports, vague surmises, and lies as empty as the space of air they occupy, we would see honest men, act like the wise men of old, we have see the star in the east and have come to worship the man child. Now ye great of the earth, without honest intention a prophet and the sprit of God, who told those 'wise men' to go and worship the babe in the manger? Would to God that, at least, a balance of this generation would 'go and do like wise.'

From the *Times and Seasons*:

NAUVOO.

As good news from a far country, like pure water to a thirsty traveller [traveler], is very refreshing, so we have thought that a little space devoted to Nauvoo, might afford some consolation to those that wish well to the cause of Zion. It is one of the few comforts of the saints in this world, to be settled in peace, and witness the raped [rapid] growth of their infant city, as a place of safety and gathering for the last days. For three or four miles upon the river and about the same distance back in the country, Nauvoo presents a city of gardens, ornamented with the dwellings of those who have made a covenant by sacrifice, and are guided by revelation, an exception to all other societies upon the earth. There is a beautiful commandment and call upon this subject in the fiftieth Psalm, as well as a prophecy of what the Lord will do when he shines, the perfection of beauty out of Zion.

The city of Nauvoo is regularly laid off into blocks, containing four lots of eleven by twelve rods each-making all corner lots. It will be no more than probably correct, if we allow the city to contain between seven and eight hundred houses, with a population of 14 or 15,000. Many of the recent built houses are brick, some one story, and some two stories high, displaying that skill, economy and industry which have always characterized intelligent minds and laudable intentions. The first habitations, as well as many now reared for the time being, in comparison with the expensive mansions of voluptuousness and grandeur in old cities, may be termed "small" but when it is recollected that a large portion of the saints have been "scattered and peeled" some two or three times: and that, also, it is the 'fashion' of the world, to 'shave' them close before they let them 'go to the land of promise,' (as hypocrites not unfrequently [sic] name the place of gathering) no apology will be needed. We can, therefore, of a truth declare, that within the same length of time, and with the same amount of means, no society on the face of the globe, has a better right to the claim of improvement by their own industry; or have offered to their surrounding neighbors, a plainer pattern of mechanical skill, domestic economy, practical temperance, common intelligence, every day virtue, and eternal religion, than the Church of Jesus Christ of Latter Day Saints.

Such a statement of facts will be considered the simple truth, when it is remembered that we are the only people upon the earth who profess to be governed and guided by direct revelation from the Lord: And in this place let us not forget to mention that important commandment which said: "And again, inasmuch as there is land obtained, let there be workmen sent forth, of all kinds, unto this land, to labor for the saints of God." Now who that has witnessed the driving of the saints from place to place, and seen them in the short space of two or three years, raise a town or a city, glowing with all the arts, improvements, and curious workmen found any where upon the earth, can doubt this revelation? One thing is certain, the elders must possess more plausibility, discernment and ingenuity, to find out wise and skilful [sic] workmen, than has ever been the lot of the world, or else the revelation is true,-and these elders are blessed with the spirit of God, to assist in bringing to pass his act, his strange act. This light is not under a bushel.

Two steam mills have been put into operation this season, and many other buildings for mechanical labor in the various branches of manufacture, are either under way or in contemplation,-while the Temple of God, a work of great magnitude, and the Nauvoo House, which when finished will hardly be surpassed in the western world, are rising up as monuments of the enterprise, industry and reverence of the commandments of God, of the saints in their banishment from Missouri.

As to mercantile business we have but little to say:-The fewer foreign goods that are consumed among the saints, the better it will be for home manufactories,-and the nearer we shall come to the word of the Lord, which says: "Thou shalt not be proud in thy heart; let all thy garments be plain, and their beauty the beauty of the work of thine own hands."
We have two presses doing as much as can be expected from the limited resources of a people twice plucked up by the roots, and plundered, even to their

177

clothes, besides the loss of a good printing establishment. As far as truth can be spread and lies contradicted by two presses, against several thousand, it is done! and we have the gratification of saying that things seem to work together for good to them that look for the second appearing of our Lord Jesus Christ.

Finally, brethren, as this world is not the place of much happiness to the saints, on account of the great prevalence of the powers of darkness upon the earth, and the wickedness and corruption of men's hearts, we think we can not do better than say, that while other cities are secretly practicing vice in its most horrid form, Nauvoo, like an infant at the breast of its mother, is deriving its nourishment from that fountain of life which invigorates youth without endangering the health; and we do sincerely hope, that we as children of the kingdom, may keep the law of God, and the law of the land, continuing steadfast in the liberty of the gospel, and ever abounding in the knowledge of the Lord, knowing this, for grace and salvation, that in the world there is no deliverance; no; nowhere but in Jerusalem, and in Mount Zion, and in the remnant whom the Lord our God shall call.

Nauvoo, at present is, figuratively, the great fish market of the earth, where all kinds, both good and bad, are gathered-where the good are preserved, and the bad cast away-for until the savior comes, there will be wise virgins and foolish;-blessed are they that continue to the end faithful, for whether they have builded a city in Ohio, or Missouri, or Illinois, they shall enter into the joys of their Lord, and inherit the kingdom prepared before the foundation of the world.

Chapter 10: Geography References

EARLY CHURCH NEWSPAPERS OFTEN CITED EXTRINSIC EVIDENCE of the Book of Mormon to promote interest. This table brings them together in one place.

Reference	Author	Excerpt	Central/ South America	North America
"The Book of Ether" 1832, Aug., EMS	Unsigned (W.W. Phelps was the only one writing for EMS at this time)	As to the Jaredites, no more is known than is contained in The Book of Ether. Perhaps "Dighton writing Rock," **in Massachusetts,** may hold an unknown tale in relation to these Pioneers of the land of liberty, which can yet be revealed.		X
[Excerpt continued] … we can not only discover the traces in artificial curiosities, and common works, and **small hills, mountain caves, and extensive prairies**, where the Jaredites filled the measure of their time, but, as they were a very large race of men, **whenever we hear that uncommon large bones have been dug up from the earth,** we may conclude, That was the skeleton of a Jaredite.				
"The Far West" 1832, Oct., EMS, p. 37.	Unsigned (W.W. Phelps)	The far west, as the section of country from the Mississippi to the Rocky Mountains may justly be styled, is not only distant from the		

		Atlantic States, but different.		

[Excerpt continued] Its principle river, running rapidly from the 48th to the 39th degree of north latitude, is always rily, always wearing away its banks and always making new channels: It is rightly named Missouri… while the eye takes in a large scope of clear field, or extensive plains, … the mind goes back to the day, **when the Jaredites were in their glory upon this choice land** above all others, and comes on till they, and even the Nephites, were destroyed for their wickedness: this beautiful region of country is now mostly, excepting Arkansas and Missouri, the land of Joseph or the Indians, as they are called, and embraces three fine climates… . **This place may be called the centre of America**; it being about an equal distance from Maine, to Nootka sound; and from the gulf of St. Lawrence to the gulf of California; yea, and about the middle of the continent from cape Horn, south, to the head land at Baffin's Bay, north. The world will never value the land of Desolation, as it is called in the book of Mormon, for any thing more than hunting ground, for want of timber and mill-seats: The Lord to the contrary notwithstanding, **declares it to be the land of Zion** which is the land of Joseph, blessed by him… When we consider that the land of Missouri is the land where the saints of the living God are to be gathered together and sanctified for the second coming of the Lord Jesus, we cannot help exclaiming with the prophet, O land be glad!

"Letter VII. To W. W. Phelps, Esq." 1835, July, M&A, pp. 155-9. [Reprinted in GR, 15 Mar. 1841; T&S 2:11 1 Apr. 1841, p. 379; The Improvement Era 2, 1899, pp. 729-734]	Oliver Cowdery	I must now give you some description of the place where, and the manner in which these records were deposited….this is the highest hill for some distance round….		

[Excerpt continued] At about **one mile west** rises another ridge of less height, running parallel with the former, leaving **a beautiful vale between**. … one reflects on the fact, that **here, between these hills, the entire power and national strength of both the Jaredites and Nephites were destroyed.** By turning to the 529th and 530th pages of the book of Mormon you will read Mormon's account of the last great struggle of his people, as **they were encamped round this hill Cumorah. In this valley fell the remaining strength and pride of a once powerful people, the Nephites… From the top of this hill, Mormon,** with a few others, after the battle, **gazed with horror** upon the mangled remains of those who, the day before, were filled with anxiety, hope, or doubt… [Mormon] deposited, as he says, on the 529th page, **all the records in this same hill, Cumorah,** and after gave his small record to his son Moroni, who, as appears from the same, finished, after witnessing the extinction of his people as a nation... **This hill, by the Jaredites, was called Ramah: by it, or around it, pitched the famous army of Coriantumr their tents.** Coriantumr was the last king of the Jaredites. The opposing army were to the west, and in this same valley, and near by, from day to day, did that mighty race spill their blood, in wrath, contending, as it were, brother against brother, and father, against son. In this same spot, in full view from the top of this same hill, one may gaze with astonishment upon the ground which was twice covered with the dead and dying of our fellowmen... In this vale lie commingled, in one mass of ruin, the ashes of thousands, and in this vale was destined to consume the fair forms and vigerous [sic] systems of tens of thousands of the human race-blood mixed with blood, flesh with flesh, bones with bones, and dust with dust!

"Evidences of the Book of Mormon" 1837, Jan., M&A	Wm. Smith	"in the Book of Mormon… a remnant of the branches or seed of Joseph are represented as crossing the sea, and settling this continent of North and South America	X	X
American Antiquities-More Proofs of the Book of Mormon 1841, June 15, T&S 2:16	Unsigned	We feel great pleasure in laying before our readers the following interesting account of the **Antiquities of Central America,**	X	

[Excerpt continued] which have been discovered by two eminent travellers who have spent considerable labor, to bring to light the remains of ancient buildings, architecture &c., which prove beyond controversy that, on this vast continent, once flourished a mighty people, skilled in the arts and sciences, and whose splendor would not be eclipsed by any of the nations of Antiquity-a people once high and exalted in the scale of intelligence, but now like their ancient buildings, fallen into ruins.

To the Editors of the Times & Seasons: 1841, Sep. 15, T&S 2:22	Chas. W. Wandell	I consider it to be a great acquisition to us **in proving the Book of Mormon to be a genuine record, by comparing it with**	X	X

		the researches of Humboldt, Raffinesque, Stephens and others. [Wandell compares Prof. Anthon's description of the characters to a description of "American glyphs" in *American Antiquities*.]		
Church History (the Wentworth Letter) 1842, Mar. 1, T&S 3:9	Joseph Smith, Jr.	In this important and interesting book the history of ancient America is unfolded, from its first settlement...		X

[Excerpt continued] to the beginning of the fifth century of the Christian era. We are informed by these records that America in ancient times has been inhabited by two distinct races of people. The first were called Jaredites and came directly from the tower of Babel. The second race came directly from the city of Jerusalem, about six hundred years before Christ. They were principally Israelites, of the descendants of Joseph. The Jaredites were destroyed about the time that the Israelites came from Jerusalem, who succeeded them in the inheritance of the country. The principal nation of the second race fell in battle towards the close of the fourth century. **The remnant are the Indians that now inhabit this country.** This book also tells us that our Saviour made his appearance upon this continent after his resurrection,

American Antiquities 1842, Jul. 15, T&S 3:18	ED.	[After quoting American Antiquities...] Stephens and Catherwood's researches in Central America abundantly testify of this thing.... **Their ruins speak of their greatness; the Book of Mormen unfolds**	X	X

		their history		
From the Bostonian. MORMONS, OR "LATTER DAY SAINTS." 1842, Sep. 1 T&S 3:21, p.	"Lover of Truth"	He introduced an account of many American antiquities together with the discoveries lately made by Mr. Stevens that all go to prove that the American Indians were once an enlightened people and understood the arts and sciences, as the ruined cities and monuments lately discovered fully prove.	X	
EXTRACT From Stephen's "Incidents of Travel in Central America." 1842, Sep. 15 T&S 3:22	Unsigned	Let us turn our subject, however, to the Book of Mormon, where **these wonderful ruins of Palenque are among the mighty works of the Nephites:-**and the mystery is solved….	X	

[Excerpt continued] Mr. Stephens' great developments of antiquities are made bare to the eyes of all the people by reading the history of the Nephites in the Book of Mormon. **They lived about the narrow neck of land, which now embraces Central America, with all the cities that can be found.** …Who could have dreamed that twelve years would have developed such incontrovertible testimony to the Book of Mormon? surely the Lord worketh and none can hinder.

"FACTS ARE STUBBORN THINGS." 1842, Sep. 15 T&S 3:22	Unsigned	From an extract from "Stephens' Incidents of Travel in Central America," it will be seen that the proof of the Nephites and	X	

		Lamanites dwelling on this continent,		

[Excerpt continued] according to the account in the Book of Mormon, is developing itself in a more satisfactory way than the most sanguine believer in that revelation, could have anticipated...When we read in the Book of Mormon...that Lehi went down by the Red Sea to the great Southern Ocean, and crossed over to this land and **landed a little south of the Isthmus of Darien,**

ZARAHEMLA 1842, Oct. 1 T&S 3:23	Unsigned	Central America, or Guatimala, is situated north of the Isthmus of Darien and once embraced several hundred miles of territory from north to south.-	X	

[Excerpt continued] **The city of Zarahemla**, burnt at the crucifixion of the Savior, and rebuilt afterwards, **stood upon this land**... It is certainly a good thing for the excellency and veracity, of the divine authenticity of the Book of Mormon, that **the ruins of Zarahemla have been found where the Nephites left them**

LETTER OF ORSON SPENCER 1843, Jan. 2 T&S 4:4	ORSON SPENCER	As you enquire after the reasons that operated to change my mind to the present faith, I only remark that **Stevens' Travels had some influence, as an external evidence of the truth of the Book of Mormon.**	X	
Ancient Records 1843, May 1 T&S 4:12	Unsigned	But when they were told of the various relics that have been found indicative of civilization, intelligence and learning;	X	

[Excerpt continued] when they were told of the wealth, architecture and splendor of ancient Mexico; when recent developements proved beyond a doubt, that **there was**

ancient ruins in Central America, which, in point of magnificence, beauty, strength and architectural design, would vie with any of the most splendid ruins on the Asiatic continent; when they could trace the fine delineations of the sculptor's chisel, on the beautiful statue, the mysterious hieroglyphic, and the unknown character, they begun to believe that a wise, powerful, intelligent and scientific race had inhabited this continent;.

| STEPHEN'S WORKS ON CENTRAL AMERICA 1843, Oct. 1 T&S 4:22 | Unsigned | We have lately perused with great interest, Stephen's works on Central America, Chiapas, and Yucatan.... | X | |

[Excerpt continued] Since the publication of this work, Mr. Stephens has again visited Central America, in company with Mr. Catherwood, and other scientific gentlemen, for the purpose of making further explorations among those already interesting ruins. This is a work that ought to be in the hands of every Latter Day Saint; **corroborating, as it does the history of the Book of Mormon. There is no stronger circumstantial evidence of the authenticity of the latter book, can be given, than that contained in Mr. Stephens' works**.... For the information of our friends who do not possess this work, we may at a convenient time collect and compare many of the important items in this work, and in the Book of Mormon, and publish them.
[Note: this comparison was never published.]

| ANCIENT RUINS 1844, Jan. 1 T&S 5:1 | Ed. and [Texas Telegraph] | Every day adds fresh testimony to the already accumulated evidence on the authenticity of the "Book of Mormon." | X | X |

[Excerpt continued] At the time that book was translated there was very little known about ruined cities and dilapidated buildings. The general presumption was, that no people possessing more intelligence than our present race of Indians had ever inhabited this continent, and the accounts given in the Book of Mormon concerning large cities and civilized people having inhabited this land, was generally disbelieved and pronounced a humbug. **Priest, since then has thrown some light on this interesting subject. Stephens in his "Incidents of Travels in Central America," has thrown in a flood of testimony, and from the following statements it is evident that the Book of Mormon does not give a more extensive account of large and populous cities than those discoveries now demonstrate to be even in existence**... there are vestiges of ancient cities and ruined castles or temples on the Rio Puerco and on the Colorado of the west. He says that one of the branches of the Rio Puerco, a few days travel from Santa Fe, there is an immense pile of ruins that appear to belong to an ancient temple.

For the *Times and Seasons* Pekin, Illinois, Dec. 1, 1843. Brother Taylor: 1844, Jan. 15 T&S 5:2, p. 406.	H. Tate	Ye men of science and literature, why does Josiah Priest's antiquities, and Stephens' Yucatan, give an account of the very things that were described in the Book of Mormon, before their discovery?	X	X

[Excerpt continued] Why does the circumstance of the plates recently found in a mound in Pike county, Ill., by Mr. Wiley, together with ethmology and a thousand other things, go to prove the Book of Mormon true?-Ans. Because it is true!

ANCIENT RUINS IN TEXAS 1844, Aug. 15 T&S 5:15, p. 622	[Texas Telegraph]	[reprinting of excerpt from 1 Jan. 1844, but without the editorial introduction]	X	X
ANCIENT RUINS 1844, Dec. 15 T&S 5:23	Unsigned	Were it necessary, in order to establish the truth of their reality, just as they are found, showing that civilized nations,	X	X

[Excerpt continued] possessing the highest attainments in the arts and sciences, once occupied this whole land, and we add, world,-we might go behind the flood of Noah, and bring in the ante-deluvians, those "men of renown," and suppose a few cases of their "ruins"-for there were "giants in the earth in those days," and put curiosity on the stretch... From many of the speculations of this age upon the grandeur of the ruins, discovered in Central and South America, ... In our last paper may be seen the "Interesting discovery in South America," and the "Disinterment of Nineveh." ... **As to the original inhabitants of the continent of America, the Book of Mormon, backs up the description of immense "ruins" in Central America, dispels all doubt. ...** After they had almost covered the land with cities, and probably made the present prairies by extensive cultivation.... **To turn the attention of such as may read the works of Stevens' upon the "ruins" of Central America, we ask a perusal of the following from the writings of Nephi in the Book of Mormon:**

CORRESPONDENCE.	Wm. Smith	Was it for revealing		

Bordentown N. J. Nov. 10th, 1844. 1845, Jan. 1 T&S 5:24		to the world a knowledge of whose lands, and by whom the foundation of these mighty cities had been laid,	X	

[Excerpt continued] and since discovered by Stephens and Catherwood; this none will doubt, yet a knowledge of the fact of these cities being built by skillful hands, hundreds of years ago, written in the Book of Mormon would be 'humbug.'

These discoveries, made by the these men, which are truly great and confirmatory [confirmation] of the truth of the Book of Mormon, and the inspiration of the prophet Joseph, was made since this book was found and published to the world in 1830; then the prophecy was made that the Indians were a remnant of the house of Israel, "had wandered through the wilderness, and came over the sea," inhabited North and South America, built large cities, and were a warlike people; that many had fallen in battle and cities had been destroyed, a remnant remained as the last vestige, to tell the sad tale and history of their fallen race. And who has proved this prophecy true? 'Stephens and Catherwood!'

THE ANSWER 1845, Jan. 1 T&S 5:24	W.W. Phelps	shall we, who have beheld prophecies fulfilled knowing that **the very bowels of the earth have hove up her "stony ruins,"** to establish the validity of the Book of Mormon, beyond a doubt		
ANOTHER MORMON WITNESS 1845, Mar. 1 T&S 6:4	Unsigned	A Relic.-A day or two ago, an oak was cut down **a short distance from Harrisburg,** (and near an old revolutionary relic, known as Paxton's church,)	X	X

[Excerpt continued] which, upon counting the growth proved to be near four hundred years old, and perfectly embedded in it, at a height of near thirty feet from the ground, was found a well shaped stone mortar and pestle, and an instrument very much resembling an axe, though much smaller in size.... About three hundred and fifty two years ago, Columbus discovered South America, and **about as long ago as any of these times, nobody but the natives lived near "Harrisburg," and thus the old stone mortar, pestle, and axe were laid up as Mormon testimony. Such relics are capital stock for the Latter-day Saints, as well as is the cities, and ruins in Central America, discovered by Mr. Stevens in the very places where the Book of Mormon left them.**

| From the Christian Reflector. THE MORMON PROPHET Remarks 1845, Apr. 1 T&S 6:6 | Unsigned | we copy the foregoing eulogy on General Joseph Smith, one of the greatest men that ever lived on the earth; | X | |

[Excerpt continued] emphatically proved so, by being inspired by God to bring forth the Book of Mormon, which gives the true history of the natives of this continent; their ancient glory and cities:-which cities have been discovered by Mr. Stevens in Central America, exactly were the Book of Mormon left them.

| ANOTHER WITNESS FOR THE BOOK OF MORMON 1845, Mar. 1 T&S 6:4 | Unsigned | A writer in the Buffalo Pilot gives us another witness for the Book of Mormon. | | X |

[Excerpt continued] It is a fine thing to have such specimens of antiquity found and then to have wise men look into the Book of Mormon and solve the mystery. ... The writer states, that **in the town adjoining Cooper, county of Allegan, Michigan, about a mile distant from the fertile banks of the Kalamazoo, is a small hamlet, commonly known as Arnold's Station. The first settlers of this little place, emigrants from the St. Joseph country, found in the township some extensive ruins of what had evidently been the work of human ingenuity**, and which they christened the Military Post.

"It consists," says the writer, "of a wall of earth, running northwest and southeast, being about the height of a man's head in the principal part of its length, but varying in some places, as if it had been degraded, either by the hands of assailants or the lapse of time.... If the neighboring Indians are questioned upon its traditionary history, the invariable answer is, that it was there when they came-more, they either do not or can not say.

That it was the labor of an extinct race is pretty evident, and it probably dates from the same era with the extensive works at Rock River.

General Conference

1857, Sep. 13 JoD 5:237-248	John Taylor [Note: this is the only mention of Stephens and Catherwood signed by Taylor]	**Stephens and Catherwood,** after examining the ruins that were found at Guatemala, in Central America, and gazing upon magnificent ruins, moldering temples, stately edifices, rich sculpture, elegant statuary, and all the traces of a highly cultivated and civilized people, said—	X	

[Excerpt continued] "Here are the works of a great and mighty people that have inhabited these ruins; but now they are no more: history is silent on the subject, and no man can unravel this profound mystery. Nations have planted, and reaped, and built, and lived, and died, that are now no more; and no one can tell anything about them or reveal their history."

Why, there was a young man in Ontario County, New York, to whom the angel of God appeared and gave an account of the whole. **These majestic ruins bespeak the existence of a mighty people. The Book of Mormon unfolds their history.**

1877, Jun. 17 JoD 19:36-45	Brigham Young	This is an incident in the life of Oliver Cowdery, but he did not take the liberty of telling such things in meeting as I take.		X

[Excerpt continued] I tell these things to you, and I have a motive for doing so. I want to carry them to the ears of my brethren and sisters, and to the children also, that they may grow to an understanding of some things that seem to be entirely hidden from the human family. Oliver Cowdery went with the Prophet Joseph when he deposited these plates. Joseph did not translate all of the plates; there was a portion of them sealed, which you can learn from the Book of Doctrine and Covenants. **When Joseph got the** plates, the angel instructed him to carry them back to the hill Cumorah, which he did. Oliver says that when Joseph and Oliver went there, the hill opened, and they walked into a cave, in which there was a large and spacious room. He says he did not think, at the time, whether they had the light of the sun or artificial light; but that it was just as light as day. They laid the plates on a table; it was a large table that stood in the room. Under this table there was a pile of plates as much as two feet high, and there were altogether in this room **more plates than probably many wagon loads; they were piled up in the corners and along the walls.** The first time they went there the sword of Laban hung upon the wall; but when they went again it had been taken down and laid upon the table across the gold plates; it was unsheathed, and on it was written these words: "This sword will never be sheathed again until the kingdoms of this world become the kingdom of our God and his Christ." **I tell you this as coming not only from Oliver Cowdery, but others who were familiar with it, and who understood it just as well as we understand coming to this meeting**, enjoying the day, and by and by we separate and go away, forgetting most of what is said, but remembering some things. So is it with other circumstances in life. I relate this to you, and I want you to understand it. I take this liberty of referring to those things so that they will not be forgotten and lost. Carlos Smith was a young man of as much veracity as any young man we had, and he was a witness to these things. Samuel Smith saw some things, Hyrum saw a good many things, but Joseph was the leader.

| 1854, Jul. 4
JoD 6:367-371 | Orson Hyde | It was by the agency of that same angel of God that appeared unto Joseph Smith, and revealed to him **the history of the early inhabitants of this country, whose mounds, bones, and remains of towns, cities, and fortifications** speak from the dust in the ears of the living with the voice of undeniable truth. | | X |
| 1868, Dec. 27
JoD 12:338-346 | Orson Pratt [He also wrote on | by the command of the Lord they [the Jaredites] collected | X | |

	the topic in various articles, pamphlets, etc.]	seeds and grain of every kind, and animals of almost every description, among which, no doubt, were the elephant and the curelom and the cumom,		

[Excerpt continued] very huge animals that existed in those days, and after traveling and crossing, we suppose, the sea that was east of where the Tower of Babel stood, and traveling through the wilderness many days, with their flocks and herds, their grain and substance, they eventually came to the great Pacific ocean, on the eastern borders of China or somewhere in that region.... He it was who guided them safely to this American shore.

They landed to the south of this, just below the Gulf of California, on our western coast. They inhabited North America, and spread forth on this Continent, and in the course of some sixteen hundred years' residence here, they became a mighty and powerful nation.... The whole nation perished. **Their greatest and last struggles were in the State of New York, near where the plates from which the Book of Mormon was translated...** After the destruction of the Jaredites, the Lord brought two other colonies to people this land. **One colony landed a few hundred miles north of the Isthmus on the western coast; the other landed on the coast of Chile, upwards of two thousand miles south of them.... A little over one century before Christ the Nephites united with the Zarahemlaites in the northern portions of South America, and were called Nephites and became a powerful nation. The country was called the land Bountiful, and included within the land of Zarahemla. But to go back to their early history. Shortly after the Nephite colony was brought by the power of God, and landed on the western coast of South America, in the country we call Chile, there was a great division among them.**

1870, Nov. 27 JoD 14:289-299	Orson Pratt	God had a people here in ancient America, there is no mistake about this, and all who want to know for certain in regard to this Continent being settled, just read the	X	X

		history of its antiquities—		

[Excerpt continued] read the works of Stevens and Catherwood and many others, on the great and mighty ancient cities whose ruins are seen on various parts of this Continent, especially in Central America and the northern part of South America. Ruins, too, that not only speak of a former civilization of the inhabitants who dwelt there, but which show that they were a people who understood the arts—understood building magnificent cities, temples and great palaces. They were a very different people from the present aboriginal inhabitants of the Continent... Only a few years ago—in 1835, thirty-eight years after the plates of the Book of Mormon were taken out of the earth by Joseph Smith, one of the great mounds in the State of Ohio was opened, near Newark, in Licking County. It was a very large mound: it measured, before they began to cart away the stones and dirt, 580 feet in circumference, and was from forty to fifty feet in height. After they had carted away from this mound several thousand loads of dirt and stones, for the purpose of canalling or fixing a canal, they found on the outer edge near the circumference of the base of this mound, just within the circle, several smaller mounds, built entirely of fire clay, that had the appearance of putty. When digging into one of these smaller mounds they came to something that had the appearance of wood, and after having removed the upper surface of it, they found a trough, and in that trough several metallic rings, probably the ancient coins of the country. They also found that the interior trough had been lined with some kind of cloth, but it was in such a state of decomposition that only the least bit of it would hold together, not even a piece as large as your thumb nail. There was also some human bones in this trough and a lock of fine black hair. Underneath this trough, still further down in the fire clay, they found a stone, and when it was taken out they found that it was hollow and that there was something inside of it. They found by inspection that it had been cemented together with hard cement. With considerable exertion they broke the stone in two. It was oval, or elliptical in form. They separated it where it was cemented together, and in the inside they found another kind of stone on which was engraven the Ten Commandments in the ancient Hebrew. This stone was immediately sent to Cincinnati, where many learned men saw it and they declared the inscriptions were in ancient Hebrew, and translated the Ten Commandments. The stone was nearly seven inches long, nearly three inches wide, and almost two in thickness. On one side of it there was a depression, and in this depression was a raised profile, the likeness of a man clothed with a robe—that is, carved out of the stone, with his left side partly facing the beholder, and the robe and girdle upon his left shoulder; he had also a turban on. Over his head was written in Hebrew, Moshe, which is the Hebrew name for Moses. They therefore represented this person, thus carved out, as Moses. Around about him, that is on the various sides of the stone, were written the Ten Commandments in ancient Hebrew.

Now what does this prove? It proves that the inhabitants of this country were acquainted with the revelations of heaven—those given to Moses; and if they understood these would they not naturally look forward to the coming of the Messiah? Would they not look for the Lord to raise up such a being, which their law indicated by types? And when that being came is it to be supposed that he would leave the inhabitants of America ignorant concerning that event? By no means. He would not forget them. **And this record—the Book of Mormon, gives us an account of that very people.**

Let me here state that I have seen this stone; with my own eyes I have seen the Hebrew engravings upon it; and though many of the characters were altered in shape from the present Hebrew, yet I had sufficient knowledge of them to understand and know how to translate the inscription. This stone was sent to the New York Ethnological Society, and while there, by the politeness of the Secretary of the Society, I had the pleasure of seeing it. Another mound was opened in the same county, in Ohio, and out of it were taken stones with other Hebrew inscriptions; and in 1860 and 1865 there were several of these antiquities exhumed with Hebrew characters on, and one with characters that were not Hebrew, and which the learned could not translate, showing that the people of this continent not only understood the Hebrew, but some other kind of an alphabet. This book—the Book of Mormon, informs us that the Lord brought the colony to this country six hundred years before Christ, and that he brought them from Jerusalem. Was there anything connected with these ancient characters that would indicate such a great antiquity? Yes. The Hebrew, since six hundred years before Christ, every learned scholar knows, has been greatly altered in the shape of its characters. It now has square characters, with vowel points; that is, the form of the Hebrew characters now is entirely different in many respects from the ancient characters, such as are found on coins and engravings lately exhumed in Palestine. Moreover since the period that colony was brought to America, not only have the forms of the Hebrew characters been changed, but some fourteen different new characters have been introduced. Now, the stones taken from these mounds, on which the Ten Commandments were engraved, had none of these new characters, which shows that the inscriptions were of a more ancient date than the modern Hebrew. Still further. The Hebrew as it now stands, has a great many of what are termed final characters that it did not have six hundred years before Christ. You do not find these characters on these stones that were taken out of the Ohio mounds. All these circumstances prove, pointedly, the great antiquity of the people who formed these mounds and wrote the characters on these stones…. On what part of this continent did Jesus appear? He appeared in what is now termed the northern part of South America, where they had a temple built.

| 1867, Oct. 7 | Orson Pratt | When I entered this | | |

JoD 19:311-321		Territory in August last, on my return from my last mission,		X

[Excerpt continued] I beheld from the mouth of Parley's Canyon the top of this building very prominent. It seemed to rear itself up above the surrounding buildings, and it was easily to be seen. **It looked very much like an artificial mountain erected here, or like some of those mounds that we see down on the Missouri River, that were made by the ancient inhabitants of our country,** only it is much larger and higher than some of them.

1870, Apr. 10 JoD 13:124-138	Orson Pratt	[The Jaredites] colonized what we call North America, landing on the western coast, a little south of the Gulf of California, in the southwestern part of this north wing of our continent....		X

[Excerpt continued] [The Lehites] went aboard of this vessel and were brought by the special providence of God across the great Indian and Pacific Oceans, and landed on the western coast of South America.... [The Mulekites] left Jerusalem the same year that the Jews were carried away captive into Babylon, were brought forth to this continent and landed somewhere north of the Isthmus. They wended their way into the northern part of South America. About four hundred years after this the two colonies amalgamated in the northern part of South America and they became one nation.

1873, May 18 JoD 16:47-59	Orson Pratt	These records were carried by Ether from the hill Ramah, afterwards called Cumorah, where the Jaredites were destroyed, as well as the Nephites. He carried them forth towards South America,		X

[Excerpt continued] and placed them in a position north of the Isthmus, where a portion of the people of King Limhi, about one hundred years before Christ, found them. I will read you a little description of their being found. On page 161, Book of Mormon, it appears that the people of Limhi were a certain colony that had left the main body of the Nephites, and had settled in the land where Nephi built and located his little colony, **soon after their landing on the western coast of South America.** After landing, and after the death of his father Lehi, Nephi was commanded of God to take those who would believe in the Most High, and flee out from his brethren. And they traveled many days' journey to the northward, and located in a land which they called the Land of Nephi, and dwelt there some four hundred years. And then because of the wickedness of the people they were threatened with a great destruction. **The Lord led Mosiah out of the Land of Nephi, and led him still further north, some twenty days' journey, and they located on the river Sidon, now called Magdalena, which runs from the south to the north. And there they found a people called the people of Zarahemla.**

1881, Feb. 6 JoD 22:17-27	John Nicholson	We claim this book is a record or history of the ancient inhabitants of America, the remnants of whom are now scattered on various portions of this continent.	X	X

[Excerpt continued] Numbers of them surround us in these valleys, and are known as the aborigines of America. It is unnecessary for me to more than allude to the fact that there did exist, in the ages of the past, peoples on this land who had arrived at an advanced stage of civilization, and who cultivated the arts and sciences. The ruins of vast cities, among which are the remains of great structures, giving ample evidence of this fact. This testimony is presented before the world and is being constantly produced for the consideration of the reading public. Then there was a people anciently upon this continent who were in a condition of advancement; this is universally acknowledged, I believe, by those who have considered this question.

Conclusion: Joseph Looks Better than Ever

FOR OVER 170 YEARS, CHURCH MEMBERS, LEADERS, and scholars have been influenced by Benjamin Winchester's articles in the *Times and Seasons*. This has led to an unfortunate focus on Mesoamerica in the search for Book of Mormon lands. Joseph Smith never described sites in Mesoamerica as places where Book of Mormon events occurred. By contrast, he did name specific places in North America.

Concluding as I have that the Mesoamerican theory originated out of misplaced missionary zeal (or a focus on the Hinterlands), I was curious about what a "correct" geography would look like. The work of Sorenson and others has been invaluable in this pursuit—but it led me to a much different conclusion. Sorenson's work *excludes* Mesoamerica as a viable setting for the Book of Mormon.

Now that the truth about the *Times and Seasons* is known, hopefully we can redirect our efforts, energy, and resources to North America. People respond to the truth. The more we learn about The Book of Mormon, the more the truth becomes apparent. A correct understanding of Book of Mormon geography and anthropology will facilitate acceptance of the book on a broader scale than ever before. Replacing Mesoamerica with North America will strengthen the faith of members, encourage missionaries, and remove an unnecessary stumbling block for investigators.

We can all look forward to a whole new world of Book of Mormon studies.

Postscript.

The issues addressed in this book have been on my mind since before I was a freshman at BYU and took a class from Professor John L. Sorenson, whom I greatly respect. I have read extensively about the various theories of

Book of Mormon geography, and I have visited many of the sites in Mesoamerica and North America. The disputes among the various proponents has been unfortunate, to say the least, but there's no doubt that these *Times and Seasons* articles have been one of the major sources of confusion and contention.

It wasn't until December 2014, when I first read the Roper article, that the role of an unknown author became apparent. Through a series of events too long to recount here, I stumbled upon Benjamin Winchester. Everything else flowed from that.

Along the way, I've had the fortune of receiving input from many friends, and I wish to thank them here. You know who you are; maybe in the future I can list your names. The one I thank above all others is my wife, Beverly.

I owe a tremendous debt to all individuals who kept records and journals in the 1800s, often under difficult circumstances, as well as to the researchers who have examined these issues from so many angles. Only a few could be cited herein. I especially appreciate the ongoing work of the Joseph Smith Papers, which has made this research feasible and accessible to the world.

Many who have believed Joseph Smith wrote or approved the 900 words have felt bound by the Mesoamerican connection they established. Hopefully, the truth will make them free.

Surely additional information will come to light in the future—possibly the near future.

Jonathan Neville, February 2015

Appendix 1: Correspondence between John Bernhisel and Joseph Smith

The seven letters between John Bernhisel and Joseph Smith are shown below with key points emphasized in **bold**.

13 April 1841

City of Nauvoo April 13, 1841

Dear Brother,

Yours of the 6th. ultimo is received, **which should have been answered before, had not I been so much engaged in the business of the conference.**

In reply, I have to say, that I allways feel glad to do all I can for the interest of the church and for individuals.

I think it will be impossible to enter any land at Congress price excepting prairie, about 4 or 5 miles from town. But there is frequently persons who want to sell lands in the neighborhood and who, would be induced to sell very low for cash.

If you were here; I think you would have plenty of oppertunities of making good bargains if you were here, but if you cannot come I will endeavour to obtain a suitable place for you if you advise me so to do.

If you were to send what means you can conveniently spare for that purpose to me, I will lay it out to the best advantage for you, and if I should not meet with a suitable purchase soon, I will allow you good interest for the same, but I have no doubt but I shall have plenty of oppertunities of laying out your money to good advantage.

I approve of your place of letting out the land you purchase, as it must soon be verey valuable indeed, and at the same time be doing a favor to some of the poor brethren whose property has been taken away from them by a ruthless mob.

Our conference is just over; we have ad a glorious time indeed; the particulars **you will see in the Times and Seasons which will be out in a few days.**

The health of the people is good, and we are expecting great blessings and enjoyments, and are anxously looking for, and expecting our

199

eastern friends to come and share in the toils and blessings

With sentiments of respect
I am yours &c in the gospel
Joseph Smith

J. M. Berishall. [John Bernhisel] M.D.

P.S. If you should send any means on, you can send it by Elders [Samuel] Bent or [George W.] Harris who I expect are somewhere in your neighborhood or with any of the twelve when they come, or a draught on New York by mail. J. S.

The Brethren in New York wrote to me sometime ago on the subject of Babtizm [baptism] for the dead please to inform them **I well attend to it as soon as I possibly can.** J. S.

12 July 1841

New York July 12, 1841.

Dear Brother,

I have received your favor of the 13th of April, informing me that it would be impossible to enter any land except prairie at Congress price, and kindly offering to procure a suitable place for me if I should advise you to do so. Enclosed you will receive a certificate of deposite for four hundred and twenty five dollars on the Greenwich bank in this city, and **you will have the goodness to purchase as soon as a a favorable opportunity offers** (for I presume it will advance rapidly in price) as large a tract of good land, with a sufficient quantity of timber, in a healthful location, and within a convenient distance, say one two or three miles of Nauvoo, as you can for about five hundred dollars, the remaining seventy five I will remit to you on or before the 1st of July of next year. Be pleased to have the deed recorded and retain it in your possession until the balance is paid, for I suppose it will not be necessary to execute a mortgage on the property for so small an amount. Of the value of the improvements I care but little as my object is to procure as large a tract of land as I can with my limited means. When you have made the purchase, you will please to rent it to such a tenant and on such terms as you would if it were your own. You will greatly oblige me by immediately acknowledging the receipt of the enclosed certificate, and writing me when you have effected a purchase.

I have delivered your Message to the Bretheren here respecting your reply to their letter on the subject of baptism for the dead. We were rejoiced to here that you were delivered out of the hands of wicked and ungodly men. It was reported that you designed making us a visit about the latter part of May, we therefore anxiously expected you, but it is superfluous to add that were disappointed. **I have for several weeks past transmitted the New York Evangelist to the Editors of the Times & Seasons, if it is of no service to them, please say to them if they will return a no. I will discontinue sending it.** Elder John E. Page arrived in this city on the 6th instant, on his way to Jerusalem, and will sail for Liverpool in a few days. Elder [Wilford] Woodruff has not yet returned from the state of Maine. We have had the pleasure of a flying visit from Elders Hiram [Hyrum] Smith, Wm [Law] & Wilson Law. I tender to you my grateful acknowledgments for your kind offer to attend to this affair, but **it is with some reluctance that I accept it, for your are no doubt almost overwhelmed with business.**

> With sentiments of the highest
> Regard I am yours in the Gospel
> John M. Bernhisel
> 176 Hudson street

P. S. Elder Page delivered three discourses yesterday to crowded congregations, and requests me to present his best respects to the authorities of the Church and desires that you would inform his family that he is in the enjoyment of good health. He gives exceedingly flattering accounts of the progress of the work where he labored during the past winter & Spring and this summer. J. M B.

3 August 1841

City of Nauvoo. Aug. 3, 1841

Dear Brother,

Your certificate of deposit of $500.— came Safe to hand a few days ago. **It shall be applied on the most advantageous purchase I can find.** If a purchase could have been made early in the spring it could have been done to much better advantage than at present, owing to the vast number of the Saints who are continually pouring in to this county— all, of course. want locations, consequently the land in the immediate vicinity had been taken up— However, I have no doubt, but that for Cash a good bargain can be had, which **I shall endeavour to effect— the first oppertunity I have,** and **shall write you on the subject as soon as I do**

With sentiments of esteem

I am Yours in the bonds

of the E. [verlasting] Covenant

Joseph Smith

J[ohn] M. Bernhisel M. D.

18 August 1841

New York August 18th. 1841

Dear Brother,

I wrote you about the 12th. Ultimo enclosing a certificate of deposite on the Greenwich bank in this city for four hundred and twenty five dollars, and **requested that you would do me the favor to purchase land for me** to the amount of about five hundred [hole in page] [d]ollars, and stated that I would remit you the remaining [s]eventy five dollars by the 1st of July next, but I shall probably be enabled to do so in the course of the ensuing winter, certainly by the first of May next. **Not having received an acknowledgment of the receipt of the certificate of deposite,** and supposing that **you were probably prevented from acknowledging <it> by the pressure of other business,** I wrote a few days since to Elder [Heber C.] Kimball, requesting him to make the inquiry and write me, as **I felt anxious to know** whether it had reached you in safety. **In my last I desired you to make the purchase within two or three miles of Nauvoo**, but I have very recently been informed that the price of land is very high in the immediate vicinity of that city, I should therefore obtain a very small tract for five hundred dollars. If this be the case, **you will have the goodness to purchase land, (if you have not already done so)** at any distance within ten miles of your city, but **you will please to act in this matter as if you were purchasing for yourself,** for you are on the spot and perfectly well acquainted with all the advantages and disadvantages of location &c &c and a small piece of ground near the city may be better than a larger one at a greater distance from it **You will greatly oblige me by writing immediately after making the purchase, if time and other avocations will permit.** Elder Henry Moore arrived here from England some ten or twelve days ago, and intends to take his departure for the west about the middle of next month— I hope you will have the kindness to excuse <me> for again trespassing on your precious time—

> [W]ith perfect respect
> I am yours in the Gospel
> John M. Bernhisel
> 176 Hudson street

8 September 1841

> New York September 8th. 1841.

Dear Brother

You will herewith receive a copy of Stephen's Incidents of Travel in Central America, Chiapas, and Yucatan, which I hope you will do me the favor to accept, as a small testimony of my gratitude to you for the valuable services you are rendering me, and as a token of my regard for you as a Prophet of the Lord.

> With sentiments of the highest consider
> ation, I am yours in the bonds of the New
> and Everlasting Covenant.
> J[ohn] M. Bernhisel

P.S. I have had the pleasure to receive your favor of the 5th ultimo, acknowledging the receipt of the certificate of deposite for four hundred and twenty five dollars, and **kindly saying that you would expend it to the best advantage.** In addition to the above Elder [Wilford] Woodruff will hand you forty dollars, and the balance I will endeavor to remit you **soon after you inform me that you have made the purchase,** but certainly before the first of May next. On the genuineness of the bills you may place the most implicit reliance, for one of them I obtained at the bank from which it was issued, and the other at the Greenwich bank. I sincerely condole with you on the death of your brother Don Carlos [Smith].

16 November 1841

Nauvoo November 16, 1841

Dear Sir

I received your kind present by the hand of Er. [Wilford] Woodruff & feel myself under many obligations for this mark of your esteem & friendship which to me is the more interesting as it unfolds & developes many things that are of great importance to this gen eration & corresponds with & supports the testimony of the Book of Mormon; I have read the volumnes with the greatest interest & pleasure & must say that of all histories that have been written pertaining to the antiquities of this country it is the most correct luminous & comprihensive.—

In regard to the land referred to by you I would simply state that I have land both in and out of the City some of which I hold deeds for and others bonds for deeds **when you come which I hope will be as soon** as convenient you can make such a selection from among those as shall best meet with your veiws & feelings. In gratefull remembrance of your kindness I remain your affectionate Brother in the bonds of the

Everlasting Covenant

Joseph Smith

To Dr. [John] Bernhisel

4 January 1842

Copy of a letter to Dr John M. Burnhisel [Bernhisel].

176. Hudson Str N. York

Nauvoo City January 4. 1842

Dear Brother

Yours of the 11th Dec. post Marked 13th. is recived & I have this day made a purchase according to your request, of 60 acres of land off the South Side, of the south east quarter, <of> Section 9. of Township six north, of range 8 west, of the 4th principal Meridian in the tract appropriated for Military bounties, for the Sum of $480. I.E. $8. per Acre, which is less than its present value, & that on account of Previous advances on your part.

The land is situated about 2 miles east by south of the Temple, and of an excellent quality though perhaps not quite so great a proportion of timber as you would have preferred, yet it was the best chance which presented itself to me at present , We do not long expect to be dependent on wood, from this immediate vicinity for firing our city, there are, unquestionably, inexaustable mines of coal in the neighborhood, not far beneath the surface, which we expect will shortly be opened, furnishing an abundance of fuel at a moderate price, & also lights for the City, as soon as means can be brought in requisition to establish Gas works.

The purchase I made of Mr Peter Hawes [Haws] & have his deed to you for the Land, & I shall improve the earliest opportunity. to forward it to the Recorders Office, for entry, and after that is accomplished I will file it away with my Deeds, holding it subject to your order.

The certificate of deposite referred to in your letter, July 12— 1841 for—$425,

together with the 8th Sept for Mr [Wilford] Woodruff. of 40
$465,

deducted from the, 480

paid for the land, leaves a balance in my favor of $15

concerning which you will act your pleasure or or convenien[c]e. I would rather it should be forwarded by the brethren, or some private conveyance, than risque it in the Post office, &c

&c—

I remain yours in the N. C.

Joseph Smith.

pr W[illard] Richards Scribe

omitted all but the business Part.

Appendix 2: Biography of Don Carlos Smith

This biography appears *in Joseph Smith's History*, 1838-1856, volume C-1 Addenda. The compilation of Joseph Smith's history involved numerous scribes and historians, with many starts and stops. This biography of Don Carlos Smith was included in the addenda to volume C-1 under the date of 7 August 1841. A full explanation of the Addenda is included the Historical Introduction in the Joseph Smith Papers at this link, which is where the 7 August 1841 account starts:

http://www.josephsmithpapers.org/paperSummary/history-1838-1856-volume-c-1-addenda&p=12.

According to the convention used by Church historians, the account is written in the first person, although this was not actually written by Joseph Smith.

Addenda - 7 August 1841

Augt. 7 -[My youngest brother Don Carlos Smith died.]- He was born 25th. March 1816, was one of the first to receive my testimony, and was ordained to the Priesthood when only 14 years of age. The evening after— — the plates of the Book of Mormon were shewn to the eight witnesses, a meeting was held, when all the witnesses, as also Don Carlos bore testimony to the truth of the Latter Day dispensation He accompanied Father to visit Grandfather and relatives in St. Lawrence Co: N.Y., in August 1830. During that mission he convinced Solomon Humphrey Jr., a licensiate of the Baptist order, of the truth of the work. He was one of the 24 Elders who laid the corner stones of the Kirtland Temple. In the fall of 1833 he entered the office of Oliver Cowdery, to learn the art of printing. On the 30th. July 1835 he married Agnes Coolbrith in Kirtland, Ohio. On the 15th. January 1836 he was ordained President of the High Priest's Quorum. He took a mission with Solomon Wilber Denton in the Spring and Summer of 1836 in Pennsylvania and New York. On the commencement of the publication of the *Elders' Journal* in Kirtland, he took the control of the establishment until the office was destroyed by fire in December 1837, when in consequence of persecution he moved his family to New Portage.

Early in the spring of 1838 he took a mission through the States of Virginia, Pennsylvania and Ohio, and raised means to assist his father; and immediately after his return he started to Missouri with his family, in company with father and family, and purchased a farm in Daviess County. [p. 12]

1841 Augt. 7. On the 26th. September he started on a mission to the States of Tennessee and Kentucky to collect means to buy out the claims and property of the Mobbers in Davies County Mo. During his absence his wife and two little children were driven by the mob from his habitation, and she was compelled to carry her children three miles through snow three inches deep, and wading through Grand River which was waist deep during the inclement weather. He returned about the 25th. of December after a very tedious mission, having travelled 1500 miles, 650 of which were on foot. I extract the following from his journal:

"On the 30th. day of September 1838, I in company with George A. Smith, Lorenzo Barnes and Harrison Sagers went on board the "Kansas", (which had one wheel broke;) the Missouri river was very low, & full of snags and sand bars. Generals Samuel D. Lucas and Moses Wilson of Jackson County, Coll. Thompson from Platte purchase, and many others of the active mobbers were on board, as also General David R. Atchison. On touching at De Witt on 1st. October for wood, we found about 70 of the brethren with their families surrounded by an armed mob of upwards of 200. The women and children there were much frightened, expecting it was a boat loaded with mobbers. We would have stopped and assisted them, but being unarmed, we thought it best to fulfil our mission. From this onward the "Mormons" were the only subject of conversation, and nothing was heard but the most bitter imprecations against them. Gen. Wilson related many of his deeds of noble daring in the Jackson mob, one of which was the following: 'I went, in company with forty others, to the house of Hiram Page, a mormon, in Jackson County. We got logs and broke in every door and window at the same instant; and, pointing our rifles at the family, we told them, we would be God d—d if we did'nt shoot every one of them, if Page did not come out. At that, a tall woman made her appearance, with a child in her arms. I told the boys she was too d—d tall. In a moment the boys stripped her, and found it was Page. I told them to give him a d—d good one. We gave him sixty or seventy blows with hickory withes which we had prepared. Then, after pulling the roof off the house, we went to the next d—d Mormon's house, and whipped him in like manner. We continued until we whipped ten or fifteen of the God d—d Mormons, and demolished their houses that night. If the Carroll boys would do that way, [p. 13]

1841 Augt. 7 they might conquer; but it is no use to think of driving them without four or five to one. I wish I could stay; I would help drive the d—d Mormons to hell, old Joe, and all the rest. At this I looked the General sternly in the face, and told him, that he was neither a republican nor a gentleman, but a savage, without a single principle of honor or humanity,. If, said I, 'the Mormons have broken the law, let it be strictly executed against them; but such anti-republican, and unconstitutional acts as these related by you, are beneath the brutes.' We were upon the hurricane deck, and a large company present were listening to the conversation. While I was speaking, Wilson placed his hand upon his pistol, which was belted under the skirt of his coat; but Cousin George A. Smith stood by his side, watching every move of his hand, and would have knocked him into the river instantly, had he attempted to draw a deadly weapon. But General Atchison saved him the trouble, by saying, "I'll be God d—d to hell if Smith aint right.' At this, Wilson left the company, crest-fallen. In the course of the conversation Wilson said, that best plan was, to rush into the 'Mormon' Settlements, murder the men, make slaves of the children, take possession of the property, and use the women as they pleased.

A gentleman present from Baltimore, Maryland, said he never was among such a pack of d—d savages before; he had passed through Far West, and saw nothing among the "Mormons" but good order. Then, drawing his pistols, he discharged them, and re-loading, said, 'if God spares my life till I get out of Upper Missouri, I will never be found associating with such devils again.'

Shortly after this we were invited to preach on board. Elder Barnes and I preached. The rest of the way we were treated more civilly; but being deck passengers, and having very little money, we suffered much for food.

We continued our journey together through every species of hardship and fatigue, until the eleventh of October, when Elder Barnes and H. Sagers left us at Paducah after our giving them all the money we had, they starting up the Ohio river, and we, to visit the Churches in West Tennessee and Kentucky. Soon after this, Julian Moses gave us a five franc piece, and bade us farewell.

We soon found that the mob spirit was in Kentucky, as well as [p. 14]

1841 Augt. 7 in Missouri;—— we preached in a small branch of the Church in Calloway Co. and staid at the house of Sister Selah Parker, which was surrounded in the night by about twenty armed men, led by John Mc.Cartney a Campbellite Priest, who had sworn to kill the first Mormon Elder who should dare to preach in that place. The family were very much terrified. After trying the doors, the mobbers finally went away. We visited a number of small branches in Tennessee; the brethren generally arranged to be on hand with their money, or lands for exchange in the spring. Bror. Samuel West,—— gave us twenty-eight dollars to help defray our travelling expenses. We also received acts of kindness from others which will never be forgotten.

About this time our minds were seized with an awful foreboding— horror seemed to have laid his grasp upon us— we lay awake night after night, for we could not sleep. Our forebodings increased, and we felt sure that all was not right; yet we continued preaching, until the Lord showed us that the Saints would be driven from Missouri. We then started home, and, on arriving at Wyatt's Mills, we were told, that if we preached there it would cost us our lives. We had given out an appointment at the house of Mrs Foster, a wealthy widow. She also advised us to give it up; but, as she had no fears for herself, her property, or family, we concluded to fulfil our appointment. The hour of meeting came, and many attended. George A. preached about an hour; during which time Captain Fitch came in at the head of twelve other mobbers, who had large hickory clubs, and they sat down with their hats on. When George A. took his seat, I arose and addressed them for an hour and a half, during which time, I told them that I was a patriot— that I was free— that I loved my country— that I loved liberty— that I despised both mobs and mobbers— that no gentleman, or Christian at heart, would ever be guilty of such things, or countenance them.

Whereupon the mob pulled off their hats, laid down their clubs, and listened with almost breathless attention.

After meeting, Mr. Fitch came to us and said that he was ashamed of his conduct, and would never do the like again; that he had been misinformed about us by some religious [p. 15]

1841 Augt. 7 bigots, and begged of us to forgive him, which we did.

We continued our journey to Columbus, Hickman county, Kentucky, and put up with Captain Robinson, formerly an officer in the army, who treated us very kindly, assuring us that we were welcome to stay at his house until a boat should come, if it were three months. We staid nine days, during which a company of thirteen hundred Cherokee Indians ferried over the river.

We went on board the Steamer Louisville, and had to pay all our money for a deck passage. About ninety miles from St. Louis our boat got aground, where it lay three days. We had nothing to eat but a little parched corn. We then went on board of a little boat, "the Return", which landed us in St. Louis the next morning. Here we found Elder Orson Pratt and learned that Joseph was a prisoner with many others, and that David W. Patten was Killed, and of the sufferings of the Saints, which filled our hearts with sorrow.

The next morning we started on foot for home; at Huntsville, about 200 miles, we stopped at the house of George Lyman to rest. George A's feet had now become very sore with walking.

We had not been long in Huntsville before the Mob made a rally to use us up as they said with the rest of the Smith's; and, at the earnest request of our friends, we thought best to push on, and started about ten at night. The wind was in our faces, the ground slippery, and the night very dark; nevertheless we proceeded on our journey. Travelling twenty-two miles, we came to the Chariton river, which we found frozen over, but the ice too weak to bear us, and the boat on the west side of the river. We went to the next ferry, but finding there was no boat, and knowing that in the next neighborhood a man's brains were beat out, for being a 'Mormon', we returned to the first ferry, and tried by hallooing to raise the ferryman on the opposite side of the river, but were not able to awake him. We were almost benumbed with the cold, and to warm ourselves we commenced scuffling and jumping; we then beat our feet upon the logs and stumps, in order to start a circulation of blood; but at last George A. became so cold and sleepy that he could not stand it any longer, and lay down. I told him he was freezing to death; I rolled him on the ground, pounding and thumping him; I then cut a stick and said I would thrash him. At this he got up, and undertook to thrash me; this stirred his blood a little, but he soon lay down again. By this time the ferryman came [p. 16]

1841 Augt. 7 over, and set us across the river, where we warmed ourselves a little, and pursued our journey until about breakfast time, when we stopped at the house of a man, who, we afterwards learned, was a leader of the mob at Haun's Hawn's Mill massacre; and started the next morning without breakfast. Our route lay through a wild prairie, where there was but very little track, and only one house in forty miles. The north-west wind blew fiercely in our faces, and the ground was so slippery that we could scarcely keep our feet, and when the night came on, to add to our perplexity, we lost our way; soon after which, I become so cold that it was with great difficulty I could keep from freezing. We also became extremely thirsty; however, we found a remedy for this by cutting through ice three inches thick with a penknife. While we were drinking, we heard a cow bell; this caused our hearts to leap for joy, and we arose and steered our course towards the sound. We soon entered Tenneys grove, which sheltered us from the wind, and we felt more comfortable. In a short time we came to the house, of Whitford G. Wilson, where—— we were made welcome and kindly entertained. We laid down to rest about two o'clock in the morning, after having travelled one hundred and ten miles in two days and two nights. After breakfast I set out for Far West, leaving George A. sick with our hospitable friend. When I arrived on the evening of Dec 25 I was fortunate enough to find my family alive, and in tolerable health; which was more than I could have expected, considering the scenes of persecution through which they had passed."

Don Carlos visited us several times while we were in Liberty Jail, and brought our wives to see us, and some money and—— articles to relieve our necessities. He took charge of father's family in his flight from Missouri, and saw them removed to Quincy, Illinois for safety.

In June 1839 he commenced making preparations for printing the *Times and Seasons*. The press and type had been resurrected by Elias Smith, Hyrum Hiram Clark and others, from its grave in Dawson's yard, Far West, where it was buried for safety the night that General Lucas surrounded the City with the mob militia. The form for a No. of the Elder's Journal was buried with the ink on it. They were considerably injured by the damp; it was [p. 17]

1841 Aug 7 therefore necessary to get them into use as soon as possible, and in order to do this, Don Carlos was under the necessity of cleaning out a cellar through which a spring was constantly flowing, as the only place where he could put up the press. Ebenezer Robinson and wife being sick, threw the entire burden on him.

As a great number of brethren lay sick in the town, on Tuesday 23rd. July 1839, I told Carlos and George A. to go and visit all the sick, exercise mighty faith, and administer to them in the name of Jesus Christ, commanding the destroyer to depart, and the people to arise and walk; and—— not to leave a single person on the bed between my house and Ebeneezer Robinson's, two miles distant; they administered to over 60 persons, many of whom thought they would never sit up again; but they were healed, arose from their beds, and gave glory to God; some of them assisted—— in visiting and administering to others who were sick.

Working in the damp cellar, and administering to the sick impaired his health, so that the first number of the Times & Seasons was not issued until November. He edited 31 numbers.

He was elected Major in the Hancock county Militia, and on the death of Seymour Brunson—— Lieutenant Colonel.

He was elected on 1st. February 1841, a member of the city Council of Nauvoo——; and took the necessary oath on 3rd. February, and on the 4th. he was elected Brigadier General of the first Cohort of the Nauvoo Legion.

He was 6 feet 4 inches high, was very straight and well made; had light hair, and was very strong and active. His usual weight when in health was—

— 200 lbs. He was universally beloved by the Saints

He left three daughters, namely Agnes C., Sophronia C., and Josephine D.

Another incident involving Don Carlos is of interest. After Joseph Smith began teaching the doctrine of baptism for the dead, the Saints in Nauvoo participated in the ordinance in the Mississippi River. Don Carlos was baptized for George Washington.[148] That he was chosen for this honor is an indication of his stature in Nauvoo society.

For some historical flavor, consider this letter written by Charlotte Haven, a non-member, in which she described a baptismal service.

We followed the bank toward town, and . . . spied quite a crowd of people, and soon perceived there was a baptism. Two elders stood knee-deep in the icy cold water, and immersed one after another as fast as they could come down the bank. We soon observed that some of them went in and were plunged several times. We were told that they were baptized for the dead who had not had an opportunity of adopting the doctrines of the Latter Day Saints. So these poor mortals in ice-cold water were releasing their ancestors and relatives from purgatory! We drew a little nearer and heard several names repeated by the elders as the victims we douched, and you can imagine our surprise when the name George Washington was called. So after these fifty years he is out of purgatory and on his way to the "celestial" heavens![149]

---

[148] Nauvoo Baptismal Record Index, microfilm #820155, Family History Library, Salt Lake City.

[149] Charlotte Haven, letter to "My dear home friends," 2 May 1843, quoted in William Mulder & A. Russell Mortensen, eds., *Among the Mormons: Historical Accounts by Contemporary Observers*, 123. Also in Michael K. Winder, *Presidents and Prophets* (Covenant Communications, 2007), p. 11.

Appendix 3: Letter from Don Carlos Smith, 3 June 1841 and Obituary

Don Carlos wrote this letter to his brother Joseph when they were both in Nauvoo. Don Carlos had purchased 160 acres of land and wanted Joseph to sell it for him. He also mentions his plan to start a weekly newspaper.

The original letter can be viewed at http://www.josephsmithpapers.org/paper-summary/letter-from-don-carlos-smith-3-june-1841/1.

Letter from Don Carlos Smith, 3 June 1841

city of Nauvoo, June 3rd, 1841

Brother Joseph

I have made a purchase of 160 acres of land as good as ever laid out of doors; it is situated Just two miles from the city on a beautiful undulating prairie and is the west half of the south half of section 3rd. I wish you would sell it for me the first opportunity, perhaps you may have an opportunity the while I am gone. Doct. [Robert D.] Foster can give all necessary information as he owns the other half Quarter of the same Section. The price is $7.00 per acre or one thousand dollars for the Quarter, one half down the balance in one, two, & three years. If you will sell this for me, Brother Joseph, you will confer a lasting favor on one that will stand by (the "Rack hay or no hay") you through time & in eternity. The Quarter is an excellent purchase for some body, and whoever gets it will get a fortune. It is wholly unconnected with Doctor Foster's as far as the contract is concerned. I have Paid one hundred dollars down on the land, and have some lenity on the balance. [p. [1]]

Bare with me Joseph while I write—I have no opportunity to converse with you—you are thronged with business—and all the time (almost) in the narrows, straining the last link, as it were, to get out of this & that Pinch &c. &c. all this I know, I am not ignorant of it—I have been, and now am in the <same> mill—when I'll. get through the hopper I know not, one thing I do know, and that is this when I got into the hopper in this place I was owing in Kirtland and elsewhere about $200,00 <or more> and <up◊◊◊ds> w [hole in page] not worth a red cent. I borrowed money to commence business—built a log cabbin—built an office—was sick upwards of 11 months with my family — have not obtained any thing on the rise of property—did not purchase any lots in the city because I knew you must have your money for them or loose the whole—I have labored hard early, and late—fared hard—received nothing by speculation, or rise of property; but in the midst of all, I have not complained, nor will I—but have tried to be content, and done the best I knew how. I have paid the best part of my old debts, [p. [2]] and have contracted new ones by borrowing of "Peter to pay Paul," (as the maxim runs) I owe about five hundred dollars in all; I have papers on hand <and accounts> to the amount of 800 or 1000 dollars, and <accounts> The printing establishment, aparatus &c. is worth $1500,00. you see by this that if I could raise five hundred dollars, to pay my debts, out of my land or in any way; it would leave me a property of $2500,00, or at least 2300,00 dollars. Now this is my exact situation, and I have written it because because I had not the opportunity of talking it, and I hope you will not think strange of this letter, because I am going away and do not know but what you could sell this land for me while I am gone. The title is good &c. &c. Would you, or could you let me have city property here, for the property which Elder [Oliver] Granger has in Kirtland that should be mine? I have reference to the house and lot. You can tell me all about these matters when I come home.

As it did <not> fall to my lot to get an interest in the store with you by selling out &c. which, after due reflection, did not appear to <be> wisdom for the present; I feel anxious to enlarge the printing business by publishing a weekly newspaper, and I think it will do well, if it should, it will be very valuable.

D. C. [Don Carlos] Smith

The *Times and Seasons* published an announcement of the death on August 16, 1841 (*Times and Seasons* Vol. 2, No. 20). It also published a poem about him written by Eliza R. Snow.

Death of General Don Carlos Smith.

With emotions of no ordinary kind, we announce the death of Don Carlos Smith, the publisher and one of the editors of this paper; which unexpected event took place at his residence, in this city, on the morning of the 7th int. at 20 minutes after 2 o'clock, in the 25th year of his age.

The deceased had been afflicted some time, but nothing serious was apprehended, and, not until a day or two before his death was he thought to be dangerous. It was then ascertained that disease had been preying upon his system in such a manner, as baffled all medical skill to check; and he gradually sunk in the arms of death.

His funeral obsequies took place on the 9th inst. amid a vast concourse of relatives and friends. He was buried with military honors, holding at the time of his death the office of Brigadier General of the 2nd Cohort of the Nauvoo Legion.

The death of Bro. Smith, so unexpected, caused a sensation, not only in the minds of his relatives, but his numerous acquaintance of friends, which will never be forgotten. Endeared to the church and to his friends by all that was virtuous, honorable, and exalted in a christain [Christian] and a man-to his partner and children by all that was affectionate, kind, and lovely, in a parent and father-to his aged mother who yet survives her youngest son, by all that was dutiful, and affectionate in a son.

In all our associations with mankind, we never knew of an induvidual [individual] who stood higher in the estimation of all, than did the deceased. His manners were courteous and bland. His disposition was kind and gentle, ever looking over the foibles of his fellow men, and puting [putting] the best construction upon their actions, at the same time, setting them such examples of integrity, sobriety, humanity, and virtue, as could not but cause very one to admire him, and consequently he secured the good will of all-their friendship and esteem.

He was just in the bloom of manhood, and bid fair to survive most of his contemporaries. But just as the sun was shining with its lustre [luster], and sheding [shedding] a radiance all around, it set in a moment-

"Lo! at day 'twas sudden night."

The hopes of relatives and friends and the entire community, who had observed with pleasure and delight the opening glories which shone around his path, who had marked his virtues, faith, and piety; and who had received council at his hands, were blasted, and sorrow and distress has taken the place of high strung hopes, and ardent anticipations.

Since our acquaintance with the deceased, we have shared his friendship, and have had opportunities of marking his character under various circumstances-we have seen him struling [struggling] against misfortune and steming [stemming] the tide of adversity, and have seen displayed, under those unpropitious circumstances, patience, resolution, and firmness-his only anxiety seemed to be for the welfare and comfort of his family and parents, who clung to him for support.-We have likewise marked his conduct while prosperity and peace filled his noble soul, and gladdened his fire side, and while honor from God and man was deservedly lavished upon him, and he remained the same kind affable, generous, and pious character.

He will be missed in the councils of the just, and as president of the High Priesthood, which office he filled with honor to himself and credit of the church. As a councillor [councilor] in the Church of God he has frequently given evidence of wisdom far beyond his years, and the aged have listened with amazement and delight at the wisdom which flowed from his lips.

He was warmly attached to the cause of truth, and in the day of triod [trial] and bitter persecution, when others wavered andturned [and turned] aside, he stood firm and immovable, trusting in the mighty God of Jacob, and fearlessly advocated the cause of suffering Zion, and ever maintained his integrity.

While writing this, so many associations crowd upon us, which give evidence of his moral worth, his kindness, his sensibility, his piety, and friendship, as entirely unman us, and we feel we must bring this notice to a close. May that God, who in the order of his providence, has called from our midst the spirit of our departed brother and friend, be a husband to the widow and a father to the fatherless, and assist us by his spirit, to follow him, as he followed Christ.

A discourse was delivered at his funeral by Elder John Taylor, which was attentively listened to by the immense concourse which assembled to pay their last respects and kind offices to the deceased.

"Now he's gone we'd not recall him
From a paradise of bliss,

Where no evil can befall him,
To a changing world like this.
His loved name will never perish,
Nor his mem'ry crown the dust;
For the saints of God will cherish
The remembrance of the JUST."

The deceased has left a wife and three children to mourn his loss.

Lines, Written on the Death of Gen. Don Carlos Smith.
By Miss E. R. Snow.

"Thy shaft flew thrice and thrice my peace was slain."
Th' insatiate archer, Death, once more
Has bath'd his shaft in human gore!
The pale fac'd monarch's crimson'd bow, Ours, is the sorrow-ours the loss!
Once more has laid a good man low! For thro' the triumphs of the Cross,
His noble part by death set free,
If tears of love could ever save On wings of immortality;
A noble victim from the grave- Tracing the steps the Savior trod,
If strong affection e'er had power Has reach'd the paradise of God.
To rescue in the dying hour- There he rejoins the ransom'd choir-
If kindred sympathy could hold There, there he hails his noble sire,
A jewel in its sacred fold- A Patriarch of these latter-days,
If friendship could produce a charm Whose goodness, mem'ry loves to trace
The heartless tyrant to disarm- With rev'rence, grattitude [gratitude] and love:
If wide acknowledg'd worth could be He left us for the courts above.
A screen from mortal destiny- There, with the Spirits of the just,
If pure integrity of heart Where Zion's welfare is discuss'd
Could baffle death's malignant dart- Once more, their kindred spirits join-
If usefulness and noble zeal- Once more, their efforts to combine
Devotedness to Zion's weal- In Zion's cause.-And shall we mourn
A conduct grac'd with purpos'd aim- For those who have been upward borne?
A reputation free from blame, And shall the "Legion's: sorrow flow:

Could save a mortal from the tomb, As if a Chieftain were laid low;
And stamp with an eternal bloom; Who threw his frail escutcheon by,
He never would have bow'd to death, To join the Legion form'd on high?
Or yielded up his mortal breath. Yes, mourn:-the loss is great to earth-
A loss of high exalted worth!

City of Nauvoo, Aug. 8th, 1841.

Appendix 4: Holographic writings of Joseph Smith

Joseph Smith's holographic writings are available online at the Joseph Smith papers at this link: http://josephsmithpapers.org/site/documents-in-joseph-smiths-handwriting. Most of them are brief journal entries, short notes, and letters to Emma. This Appendix includes Joseph's longest holographic writings, indicated by * on the list below.

Documents in Joseph Smith's Handwriting

Book of Mormon Manuscript Excerpt, circa May 1829 [Alma 45:22]
*History, circa Summer 1832
Entries from Journal, 1832–1834
27 November 1832
28 November 1832
29 November 1832
30 November 1832
1 December 1832
2 December 1832
3 December 1832
4 December 1832
5 December 1832
6 December 1832
4 October 1833
5 October 1833
6–12 October 1833
13 October 1833
14–18 October 1833
20–25 October 1833
26 October 1833
29 October 1833
30–31 October 1833
5–13 November 1833

*14–19 November 1833
16 January 1834
26–28 February 1834
1–2 March 1834
3 March 1834
14 March 1834
15 March 1834
16 March 1834
17 March 1834
18 March 1834
19 March 1834
20 March 1834
21 March 1834
22 March 1834
23 March 1834
24 March 1834
25 March 1834
26 March 1834
27 March 1834
28 March 1834
29 March 1834
30 March 1834
31 March 1834
1 April 1834
Entries from Journal, 1835–1836
[22] September 1835
23 September 1835
24 September 1835
19 December 1835
20 December 1835
21 December 1835
22 December 1835
*Letter to Hyrum Smith, 3–4 March 1831
Letter to Emma Smith, 6 June 1832
Letter to Emma Smith, 13 October 1832
*Letter to William W. Phelps, 27 November 1832
*Letter to Church Leaders in Jackson County, Missouri, 18 August 1833
*Note to Newel K. Whitney, circa October 1833—Early 1834
Letter to Emma Smith, 18 May 1834

Letter to Almira Mack Scobey, 2 June 1835 (at end of Letters to John Burk, Sally Phelps, and Almira Scobey, 1—2 June 1835)
Letter to Sally Waterman Phelps, 20 July 1835
Letter to Emma Smith, 19 August 1836
Letter to Emma Smith, 4 November 1838
Letter to Emma Smith, 12 November 1838
Letter to Emma Smith, 1 December 1838
Letter to Emma Smith, 21 March 1839
Letter to Emma Smith, 4 April 1839
Letter to Henry G. Sherwood, 7 November 1839
Letter to Emma Smith, 9 November 1839
Letter to Emma Smith, 20 January 1840
Statement, February 1840
Letter to Oliver Granger, 15 April 1840
*Letter to Newel K. Whitney, 12 December 1840
Agreement with Ebenezer and Elender Wiggins, 14 May 1841
Note of Authorization, 24 February 1842
Complaint against William Thomas, 2 August 1842
Letter to Newel K. and Elizabeth Smith Whitney, 18 August 1842
Letter to Lucien Adams, 2 October 1843
Note to William Clayton, 9 December 1842
Autograph to Barbara Matilda Neff, May 1844
Letter to Emma Smith, 27 June 1844 (postscript)

Longest holographic writings

History, circa Summer 1832

http://josephsmithpapers.org/paperSummary/history-circa-summer-1832

the Kees of the Kingdom of God confered upon him and the continuation of the blessings of God to him &c   I was born in the town of Charon [Sharon] in the <State> of Vermont North America on the twenty third day of December AD 1805 of goodly Parents who spared no pains to instructing me in \<the\> christian religion at the age of about ten years my Father Joseph Smith Siegnior moved to Palmyra Ontario County in the State of New York and being in indigent circumstances were obliged to labour hard for the support of a large Family having nine chilldren and as it required the exertions of all that were able to render any assistance for the support of the Family therefore we were deprived of the bennifit of an education suffice it to say I was mearly instructid in reading and writing and the ground \<rules\> of Arithmatic which constuted my whole literary acquirements. At about the age of twelve years my mind become seriously imprest [p. 1] with regard to the all importent concerns for the wellfare of my immortal Soul which led me to searching the scriptures believeing as I was taught, that they contained the word of God thus applying myself to them and my intimate acquaintance with those of different denominations led me to marvel excedingly for I discovered that \<they did not -adorn-\> -instead- of adorning- their profession by a holy walk and Godly conversation agreeable to what I found contained in that sacred depository this was a grief to my Soul thus from the age of twelve years to fifteen I pondered many things in my heart concerning the sittuation of the world of mankind the contentions and divi[si]ons the wicke[d]ness and abominations and the darkness which pervaded the -of- the- minds of mankind my mind become excedingly distressed for I become convicted of my sins and by searching the scriptures I found that

-mand- \<mankind\> did not come unto the Lord but that they had apostatised from the true and liveing faith and there was no society or denomination that built upon the gospel of Jesus Christ as recorded in the new testament and I felt to mourn for my own sins and for the sins of the world for I learned in the scriptures that God was the same yesterday to day and forever that he was no respecter to persons for he was God for I looked upon the sun the glorious luminary of the earth and also the moon rolling in their magesty through the heavens and also the stars shining in their courses and the earth also upon which I stood and the beast of the field and the fowls of heaven and the fish of the waters and also man walking forth upon the face of the earth in magesty and in the strength of beauty whose power and intiligence in governing the things which are so exceding great and [p.

2] marvilous even in the likeness of him who created -him- <them> and when I considered upon these things my heart exclaimed well hath the wise man said -the- <it is a> fool <that> saith in his heart there is no God my heart exclaimed all all these bear testimony and bespeak an omnipotant and omnipreasant power a being who makith Laws and decreeeth and bindeth all things in their bounds who filleth Eternity who was and is and will be from all Eternity to Eternity and when I considered all these things and that <that> being seeketh such to worship him as worship him in spirit and in truth therefore I cried unto the Lord for mercy for there was none else to whom I could go and to obtain mercy and the Lord heard my cry in the wilderness and while in <the> attitude of calling upon the Lord <in the 16th year of my age> a piller of fire light above the brightness of the sun at noon day come down from above and rested upon me and I was filled with the spirit of god and the <Lord> opened the heavens upon me and I saw the Lord and he spake unto me saying Joseph <my son> thy sins are forgiven thee. go thy <way> walk in my statutes and keep my commandments behold I am the Lord of glory I was crucifyed for the world that all those who believe on my name may have Eternal life <behold> the world lieth in sin - and- at this time and none doeth good no not one they have turned asside from the gospel and keep not <my> commandments they draw near to me with their lips while their hearts are far from me and mine anger is kindling against the inhabitants of the earth to visit them acording to th[e]ir ungodliness and to bring to pass that which <hath> been spoken by the mouth of the prophets and Ap[o]stles behold and lo I come quickly as it [is] written of me in the cloud <clothed> in the glory of my Father and my soul was filled with love and for many days I could rejoice with great Joy and the Lord was with me but [I] could find none that would believe the hevnly vision nevertheless I pondered these things in my heart -about that time my mother and- but after many days

[pages written by Frederick G. Williams omitted]

and <he> imediately came to Su[s]quehanna and said the Lord had shown him that he must go to new York City with some of the caracters so we proceeded to coppy some of them and he took his Journy to the Eastern Cittys and to the Learned <saying> read this I pray thee and the learned said

I cannot but if he would bring the plates they would read it but the Lord had fo<r>bid it and he returned to me and gave them to <me to> translate and I said I said [I] cannot for I am not learned but the Lord had prepared spectticke spectacles for to read the Book therefore

[continues in Williams' handwriting]

14-19 November 1833 · Tuesday

November 19th from the 13th u[n]till this date nothing of note has transpired since the great sign in the heavins this day my <h[ea]rt> is somewhat sorrowfull but feel to trust in the Lord the god of Jacob I have learned in my travels that man is treche[r]ous and selfish but few excepted Brother <Sidney> is a man whom I love but is not capa[b]le of that pure and stedfast love for those who are his benefactors as should posess p<o>sess the breast of a man <a Pred> Presedent of the Chu[r]ch of Christ [p. 20] this with some other little things such as a selfish and indipendance of mind which to often manifest distroys the confidence of those who would lay down their lives for him but notwithstanding these things he is <a> very great and good man a man of great power of words and can <gain> the friendship of his hearrers very quick he is a man whom god will uphold if he will continue faithful to his calling O God grant that he may for the Lords sake Amen [p. 21] the man who willeth to do well we should extoll his virtues and speak not of his faults behind his back a man who willfuly turneth away from his friend without a cause is not lightly to be forgiven <easily forgiven> the kindness of a man <should> is never to be forgotten that person who never forsaketh his trust should ever have the highest place for regard in our hearts and our love should never fail but increase more and more and this [is] my disposition and sentiment &c Amen [p. 22] Brother Frederick [G. Williams] is a man who <is one of those men> in whom I place the greatest confidence and trust for I have found him ever full of love and Brotherly kindness he is not a man of many words but is ever wining because of his constant mind he shall ever have place in my heart and is ever intitled to my confiden<ce>

Letter to Hyrum Smith, 3-4 March 1831

Kirtland Geauga County Ohio
March 3th 1831
Brother Hyram

we arived here safe and are all well I hav[e] been engageed in regulating
the Churches here as the deciples are numerous and the devil has made many
att<e>mpts to over throw them it has been a serious Job but the Lord is
with us and we have overcome and have all things regular the work is
brakeing forth on the right hand and on the left and there is a great Call for
Elders in this place we hav[e] recieved a leter from Olover [Oliver Cowdery]
dated independence Jackson County Missouri January the 29th 1831 these
are the words which he has written saying My dealy dearly beloved
bretheren after a considerable lengthy journy I arived avail myself of the first
opertunity of communicating to you a knowledge of our situation that you
may be priviledged of writing to us for we have not heard any thing from
you since we left you last fall we arived here at this place a few days since
which is about 25 miles from the Shawney indians on the south side of the
Kansas River at its mouth & delewares on the north I have had two
intervi<e>ws with the Chief of [-] that the delewares who is a very old &
venerable looking man after haveing laying before him & eighteen or twenty
of the Council of that nation the truth he said that <he> hand they he and
they were very glad for what I their Brother had told them and they had
recived it in their hearts &c But how the matter will go with this tribe to me
is uncirtain nether Can I at presen<t> Conclude mutch about it the wether is
mutch is quite severe and the snow is Considerable deep which makes it at
present quite dificcult traveling about I have but a short time to write to you
my bloved Bretheren as the mail leves thi[s] place in morni the morning [p.
1] but I wish some of you to write <to> me immediately a full letter of all
your affairs and then I will write to you the situation of all the western tribes
&c thus reads most of the letter Saying to us the god of my father Jacob be
with you all amen I remain in Christ your Brother forever
    Oliver

My Dearly Beloved Brother Hyrum

I <have> had much Concirn about you but I always remember you in your <my> prayers Calling upon god to keep <you> Safe in spite <of> men or devils I think <you> had better Come into this Country immediately for the Lord has Commanded us that we should Call the Elders of this Chursh to gether unto this plase as soon as possable

March forth this morning after being Colled out of my bed in the night to go a small distance I went and had and an awful strugle with satan <but> being armed with the power of god he was cast out and the woman is Clothed in hir right mind the Lord worketh wonders in this land

I want to see you all may the grace of God be and abide with you all even so Amen

your Brother forever

Joseph Smith Jr

PS if you want to to write to Oliver direct your letter direct your to independence Jackson County misouri [p. 2]

Harrison and O[r]son prat arrived here on Feb 27th they left our folks well David Jackways has threatened to take father with a supreme writ in the spring you had <beter> Come to fayette and take father along with you Come in a one horse wagon if if you Can do not Come threw Bufalo for th[e]y will lie in wait for you God protect you I am

Joseph [p. 3]

Mr. Hyram Smith

Harpers Vill B<r>oom Co. N. Y.

Letter to William W. Phelps, 27 Nov 1832

[Portions written in Frederick G. Williams handwriting omitted]

yea thus saith the still small voice which whispereth through and pierceth all things and often times it maketh my bones to quake while it maketh manifest saying and it shall come to pass that I the Lord God will send one mighty and strong holding the scepter of power in his hand clothed with light for a covering whose mouth shall utt utter words Eternal words while his bowels shall be a fountain of truth to set in order the house of God and to arange by lot the inheritance of the saints whose names are found and the names of their fathers and of their children enroled in the Book of the Law of God while that man who was called of God and appointed that puteth forth his hand to steady the ark of God shall fall by the shaft of death like as a tree that is smitten by the vivid shaft of lightning and all they who are not found writen in the book of remmemberance shall find none inheritence in that day but they shall be cut assunder and their portion shall be appointed them among unbelievers where is wailing and gnashing of teeth these things I say not of myself therefore as the Lord speaketh he will also fulfill and they who are of the high Priesthood whose names are not found writen in the book of the Law or that are found to have appostitised or to have been cut off out of the church as well as the lesser Priesthood or the members in that day shall not find an inheritance among the saints of the most high therefore it shall be done unto them as unto the children of the Priest as you will find recorded in the second chapter and sixty first and second verses of Ezra now Broth William if what I say have said is true how careful then had men aught to be what they do in the last days lest they are cut as-sunder short of their expectations and they that think [they] stand should fall because they keep not the Lords commandments whilst you who do the will of the Lord and keep his commandments have need to rejoice with unspeakable Joy for such shall be exalted very high and shall be lifted up in triu [p. 3] triumph above all the kingdoms of this world but I must drop this subject at the begining Oh Lord when will the time come when Brother William thy Servent and myself sha behold the day that we may stand together and gase upon Eternal wisdom engraven upon the hevens while the magesty of our God holdeth up the dark curtain <until> we may read the round of Eternity to the fullness and satisfaction of our immortal souls Oh Lord God deliver us in thy due time from the little narrow prison almost as it were totel darkness of paper pen and ink and a crooked broken scattered and imperfect language I would inform you that I have obtained ten subscribers for the Star and received pay their names and place of residence [are] as follows, John McMahhan, James McMahhan, James White, William Brown, Henry

Kingery, Micayer Dillions, Abraham Kingery, John A Fisher, David
Houghs, Thomas Singers, the papers and and all to be sent to Guyndotte the
paper are all to be sent to Post office Verginea except David Houghs his is to
be sent to Wayne <County> Township Worster County <Township> Ohio,
Vienna Jaqis [Jacques] has not rceived her Papers pleas inform her Sister
<Hariet> that Shee is well and give my respects to her tell her that Mrs
Angels Brother came after her and the child soon after she went from here all
he wanted wanted was the child No more <my> love for all the Brotheren
yours in bonds Amen

    Joseph Smith Jr
    William W Phelps

Letter to Church Leaders in Jackson County, Missouri, 18 August 1833

Kirtland, August 18, 1833.
Brother William [W. Phelps],John [Whitmer], Edward [Partridge],Isaac
[Morley], John [Corrill] andSidney [Gilbert].

O thou disposer of all Events, thou dispencer of all good! in the name of
Jesus Christ I ask thee to inspire my heart indiht [indite] my thaughts guide
my peen [pen] to note some kind word to these my Brothercn in Zion that
like the rays of the sun upon the Earth wormeth [warmeth] the face thereof
so let this word I write worm [warm] the hearts of my Brotheren or as the
gentle rain deceneth [descendeth] upon the earth or the dews upon the
mountanes refresheth the face of nature and Causeth her to smile so give
unto thy servent Joseph have a word that shall refresh the hearts and revi[v]e
the spir[i]ts yea souls<of> those afflicted ones who have been called to leave
their homes and go to a strange land not knowing what should befall them
behold this is like Abraham a strikeing <evidence> of their acceptance before
the <Lord> in this thing but this is not all <they are> but called to contend
with the beast of the wilderness for a long time whos[e] Jaws <are> were
open to devour them thus did Abraham and also Paul at Ephesus b[e]hold
thou art like him <them>and again the affliction of my Brotheren reminds
me of Abraham offering up Isaac his only son but my Brotheen [brethren]

have have been called to give up even more than this their wives and their children yea and their own life also O Lord what more dost thou require at their hands before thou wilt come and save them may I not say thou wilt yea I will <say> Lord thou wilt save them out of the hands of their enemies thou hast tried them in the fu[r]nace of affliction a furnace of thine own choseing [choosing]and couldst thou have tried them more then thou hast O Lord then let this suffice and from henceforth <let> this<be> reco[r]ded <be> in heaven for thine angels to look upon and for a testimony against all those ungodly men who have commited those ungodly deeds forever and ever and <yea> let thine anger <is> beenki ndled against them and <let> them <and they shall> be consumed before thy face and be far removed from Zion O <they will go> letthem go down to <the> pit and give pl[a]ce for thy saints for thy spirit will not always strive with man therefore I fear for all these things yet O Lord glorify thyself thy will be done and not mine but I must conclude my pray[er] my heart being full of real desire for all such are not reprobate that they cannot be saved——

Dear Brotheren in fellowship and <love>towards you and with a broken heart and a contrite Spirit I take the pen to address you but I know not what to——say to you and the thaught <that> this <of> letter will be so long coming to you my heart faints within me I feel to exclaim O Lord let the desire of my heart be felt and realizied this moment <upon you hearts> and teach you all things thy servent would communicate to would you my Brotheren since the intel igence of the Calamity of Zion has reached the ears of the wicked there is no saifty for us here but evevery man has to wa[t]ch their houses every night to keep off the Mob[b]ers Satan has Come down in Great wrath upon all the Chirchof God and the[re] is no saifty only in the arm of Jehovah none else can deliver and he will not deliver unless we do prove ourselves faithful to him in the severeest trouble for he that will have his robes washed in the blood of the Lamb must come up throught great tribulation even the greatest of all affliction but know this when men thus deal with you and speak all maner of evil of you falsly for the sake of Christ that he is your friend and I verily know that he will spedily deliver Zion for I have his immutible covenant that this shall be the case but god is pleased to keep it hid from mine eyes the means how exactly the thing will be done the chirch in Kirtland concluded with one accord to die with you or redeem you and never at any time have I felt as I now feel that pure love and for you my Brotheren the wormth [warmth] and Zeal for you saf[e]ty that we can scarcely hold our spirits but wisdom I trust will keep us from madness and desperation and the power of the Go[s]pel will enable us to stand and [p. 1]

and bear with patience the Great affliction that is falling upon us on all side[s] for we <are> no safer here in Kirtland then you are in Zion the cloud is gethering arou[nd] us with great fury and all pharohs host or in other words all hell and the com[bined] pow[e]rs of Earth are Marsheling their forces to overthrow us and we like the chilldr n [children] of Issarel [Israel]with the red Sea before us them and the Egyptions ready to fall upon them to distroy them and no arm could deliver but the arm of God and this is the case with us we must wait on God to be gratious and call on him with out ceaseing to make bare his arm for our defence for naught but the arm of the almighty can Save us we are all well here as can be expe cted yea altogether so with the exception of some little ailments feavers &c.——

Brother Oliver [Cowdery] is now Sitting before me and is faithful and true and his heart bleeds as it were for Zion yea never did the hart pant for the cooling streem as doth the heart of thy Brothe[r] Oliver for thy salvation yea and I may may say this is the Case with the whole Chirch and all the faithful Oliver will or aught rather to stay with me or in this land until I am permitted to Come with him for I know that if God shall spare my life that he will permit me to settle on an inhe[r]i tance on the land of Zion <in due time> but when I do not know but this I do know that I have been keept from going <up> as yet for your sa[k]es and the day will come that Zion will be keept for our sakes therefore be of good cheer and the cloud shall pass over and the sun shall shine as clear and as fair as heaven itself and the Event shall be Glorious Oliver can stay here to good advantage and have his wife come to him and he can be instrumental of doing great good in this pla[ce] and god will <give>Brother william [W. Phelps] more help and Grace to stand as and ensign to the people for it must be lifted up— and cursed sha[ll] every man be that lifts his arm to <hinder> this great work and god is my witness of this truth it shall be done and let all the saints say amen——

Dear Brotheren we must wait patiently until the Lord come[s] and resto[res] unto us all things and build the waist places again for he will do it in his time and now what shall I say to cumfort your hearts well I will tell you that you have my whole confidence yea there is not one doubt in <my heart> not one place in me but what is filld with perfect confidence and love for you and this affliction is sent upon us not for your sins but for the sins of the chirch and that all the ends of the Earth may know that you are not speculiting [speculating] with the◊◊ for Lucre but you are willing to die for the cause you have espoused you know that the chirch have tre[a]ted lightly thecom mandments of the Lord and for this cause they are not worthy to receive them yet god has suffered it not for your sins but that he might preprare you for a grateer [greater] work that you might be prepared for theendowment from on high we cast no reflections upon you we are of one heart and one mind on this subject which I speak in the name of the chirch all seem to wax strong as th[e]y see the day <of> tribulation approcing [approaching]and if our kingdom were of this world then we would fight but our weapons are not carnal yet mighty and <will> bind satan ere long under our feet we shall get a press immediately in this place and print th[e] Star until you can obtain deliverence and git up again if god permit and we believe he will we think it would be wise in yo[u] to try to git influence by offering to print a paper in favor of the goverment as you know we are all friends to the Constitution yea true friends to that Countrywe hea for which our fathers bled in the mean time god will send Embasadors to the authorities of the government and sue for protection and redress that they may be left with out excuse that a ritious [righteous]Judgement might be upon them [p. [2]]

and thus the testimony of the Kingdom must go unto all and there are many ways that God designs to bring about his ritious purposees and in the day of Judgement he designs to make us the Judges of the whole world generation in which we live O how unsearchable are the depths of his mysteries and his ways past finding out Brotheren the testamony which you have given of your honesty and the truth of this work will be felt Eteaaly [eternally] by this generation for it will be proclaimed to Ends of the Earth that there are men now liveing who have offered up their lives for this as a testimony of their religion our Brotheren in the East will handle this

233

testimony to good advantage it seems to inspire every heart to a lively sence of faith and to arm them <with>double fortitude and power and the harder the persicution the greater the gifts of God upon his chirch yea all things shall work together for good to them who are willing to lay down their lives for Christ sake we are suffering great persicution on account of one man by the name ofDocter Hurlburt [Doctor Philastus Hurlbut] who has been expeled from the chirch for lude and adulterous conduct and to spite us he is lieing in a wonderful manner and the peapl [people]are running after him and giveing him mony to b[r]ake down mormanism which much endangers <our lives> at pre asnt [present] but god will put a stop to his carear soon and all will be well my heart this moment <is made> glad for Zion we have just receivd you[r] letter containing the bond with which our enemies bound themselves and to distroy Zion and also the blessing <of> god in poreing out upon his spirit upon you and we have had the word of the Lord that you shall [be] deliverd from you[r] dainger and <shall> again flurish in spite of hell [that i]s god has communicated to m[e]by the gift of the holy ghost that this should be<the case> after much p[rayer] and suplication and also that an other printing office must be built the Lord knows how and also it is the will of the Lord that the Store shud [should] be kept and that <not> one foot of <land> theperchased should <be> given to the enimies of God or sold to them but if any is sold let it be sold to the chirch we cannot git the consent of the Lord that we shall give the ground to the enemies yet let those who are bound to leave the land to make a show as if to do untill the Lord delivr[.] a word to the wise is sufficient therefore Jud[g]e what I say for know assuredly that every foot of ground that falls into the hands of the enimies with consent is not easy to be obtained again O be wise and not let the knowledge I give unto <you> be known abroad for your sak[e]s hold fast that which you have received trust in god considder Elijah when he prayed for rain go often to your holy plases and <look> for a cloud of light to apper to your help O God I ask thee in the name of Jesus of nazereth to Save all things concerning Zion and build up her wai t [waste]places and restore all things O god send forth Judge ment unto victory O come down and cause the mou tans [mountains] to flow down at thy presance and now I conclude by telling you that we w[a]it the Comand of God to do whatever

234

we he ple[a]se and if <he> shall say go up to Zion and defend thy Brotheren by <the sword> we fly and we count not dear our live dear to us I am your Brother in Christ

Joseph Smith Jr [p. [3]]

Note to Newel K. Whitney, circa October 1833—Early 1834

Brother Whitney

I write this because I forgot to tell you of some things that you <ought to> know wer Docter P. Hurlbut is commenceing an unjust suit against Brother Hyram to git the propety of this farm which belongs to the firm Brother Hyram <or> mot father has <not got> any property here but one cow a peace each I have a <bill> for all the rest made over to me more than one year ago for Books and what they owed me and it will involve me in or the firm if we let them take this property which you <may> rest asured belongs to us a word to the wise is sufficie<nt>

Joseph Smith Jr

Note from Joseph Smith to Newel K. Whitney, Dec. 12, 1840

Nauvoo Dec. 12th 1840
Brother Whitney
       Dear Sir
              I am at work
in my office am under the ne-
cesity to have some help from
time to time to help me along
in my calling I therefore desire
you to let the bearer of this hav[e]
<some> of that dry wood to burn in the
stove of my office and obliege
your hum[b]le servent
              Joseph Smith

Jonathan Neville

Appendix 4: Editors' Comments

A standard practice for editors of 1800s newspapers was to introduce themselves in their first issue, and to write a "Valedictory" in their final issue. This Appendix includes introductions and valedictories of all the editors of Church newspapers between 1832 and 1844.

Oliver Cowdery, *Messenger and Advocate*, May, 1835

ADDRESS

To the Patrons of the Latter Day Saints'
Messenger & Advocate.

It is proper for me to inform you, that in consequence of other business and other duties, in which my services are requisite, my editorial labors on this paper will close with the present number; and as this is the case, I hope to be indulged in a few remarks, as I take leave of this responsibility. And I will take the occasion to add, here, that for a liberal patronage, so gratuitously bestowed upon unmerited talents, you have my heart felt gratitude, and still hope, that though the Advocate is to be transferred into other hands, that it may continue to receive its present support, and as rapid an increase to its subscription list as has been its good fortune to receive, since its commencement.

The Evening and the Morning Star was commenced at Independence, Jackson County, Missouri, June, 1832, by W. W. PHELPS, who edited fourteen numbers of that paper. It is known that in July, 1833, that office was demolished by a mob, and that the Star was resuscitated in this place in December of the same year. After closing the two first volumes it was deemed advisable to discontinue it and issue the present paper. For eight numbers I have to acknowledge a rapid increase of subscriptions, which has shown, in some degree, the estimation others made of its worth. It will be conducted hereafter by Elder JOHN WHITMER, late from the State of Missouri. It is proper for me to say, that wherever Elder Whitmer is personally known, a commendation from me would be uncalled for and superfluous; and I hardly need to add, that those to whom he is unknown will find him to be a man of piety, uprightness and virtue, such as adorns the walk of the professor of the religion of the Lord Jesus, and one bearing testimony to the truth of the great work of God.

It is with no ordinary feeling that I take leave of the editorial department of this paper. There is such a complicated mass of reflection crowding itself upon the mind that no common phraseology can express. To realize that one year and eight months' labor is now before the public; that whether truth or untruth has been disseminated in the same, it must remain, calls for the serious consideration of a candid heart, full with the expectation and assurance, that before the Judge of all, and an assembled universe I must answer for the same. Some may say that these reflections ought to have been pondered previously-before stepping forward to give my views to the public-to which I conscientiously reply, that they were; and were I now sensible that I had erred from the strict principles of righteousness, in the main, it should be my first object, and business, to retract.

Men, at times, depend upon the say of others, and are influenced by their persuasions to embrace different systems; and though weak may have been my arguments and feeble my exertions to persuade others to believe as myself, some may have been disposed to listen; and I will now repeat the reflections which from the beginning have occupied my heart, and which I have endeavored to have before my mind continually.-How can I meet a fellow-being before the throne of that God who has framed the heavens and the earth, and there, if not till then, learn, that through my influence or persuasion he had been led into error and was doomed to suffer the wrath of the same? (page 120) It is no trifling matter to sport with the souls of men!-they must exist eternally, and where is the being who can save them from suffering? On certain principles, and certain ones only can they escape, whatever others may suppose, or conjecture, to the contrary notwithstanding. Agreeably to those principles, I may say in conscience, I have endeavored to have my work correspond, and if there is a lack it is a want of that perfect meekness which adorned the walk of the Savior and is left as a pattern for those who profess his gospel; and wherein I may have erred in this respect, I look for forgiveness through the merits of him who knows the integrity of my heart.

I have given extracts of letters, from time to time, showing the increase and spread of this gospel, and it is unnecessary to re-insert them, or say that the work is still progressing. The numerous obstacles which have opposed the truth have hitherto been unable to overthrow it; the mighty machinery, so artfully managed, has endeavored in vain to prevent men from obeying the gospel, and the contaminating influence of vice and folly have failed, in their attempts, to darken the minds of the honest, and turn them aside from the path of salvation; and on closing my editorial labors, it is with an increased joy as the satisfaction is redoubled, that that which was as a "grain of mustard seed" a few years since, is now beginning to enlarge its branches that the "fowls of heaven are lodging in its boughs;" and with a proportionable [proportional] increase the mild rays of peace and love will soon enlighten the dark corners of the globe, and Israel's sons will be seen wending their way to their promised home. With these prospects before me, I take this, and perhaps my last leave of my friends, as an editor of any paper whatever. In this, however, I give no pledge, as I know not what circumstances time may bring forth.

As my principles are fully known, it is unnecessary to repeat them here: I shall only add a few reflections and then close.

There is an eternity, and you, with myself, reader, are fast approaching it. There is no stay with time-it flies-it hastens-it will soon close. The sound of that trump which will awake the sleeping millions, will ere long be heard, and all nations, kindreds and tongues be brought to stand before the judgment seat of Christ-The wise and the foolish, the righteous and the wicked-no excuse can be offered to prolong the summons, or a show of righteousness, clothed with deception, escape the scrutinizing eye of "him with whom we have to do." These are realities without the least shadow of fiction.

To those who have contributed to the columns of the Advocate, I tender my thanks, and hope, that, at least, a consciousness that they have done their Master's will, and set truth before the world, will continue to cheer their hearts as they advance down the stream of time to the day of the reward of the just.

To the elders of this church who have distinguished themselves in circulating this paper, by obtaining subscribers, I also owe a thankful acknowledgement [acknowledgment], and the reflection of their kindness shall ever occupy a conspicuous portion of my gratitude. Their labors, I know, are many and fatiguing, but while they are, in many instances considered the "off-scorings" of the earth, they may know that their reward is sure, and that he whom they have served will yet give them a place in his kingdom where the glory and the power is eternal.

And that holiness may prevail until (page 121) the knowledge of the Lord covers the earth as the waters cover the sea, and that we may have an inheritance among the sanctified in that day, is the prayer of your unworthy servant and friend.

OLIVER COWDERY.

John Whitmer, *Messenger and Advocate*, June, 1835

TO THE PATRONS OF THE LATTER
DAY SAINTS' MESSENGER
AND ADVOCATE.

On assuming the editorship of this paper, its patrons, no doubt, will expect me to give them an outline of the course I intend to pursue while conducting its columns in future.

The labors of this station, to those acquainted with them, are known to be many and complicated; the responsibility resting upon an individual who steps forward in our religious country, at this day, and assumes to teach others the gospel of the Lord Jesus, and point the path to holiness, is fraught with so many reflections of importance, that one would scarce venture forward without faltering, were it not for the fact, that good may be done, the field being wide, the harvest great and the laborers few. Not that all men are pursuing the right way, and are walking before God according to his holy commandments, do I say religious world-far from this. Were I sensible that all religions were one religion, and that one the true, it would be foreign from my heart to think that my feeble exertions could benefit mankind: for if it were thus, my labors would be uncalled for. But while we discover so many, one is led to enquire [inquire], which is right? Has the Lord ordained so many ways for the salvation of his people? Does this, almost numberless train of professions, comport with the scriptures? Does it show one Lord and one faith? And amid so many professed gospels, where is the one (page 135) which is correct, and where is that order of things which the Lord approbates and acknowledges his? If all are not one, and if these, or a part are incorrect, to convince men of the correct one, needs labor-and that mine may bear the strict scrutiny of my Master, in the great day approaching, I shall endeavor to have it correspond with the strictest principles of virtue and holiness.

Yet, another reflection, that one is destined to labor for some thousands, and suit matter for all, would be a sufficient excuse to urge on my own part, to my friend and brother,-who has conducted this paper since its commencement with so much talent and ability, for him to select another person, were it not that every man is to be rewarded for his diligence and perseverance in attempting to do good, by one who knows the thoughts and intents of the hearts of all.

In this introduction, then, I take the occasion to say, that I shall not labor to please men, any farther than a relation of sacred principles will be satisfactory. The applause of this world may be courted by whom it may, and enjoyed, (if enjoyment it can be called) by whoever possesses it, but with me it will be regarded as worthless as the idle wind or the vainly attempted allurements of fabled vision. So with the frowns and scoffs of men their worthlessness alike shall be considered as a parallel of the beating waves against the rocks in the distant ocean, and the rushing tornado in the trackless wilderness-one may foam its anger in perpetual solitude, and the other discharge its fury and its wrath without injury-they lose their force and spend their violence in fruitless attempts to harm in vain.

There is a way of salvation,-a path to heaven-a crown for the pure in heart, and principles teaching men how to escape the evil and enjoy the good. One way, and only one has the Lord pointed out for me to pursue in order to obtain eternal life, and it shall be my duty to set forth such facts as are calculated to inform the mind on those principles. That they are plainly written will not be doubted by those who have made themselves acquainted with all the revelations extant, notwithstanding a majority of the professing inhabitants of our country, doubt there being any other than the one given to the Jews, and a few churches among the Gentiles, by a part of the apostles.

The last item is one that has been, and still is a matter of much controversy. Such as profess to be in the right way and enjoy the true light, are disturbed, while those who fear for the safety and profits of their craft, are trembling lest the world will be dissuaded from following them.

No man, possessing his common faculties of understanding, unconnected with, or influenced by sectarian prejudice, will hesitate to say that something is wrong; and how is the evil to be remedied? Men act for themselves, choose for themselves, and if saved are saved for themselves, and not for another they cannot be driven into salvation, as compulsion would at once destroy their agency; and if that is taken away, why was it ever spoken "Whosoever will may take of the water of life freely?" Correct reasoning, plain facts, and undeniable assertions, on the plan of redemption, when presented to the mind, will, if any thing, call up that serious enquiry [inquiry] which is requisite in all. How often do we see men of first moral characters, bountiful to the poor, and filled with compassion toward the afflicted, enquiring [inquiring] for the "old paths" wherein Israel used to walk, standing with deep anxiety and concern for their souls, and say, "If I could but see the consistent order of which the (page 136) revelations of the Lord teach, how gladly would I embrace it." How frequently do we also hear those whose names are registered with a church, say they are dissatisfied? and only continue because they have been made to believe it important that they should belong to some church?

The great point at issue, is, whether the Lord ever promised to bring back an order, in the last days, like the one in former times, and set free those who are in bondage to the systems and crafts of men; and from this another would necessarily arise, whether the situation of the world in this day requires it? And if so, has it been ushered in? These cannot be considered any other than items of deep moment to the human family, and worthy the careful investigation of all. If our opinion is based upon the rock, it is worth believing, and if it is a fable, it is unworthy the notice of the intelligent and the concern of the sure; but till these facts are settled, it may be well to investigate.

The principles of my predecessor have been faithfully written and ably defended; and it is only necessary to add, that the patrons of this paper will find mine to correspond with his.

The former correspondents of the Messenger and Advocate, are respectfully solicited to continue to write for its columns; and the elders abroad and travelling [traveling] brethren, earnestly desired to give us accounts of their prosperity and travels.

With its former, and increasing correspondents, it is hoped that this paper will continue to be worthy of patronage; and as it continues to circulate and receive accounts of the increase and spread of truth, to be interesting to every family wherever it may appear.

The elders and brethren generally are requested to obtain and forward subscribers, who will be entitled to their numbers gratis according to the conditions on the last page.

One reflection more, and only one-If, in the performance of the duties which now devolve upon me, I so discharge them as to meet the approbation of the pure in heart, and still maintain the present respectability of this paper, and above all to have my work correspond with the principles of holiness, that at the great day of the Lord Jesus, I may but receive the reward of the just and the approbation of the same, that a crown of righteousness may be placed upon my head, I shall be satisfied and give the praise and glory to the exalted name of the Most High.

JOHN WHITMER

John Whitmer, *Messenger and Advocate*, March 1836

Address

To the patrons of the Latter Day Saints' Messenger and Advocate.

It becomes my duty to inform you, that in consequence of other business, and other duties which all my immediate attention, my labors in the editorial department of this paper must cease for the present; and as this is the case, I must beg leave to make some remarks, as I am about being freed from this great responsibility. I will here say that for the increase of patronage for nine months past, so gratuitously bestowed upon unmerited talents, you have necessarily obliged me to tender you my deepest-heart felt gratitude. I still indulge a hope, notwithstanding the advocate is about being transferred into other hands, that it will continue to receive its present support, and a rapid increase to its present subscription list, inasmuch as the prospects are flourishing, and the future editor's talents are deserving of patronage; I indulge a hope, that great good may be done by this means: and more especially in these last days, while "Darkness covers the earth and gross darkness the people."

Almost six years have passed since the church of Christ has been established: many and various are the scenes, that have passed before my eyes, since its commencement, during which time, we have been favored with the privilege, of making known to the world our belief in regard to salvation.

I take occasion here to add, that I rejoice exceedingly that this Herald of truth is in being, and I enjoy the privilege of resigning it into so good and able hands as Pres. O. Cowdery whose character and standing in society need no commendation from me where he is personally known: for he is known to be a man of piety, of candor, of truth, of integrity, of feeling for the welfare of the human family, and in short, he is a man of God: God acknowled ge [acknowledge] him as such in his revealed will: and should we not do so too?

While I reflect on leaving the editorial department, such a complicated mass of ideas burst upon my mind, that it is not possible to communicate them all. The great and responsible relation which a man sustains in occupying this station, to his fellow man, will have a tendency to humble, rather than exalt him in his own eyes; for he truly becomes a servant of all; and his words are left on record for present and future generations to scrutinize.

However there is consolation attached to these responsibilities, that gladdens the heart of an honest and humble saint, even a servant of servants: For after that in he [the] wisdom of God the world by wisdom knew not God, it pleased God by the foolishness of preaching to save them that believe.-It is those things, which the world by their wisdom count foolishness, which converts the soul, and will prepare it to dwell in the presence of God, in the day of the Lord Jesus. "God has chosen the foolish things of the world to confound the things which are mighty; and base things of the world, and things which are despised, hath God chosen, yea; and things which are not, to bring to nought things that are."

While I reflect on the above sayings of the holy writer, it gladdens my heart, that I enjoy the privilege of living in this age of the world, when God in his kind providence, has began to work for the good of his long dispersed covenant people; when he has again made manifest his will, and has called servants by his own voice out of the heavens, and by the ministering of angels, and by his Holy Spirit; and has chosen the weak and simple to confound the wisdom of the wise: and to raise up and bring the church of the Lamb up out of the wilderness of wickedness, fair as the sun and clear as the moon. Which church took its rise April 6, 1830; and has thus far come up through much persecution and great tribulation.

It may not be amiss in this place, to give a statement to the world concerning the work of the Lord, as I have been a member of this church of Latter Day Saints from its beginning; to say that the book of Mormon is a revelation from God, I have no hesitancy; but with all confidence have signed my named to it as such; and I hope, that my patrons will indulge me in speaking freely on this subject, as I am about leaving the editorial department-Therefore I desire to testify to all that will come to the knowledge of this address; that I have most assuredly seen the plates from whence the book of Mormon is translated, and that I have handled these plates, and know of a surety that Joseph Smith, jr. has translated the book of Mormon by the gift and power of God, and in this thing the wisdom of the wise most assuredly has perished: therefore, know ye, O ye inhabitants of the earth, wherever this address may come, that I have in this thing freed my garments of your blood, whether you believe or disbelieve the statements of your unworthy friend and well-wisher.

It is no trifling matter to sport with the souls of men, and make merchandise of them; I can say, with a clear conscience before God and man, that I have sought no man's goods, houses or lands, gold or silver; but had in view for my chief object, the welfare of the children of men, because I know that I have been called of God, to assist in bringing forth his work in these last days, and to help to establish it, that as many souls as would believe, and obey the truth, might be saved in his kingdom; and also assist in bringing about the restoration of the house of Israel, that they might magnify his name, for what he has done and is doing for the fulfilment [fulfillment] of the prophecies of all the holy prophets that have written on this great and important subject, since the days of Adam, to this present time: and while I have been in the editorial department, I have endeavored to write, obtain and select such matter as was calculated to promote the cause of God, as far as my judgment was capable of discerning: and wherein I may have erred, I am conscientious and innocent; but do cheerfully and humbly ask pardon of those whose feelings in any wise I may have injured; by digressing in the least, from the strictest path of rectitude.

I would do injustice to my own feelings, if I did not here notice, still further the work of the Lord in these last days: The revelations and commandments given to us, are, in my estimation, equally true with the book of Mormon, and equally necessary for salvation, it is necessary to live by every word that proceedeth from the mouth of God: and I know that the Bible, book of Mormon and book of Doctrine and Covenants of the church of Christ of Latter Day Saints, contain the revealed will of heaven. I further know that God will continue to reveal himself to his church and people, until he has gathered his elect into his fold, and prepared them to dwell in his presence.

Men at times depend upon the say of others, and are influenced by their persuasions to embrace different systems. This is correct, inasmuch as the principle is a just one: God always commissioned certain men, to proclaim his precepts to the remainder of the generation in which they lived; and if they heeded not their sayings, they were under condemnation.

Though weak may have been my arguments and feeble my exertions, to persuade others to believe as myself, the few months I have labored in this department, I trust, I have been the means of doing some good to my fellow men. If I were not sensible that I have been doing the will of my heavenly Father, I should regret, that I have ever suffered my name to become public; I could not endure the idea of having been the means of persuading men to detract from truth, and embrace error: it has been a principle in my heart to embrace truth, and reject error; and I trust it will remain in my heart forever.

I feel it my duty to say, to the Elders who have been laboring in the cause of our blessed Redeemer, and have taken the trouble, to procure subscribers for the Messenger and Advocate, they have my sincere thanks, (page 287) and shall ever occupy a conspicuous portion of my gratitude. There are others who have been somewhat negligent in this thing, which is owing perhaps, in part, for want of proper instruction upon this point; not realizing that this periodical is opening and preparing many places, for such as are travelling [traveling] to proclaim the gospel of our blessed Redeemer; whereas, if it had not been for this means, would have been closed and impenitrable [impenetrable]. I desire therefore, that the Elders of the church of Latter Day Saints will avail themselves of every opportunity that presents itself of procuring subscribers for this paper, not for pecuniary interests, but for the welfare of the children of men. I hope that the Elders will do all the good in their power, as this is a day of "Warning and not of many words." Therefore, I trust you will have the spirit of God in your hearts to guide you into all truth, until the knowledge of God shall cover the earth as the waters cover the great deep, and the saints of God are gathered together, and Zion becomes the joy of the whole earth.

John Whitmer.

Although Oliver became the nominal editor of the *Messenger and Advocate* following John Whitmer, he did not write an introduction. Nor did he sign editorials as he had previously. Some editorials were signed "ED." beginning with Oliver's second assumption of the editorial role. The changed approach corroborates Warren Cowdery's claim that he did most of the work.

Nevertheless, Oliver gave his own Valedictory in August, the month before Warren gave his own in the last issue of the *Messenger and Advocate*.

Oliver Cowdery, Messenger and Advocate, August 1837

VALEDICTORY.

In the 8th number, Vol. first of the Messenger and Advocate, I addressed its readers, as I then supposed, for the last time as its Editor. From considerations of duty, on the departure of brother Whitmer to the west, I again assumed the conduct of its columns, during which interval pecuniary circumstances have compelled me almost wholly from home, and when there, a feeble state of health prevented that strict attention, after fulfilling paramount duties, necessary to render such a periodical interesting, instructing and useful. How far under those circumstances, my labors have been approved by my heavenly Master, remains to be revealed when all things are openly proclaimed: and to what extent I have answered the expectations of my friends, I do not stop here to ask, as I presume they are quite willing to exchange my labors for the labors of another, and in that change expect a more faithful servant, without venturing any hazzard [hazard].

But, lest these remarks should create an unreasonable expectation, and an unwarranted call for labor on the part of my brother who succeeds me. I will here add, **that were he tnumerous [the numerous] readers of the Messenger aware, while perusing its columns, how many, very many constitutions are impaired, ruined,-worn out, by writing matter for others to read, they would be ready to excuse, when a number appeared not quite as full of editorial matter as their fancies could wish. It may be thought a small task to fill a small monthly sheet; to such I only recommend that they engage in it for one year. And besides, a man is responsible to God for all he writes. If his communications are not according to the truths of heaven, men may follow incorrect principles, and digress, step after step from the straight path, till arguments, persuasions and facts, are as unheeded as the idle vision, when darkness and death rivet their destructive chains to be beaten off no more.**

When this last reflection rises in the mind, **the heart almost sinks within this bosom, lest in consequence of some darkness over the intellect, or some deep anxiety and concern, occasioned by inevitable and irresistable [irristable] pecuniary embarrassment, I may have dropped an item, or left unintelligible some important fact, which has occasioned an incorrect understanding on matters of eternal life.** Those who are yet here, if such should be the case, relative to the principles which I have promulgated, may retrace and correct, but what adds keenly to the reflection is the fact, that many have gone no more to return till the purposes of God are accomplished in the restoration of all things. Those are beyond my admonition, and a few more seasons round, at most, will release me from this burthensome [burdensome] tenament [tenement] and I be permitted to fly away to receive my own reward.

Those whose feelings I may have unjustly injured if any, I now ask their forgiveness and hope, through the mediation of the Son of God to find also, in his blood, a propitiation for all my sins, that I may retire with a conscious heart that He who died for me is yet my friend and advocate, and that through all my future life I may live to his glory, walk in his paths, adorn his doctrine, and meet him in peace.

I have not time, neither is it necessary to go into detail on the subject of the gospel or prophets: these have been leading topics during the entire course of both Star and Messenger, and will of necessity continue so to be while unrighteousness has dominion on the earth. It is only requisite for me to add that the doctrines which I commenced to preach some seven years since are as firmly believed by me as ever; nd [and] though persecutions have attended, and the rage and malice of men been heaped upon me, **I feel equally as firm in the great and glorious cause as when first I received my mission from the holy messenger.** And such has been the opposition generally manifest against the progress and influence of this gospel, that **it amounts to a miracle that any should distrust its divine authenticity, with these facts daily presented before them.**

One sentence more, my friends, and I have done-I need not prolong the time. Range through all the revelations of God, search them from beginning to end, and if you do not find that the Lord would do marvelous things in the last days-reveal his glorious arm, set up his kingdom, scatter light, send forth intelligence and gather Israel, the literal descendants of Jacob from the four winds, endow and prepare hasty messengers and talk with his people face to face, I say adieu to that record, it is worse than a fable, it has not the intelligence of a common news-paper! Alas! how disappointed will be the man who turns from these in unbelief. The day is near when all will be verified-the day is near when all eyes will see and every heart be penetrated, and the day is near when you and I shall meet in the presence of God.

Farewell.

OLIVER COWDERY.

Warren A. Cowdery, *Messenger and Advocate*, September 1837
VALEDICTORY.

Every period of man's existence is marked with some event differing from others of his life, and peculiar to itself and to the time and circnmstance [circumstance] under which it occurred. The little minutiæ of a man's life, however unimportant to others, constitute links in the chain of events, that in the divine mind, stamp him with infamy, or fix on him the seal of aprobation [approbation]. Man in the private walks of life may pursue the paths of virtue and peace, worship the God who made him in sincerity and truth, go down to the grave in peace, and almost unknown, and his posterity rise up and call him blessed. But not so the man that takes upon him the conducting of a public periodical, however innocent, however pure he may be. His motives are scanned, his intentions sometimes perverted and his virtues assailed, but in the main he has little cause of complaint. He will be censured, perhaps, when he least deserves it in his own estimation, and praised when he merits rebuke: but there is one other consideration that detracts from the sympathy which at first view he seems to merit: He, by his voluntary consent has placed himself before the public and submitted his happiness to the caprice of a multitude of individuals, each and every one of whom, he could never hope to please.

The editorial charge of the *Messenger and Advocate* has rested more or less on us for a period of sixteen months past, but nominally it has rested solely on us, but eight months. It is useless to say we entered with diffidence and distrust of our own abilities, upon the duties of the station we now resign.

Although our head began to be silvered o'er with age, we had not the benefit of experience like some of our poedecessors [predecessors], in this employment.-The little talent we possessed, had been cultivated for one of the liberal professions, to know the vis medica trix naturæ, and learn the modus operandi of materia medica on the human system. Therefore under circumstances thus unpropitious, we now resign our charge with as little censure, and less regret, than we could have reasonably hoped we should when we assumed the important trust.

We had one hope on which we relied when we entered upon the duties of our new calling: (viz.) that by diligence and perseverance we should overcome many of the minor obstacles that presented themselves before us, and contribute our share in promoting the great cause for which this periodical was established. How far we have succeeded, and our hopes been realized, is not for us to say; time only will determine it.

We have not at all times seduously [sedulously], pursued the plan we first marked out for ourselves, in point of diligence and assiduity, but we feel that we have, at no time shrunk with sluggish indifference, from the responsibility or duty of our station. Our time and talents have been put in requisition, and our most ardent desires are, that the saints and others, should derive a benefit commensurate (page 569) at least, with the exertions we have made to do them good.

The lapse of time since we commenced, has seemed almost imperceptible, yet when we reflect, we know of a truth months and seasons have rolled away into that vast ocean of eternity from whence there is no return. We are daily and hourly admonished of this fact, not only from the increasing dimness of our sight, the growing flaccidity of our muscles, the tottering weakness of our limbs, but the yellow autumnal hue of all surrounding nature.

A few short months, sometimes produce radical changes in the history of human affairs, and form epochs in the annals of time which are never to be forgotten. The time recently passed and now passing, is marked with no peculiarity in the religious world, only that sects and parties are divided and dividing, with the hate and animosity peculiar to religious bigots and the blinded devotees of party zeal. A combination of causes has contributed to increase the strife, and fan the flame of discord and disunion among them. The infidel has doubtless laughed at the folly of such religionists as, through party rage and discontent, have been biting and devouring each other. Notwithstanding all the fears of the pious worshiper [worshipper], the forebodings of the ignorant ones, or the slow moving finger of scorn pointed by the infidel: truth is mighty and will prevail. The faithful servants of the

Most High in the East, West, North and South are proclaiming the words of life and salvation, and the honest and unprejudiced, lend a listening ear, so that we can truly say "the word of God grows & multiplies."

We are aware there are honest differences of opinion in religion as well as politics; and there are conflicting interests in all communities, and every consideration that ought to actuate an individual occupying the station we are now about to resign, urges him to use all he may have of talent, all he may have of influence, all he may have of weight of character, to calm unruly passions, ally dissensions and restore peace, at the same time, he should not compromise the dignity and honor of a man of God, nor sacrifice the cause of truth. Peace is desireable [desirable], but should never be sought at the expense of truth. The peacemaker shall be called the child of God, but no peace will be durable, nor any happiness lasting, that is not based upon truth and righteousness. He who caters for the public should be doubly guarded in all he spreads before the eye of his readers. He should realize that extemporaneous praise or censure, salute the ear, they are words, and words are wind which soon passes away and is forgotten. But not so with his productions, they are spread out before the public, they remain to be seen when the sensorium that matured them, has ceased to combine and compare. They are become matter of history, and numbered among things which have been; and still we can look on them and they, as if by the power of magic, are present with all the train of reflections that produced them. With these views and under these circumstances, with our humble talent, we had no just right to expect we should escape censure.

We are well aware that the wise and good, as well as the crafty sycophant, in passing the ordeal of public opinion, feel the lash of censure or the stroke of keen rebuke. If vice, immorality and crime, are passed over with impunity, virtue stands aghast and abashed, hiding her head with shame. If religion, truth and virtue occupy the foreground, then all the votaries of vice and crime are ready to cry out away with him!-crucify him! We can truly say then, that our object has been to do the greatest possible good, with the least possible evil, reckless of consequences to ourselves. How far we have succeeded, God only knows, time alone can disclose the secret to us, and to our fellow mortals. He who knows our heart, knows that we entered upon our charge with (as we have before remarked,) diffidence and distrust of our own abilities, and now as we are to resign it, if we could flatter ourselves that we had done well, if our heavenly Father approbated our labors, we should rejoice that we had done some good, that we had intensely pursued the object at which we aimed in the beginning, and that the world would be the better that we have lived in it. But if we have done but indifferently well, and pleased but few, it is all with our weak capacity, we had any just right to expect; and if we have failed entirely, we mourn not that our lot is hard, for it is no harder, and we had no right (page 570) to expect any thing better, in the issue than frequently happens to better men than ourselves.

To our readers who differ from us in matters of religion we say, we have at no time since the commencement of our editorial career, dipped our pen in gall to wound your feelings or mar your peace, although we differ from you, it does not necessarily follow that we are your enemies. We have endeavored to advocate the truth as we understood it and to persuade others to believe and embrace it.

"We have endeavored, nothing to exaggerate, or to set down ought in malice."

But if at any time we have done so either intentionally or inadvertantly [inadvertently], we sincerely ask pardon.

If in the course of our editorial charge, we have unjustly impaired the confidence of our brethren, in the saints in this place, so that the poor and innocent have suffered and the progress of the work of the Lord been retarded, we most sincerely and deeply deplore it. But if on the contrary the warnings we have given, have prevented more ruin, regret and misery, than a natural, unsuspecting or unjust confidence would have produced, so that more good than evil has been the result, and the good shall finally preponderate in eternity, we trust the wise, the good, the philrnthropic [philanthropic] here and elsewhere, (partial evil to the contrary notwithstanding,) will duly appreciate our labors and approbate our course.

Of God and our brethren we sincerely ask pardon for all errors of principle, we may have in inculcated: and we most sincerely hope, they with ourselves will in future be blessed with a greater portion of that Spirit which leads into all truth, and be disposed in our hearts to embrace it and reject error. But we crave no pardon, we ask no forgiveness, for having promulgated the truth, however reprehensible it may have been to the wicked and unbelieving. Truth we believe, can never operate to the injury of a good cause, for the simple reason, that such a cause must have truth for its basis, and truth for its superstructure. We will further add, what we deem an axiom that truth, however inconsistent or irreconcilable it may appear, to other truth, will never counteract, but run parallel with other truth on which a proposition rests or a principle is based. Therefore, should be eagerly sought by all who cater for the public, regardless of consequences to themselves.

We consider the conductor of a religious periodical under as much stronger obligations to seek after and publish the truth, as eternity is longer than any portion of time of which we have any conception, or as the soul is more valuable than the mortal tenement in which it now dwells.

Once more and we have done, perhaps forever: We ask pardon of all we have unjustly injured and pray God to forgive us. We think we are willing to forgive as we hope to be forgiven. We are willing that time or eternity should disclose the motives from which we have acted, and to leave the result of our labors, to him who overrules all for his own glory. May the Lord add his blessing to our feeble labors; may they yet do the saints good, may the wicked forsake his way and embrace the truth, and we all meet in the presence of our God in peace.

To our successor in the editorial chair we say, though he may have more of talent, more of popularity than we possess, more will justly be required of him, all his talents, all his popularity, will have to be put in requisition to manage the ship across the tempestuous sea that lies before him. We most ardently wish him a prosperous voyage and safe mooring in the haven of everlasting rest.

To his readers we say show your faith by your works? pray for him in secret, and pay him in public, and then shall your works prove your faith and both be made perfect and be counted to you for righteousness. Farewell.

W. A. COWDERY.

Kirtland, Sept. 1837.

Appendix 5: Joseph Smith's letters to the editor

Over the years, Joseph Smith occasionally wrote letters to the editor that were published in the Church magazines. The most well-known now are the letters that have been canonized as D&C 127 and 128. In September 1842, he sent those to the editor of the *Times and Seasons* for publication in the paper—a very strange procedure if he was himself acting as editor at the time.

This Appendix shows other letters that Joseph wrote to editors for publication in Church magazines, showing a prior course of action that makes sense of D&C 127 and 128.

The handwritten originals of these letters are not extant, so there is no way to know if Joseph wrote these himself, if he dictated them, or if he asked someone to write them based on his general thoughts, in which case he may or may not have edited the final product.

Joseph Smith letter to the Oliver Cowdery, September 1835

TO OLIVER COWDERY.

To the elders of the church of Latter Day Saints.

After so long a time, and after so many things having been said, I feel it my duty to drop a few hints, that, perhaps, the elders, traveling through the world to warn the inhabitants of the earth to feel the wrath to come, and save themselves from this untoward generation, may be aided in a measure, in doctrine, and in the way of their duty. I have been laboring in this cause for eight years, during which time I have traveled much, and have had much experience. I removed from Seneca county, N. Y. to Geauga county, Ohio, in February, 1831.

Having received, by an heavenly vision a commandment, in June following, to take my journey to the western boundaries of the State of Missouri, and there designate the very spot, which was to be the central spot, for the commencement of the gathering together of those who embrace the fulness [fullness] of the everlasting gospel-I accordingly undertook the journey with certain ones of my brethren, and, after a long and tedious journey, suffering many privations and hardships, I arrived in Jackson county Missouri; and, after viewing the country, seeking diligently at the hand of God, he manifested himself unto me, and designated to me and others, the very spot upon which he designed to commence the work of the gathering, and the upbuilding of an holy city, which should be called Zion:-Zion because it is to be a place of righteousness, and all who build thereon, are to worship the true and living God-and all believe in one doctrine even the doctrine of our Lord and Savior Jesus Christ.

(page 179) _____

"Thy watchmen shall lift up the voice; with the voice together shall they sing: for they shall see eye to eye, when the Lord shall bring again Zion."-Isaiah 52:8.

Here we pause for a moment, to make a few remarks upon the idea of gathering to this place. It is well known that there were lands belonging to the government, to be sold to individuals; and it was understood by all, at least we believed so, that we lived in a free country, a land of liberty and of laws, guaranteeing to every man, or any company of men, the right of purchasing lands, and settling, and living upon them: therefore we thought no harm in advising the Latter Day Saints, or Mormons, as they are reproachfully called, to gather to this place, inasmuch as it was their duty, (and it was well understood so to be,) to purchase, with money, lands, and live upon them-not infringing upon the civil rights of any individual, or community of people: always keeping in view the saying, "Do unto others as you would wish to have others do unto you." Following also the good injunction: "Deal justly, love mercy, and walk humbly with thy God."

These were our motives in teaching the people, or Latter Day Saints, to gather together, beginning at this place. And inasmuch as there are those who have had different views from this, we feel, that it is a cause of deep regret: For, be it known unto all men, that our principles concerning this thing, have not been such as have been represented by those who, we have every reason to believe, are designing and wicked men, that have said that this was our doctrine:-to infringe upon the rights of a people who inhabit our civil and free country: such as to drive the inhabitants of Jackson county from their lands, and take possession thereof unlawfully. Far, yea, far be such a principle from our hearts: it never entered into our mind, and we only say, that God shall reward such in that day when he shall come to make up his jewels.

But to return to my subject: after having ascertained the very spot, and having the happiness of seeing quite a number of the families of my brethren, comfortably situated upon the land, I took leave of them, and journeyed back to Ohio, and used every influence and argument, that lay in my power, to get those who believe in the everlasting covenant, whose circumstances would admit, and whose families were willing to remove to the place which I now designated to be the land of Zion: And thus the sound of the gathering, and of the doctrine, went abroad into the world; and many we have reason to fear, having a zeal not according to knowledge, not understanding the pure principles of the doctrine of the church, have no doubt, in the heat of enthusiasm, taught and said many things which are derogatory to the genuine character and principles of the church, and for these things we are heartily sorry, and would apologize if an apology would do any good.

But we pause here and offer a remark upon the saying which we learn has gone abroad, and has been handled in a manner detrimental to the cause of truth, by saying, "that in preaching the doctrine of gathering, we break up families, and give license for men to leave their families; women their husbands; children their parents, and slaves their masters, thereby deranging the order, and breaking up the harmony and peace of society." We shall here show our faith, and thereby, as we humbly trust, put and end to these faults, and wicked misrepresentations, which have caused, we have every reason to believe, thousands to think they were doing God's service, when they were persecuting the children of God: whereas, if they could have enjoyed the true light, and had a just understanding of our principles, they would have embraced them with all their hearts, and been rejoicing in the love of the truth.

And now to show our doctrine on this subject, we shall commence with the first principles of the gospel, which are repentance, and baptism for the remission of sins, and the gift of the Holy Ghost by the laying on of the hands. This we believe to be our duty, to teach to all mankind the doctrine of repentance, which we shall endeavor to show from the following quotations:

"Then opened he their understanding, that they might understand the scriptures, and said unto them, thus it is written, and thus it behoved [behooved] Christ to suffer, and to rise from the dead, the third day; and that repentance and remission of sins should be preached in his name among all nations, beginning at Jerusalem."- Luke 24:45,46,47.

By this we learn, that it behoved [behooved] Christ to suffer, and to be crucified, and rise again on the third day, for the express purpose that repentance and

(page 180) _____

remission of sins should be preached unto all nations.

"Then Peter said unto them, repent, and be baptized every one of you, in the name of Jesus Christ, for the remission of sins, and ye shall receive the gift of the Holy Ghost. For the promise is unto you, and to your children, and to all that are afar off, even as many as the Lord our God shall call."-Acts 2:38, 39.

By this we learn, that the promise of the Holy Ghost, is unto as many as the doctrine of repentance was to be preached, which was unto all nations. And we discover also, that the promise was to extend by lineage: for Peter says, "not only unto you, but unto your children, and unto all that are afar off." From this we infer that it was to continue unto their children's children, and even unto as many generations as should come after, even as many as the Lord their God should call.- We discover here that we are blending two principles together, in these quotations. The first is the principle of repentance, and the second is the principle of remission of sins. And we learn from Peter, that remission of sins is obtained by baptism in the name of the Lord Jesus Christ; and the gift of the Holy Ghost follows inevitably: for, says Peter, "you shall receive the gift of the Holy Ghost." Therefore we believe in preaching the doctrine of repentance in all the world, both to old and young, rich and poor, bond and free, as we shall endeavor to show hereafter-how and in what manner, and how far it is binding upon the consciences of mankind, making proper distinctions between old and young men, women and children, and servants.

But we discover, in order to be benefitted [benefited] by the doctrine of repentance, we must believe in obtaining the remission of sins. And in order to obtain the remission of sins, we must believe in the doctrine of baptism, in the name of the Lord Jesus Christ. And if we believe in baptism for the remission of sins, we may expect a fulfilment [fulfillment] of the promise of the Holy Ghost: for the promise extends to all whom the Lord our God shall call. And hath he not surely said, as you will find in the last chapter of Revelations:

"And the Spirit and the bride say, Come. And let him that heareth, say, Come. And let him that is athirst, come. And whosoever will, let him take the water of life freely." Rev. 22:17.

Again the Savior says:

"Come unto me, all ye that labor, and are heavy laden, and I will give you rest.

Take my yoke upon you, and learn of me; for I am meek and lowly in heart; and ye shall find rest unto your souls. For my yoke is easy, and my burden is light." Matt. 11:28, 29, 30.

Again Isaiah says:

"Look unto me, and be ye saved, all the ends of the earth: for I am God, and there is none else. I have sworn by myself, the word is gone out of my mouth in righteousness, and shall not return, that unto me every knee shall bow, every tongue shall swear. Surely, shall one say, in the Lord have I righteousness and strength: even to him shall men come; and all that are incensed against him shall be ashamed." Isaiah 45:22, 23, 24.

And to show further connections in proof of the doctrine above named, we quote the following scriptures:

"Him hath God exalted with his right hand, to be a Prince and a Savior, for to give repentance to Israel, and forgiveness of sins. And we are his witnesses of these things; and so is also the Holy Ghost, whom God hath given to them that obey him." Acts 5:31,32.

"But when they believed Philip, preaching the things concerning the kingdom of God, and the name of Jesus Christ, they were baptized, both men and women. Then Simon himself believed also; and when he was baptized, he continued with Philip, and wondered, beholding the miracles and signs which were done. Now when the apostles, which were at Jerusalem, heard that Samaria had received the word of God, they sent unto them Peter and John; who, when they were come down, prayed for them, that they might receive the Holy ghost. (For as yet he was fallen upon none of them: only they were baptized in the name of the Lord Jesus.)-Then laid they their hands on them, and they received the Holy ghost. * * * And as they went on their way, they came unto a certain water; and the eunuch said, See, here is water; what doth hinder me to be baptized?-And Philip said, If thou believest with all thine heart thou mayest. And he answered and said,, I believe that Jesus Christ is the Son of God. And he commanded the chariot to stand still: and they went down both into the water, both Philip and the eunuch; and he baptized him. And, when they were come up out of the water, the Spirit of the Lord caught away Philip, that the eunuch saw him no more: and he went on his way rejoicing. But Philip was found at Azotus; and, passing through, he preached in all the cities, till he came to Cesarea [Ceasarea]."-Acts 8:12, 13, 14, 15, 16, 17,-36, to the end.

"While Peter yet spake these words, the Holy Ghost fell on all them which heard the word. And they of the circumcision, which believed, were astonished, as many as came with Peter, because that on the Gentiles also was poured out the gift of the Holy Ghost: for they heard them speak with tongues, and magnify God. Then answered Peter, Can any man forbid water, that these should not be baptized, which have received the Holy Ghost as well as we? And he commanded them to be baptized in the name of the Lord. Then prayed they him to tarry certain days." Acts 10:44, 45, 46, 47, 48.

"And on the Sabbath, we went out of the city, by a river side, where prayer was wont to be made; and we sat down, and spake unto

(page 181) _____

the women that resorted thither. And a certain woman, named Lydia, a seller of purple, of the city of Thyatira, which worshipped God, heard us: whose heart the Lord opened, that she attended unto the things which were spoken of Paul. And when she was baptized, and her household, she besought us, saying, If ye have judged me to be faithful to the Lord, come into my house, and abide there. And she constrained us. * * * * And at midnight Paul and Silas prayed, and sang praises unto God: and the prisoners heard them. And suddenly there was a great earthquake, so that the foundations of the prison were shaken; and immediately all the doors were opened, and every one's bands were loosed. And the keeper of the prison awaking out of his sleep, and seeing the prison doors open, he drew out his sword, and would have killed himself, supposing that the prisoners had been fled. But Paul cried with a loud voice, saying, Do thyself no harm; for we are all here. Then he called for a light, and sprang in, and came trembling, and fell down before Paul and Silas; and brought them out, and said, Sirs, what must I do to be saved? And they said believe on the Lord Jesus Christ, and thou shalt be saved and thy house. And they spake unto him the word of the Lord, and to all that were in his house. And he took them the same hour of the night, and washed their stripes, and was baptized, he and all his, straightway. And when he had brought them into his house, he set meat before them, and rejoiced, believing in God with all his house." Acts 16:13, 14, 15.-25, to 35.

"And it came to pass, that, while Apollos was at Corinth, Paul, having passed through the upper coasts, came to Ephesus; and finding certain disciples, he said unto them, Have ye received the Holy Ghost since ye believed? And they said unto him, We have not so much as heard whether there be any Holy Ghost. And he said unto them, Unto what then were ye baptized? And they said, Unto John's baptism. Then said Paul, John verily baptized with the baptism of repentance, saying unto the people, that they should believe on him which should come after him, that is, on Christ Jesus. When they heard this, they were baptized in the name of the Lord Jesus. And, when Paul had laid his hands upon them, the Holy Ghost came on them; and they spake with tongues, and prophesied."-Acts 19:1, 2, 3, 4, 5, 6.

And one Ananias, a devout man, according to the law, having a good report of all the Jews which dwelt there, Came unto me, and stood, and said unto me, Brother Saul, receive thy sight, And the same hour I looked up upon him. And he said, the God of our fathers hath chosen thee, that thou shouldst know his will, and see that Just One, and shouldst hear the voice of his mouth. For thou shalt be his witness unto all men, of what thou hast seen and heard. And now why tarriest thou? arise, and be baptized, and wash away thy sins, calling on the name of the Lord." Acts 22:12, 13, 14, 15, 16.

"For, when for the time ye ought to be teachers, ye have need that one teach you again which be the first principles of the oracles of God; and are become such as have need of milk, and not of strong meat. For every one that useth milk, is unskillful in the word of righteousness; for he is a babe. But strong meat belongeth to them that are of full age, even those who by reason of use, have their senses exercised to discern both good and evil."-Heb. 5:12, 13, 14.

"Therefore, leaving the principles of the doctrine of Christ, let us go on unto perfection; not laying again the foundation of repentance from dead works, and of faith towards God, of the doctrine of baptisms, and of laying on of hands, and of resurrection of the dead, and of eternal judgment. And this will we do, if God permit. For it is impossible for those who were once enlightened, and have tasted of the heavenly gift, and were made partakers of the Holy Ghost, and have tasted the good word of God, and the powers of the world to come, if they shall fall away, to renew them again unto repentance; seeing they crucify to themselves the Son of God afresh, and put him to an open shame. Heb. 6:1, 2, 3, 4, 5, 6.

These quotations are so plain, in proving the doctrine of repentance and baptism for the remission of sins, I deem it unnecessary to enlarge this letter with comments upon them-but I shall continue the subject in my next.

In the bonds of the new and

everlasting covenant,
JOSEPH SMITH, jr.
JOHN WHITMER, Esq.

Joseph Smith letter to the *Messenger and Advocate*, November 1835

To the elders of the church of the Latter Day Saints.

At the close of my letter in the September No. of the "Messenger and Advocate," I promised to continue the subject there commended: I do so with a hope that it may be a benefit and a means of assistance to the elders in their labors while they are combating the prejudices of a crooked and perverse generation, by having in their possession, the facts of my religious principles, which are misrepresented by almost all those whose crafts are in danger by the same; and also to aid those who are anxiously inquiring, and have been excited to do so from rumor, in ascertaining correctly, what my principles are.

I have been drawn into this course of proceeding, by persecution, that is brought upon us from false rumor, and misrepresentations concerning my sentiments.

But to proceed, in the letter alluded to, the principles of repentance and baptism for the remission of sins, are not only set forth, but many passages of scripture, were quoted, clearly illucidating [elucidating] the subject; let me add, that I do positively rely upon the truth and veracity of those principles inculcated in the new testament; and then pass from the above named items, on to the item or subject of the gathering, and show my views upon this point: which is an item which I esteem to be of the greatest importance to those who are looking for salvation in this generation, or in these what may be called "the latter times," as all the prophets that have written, from the days of righteous Abel down to the last man, that has left any testimony on record, for our consideration, in speaking of the salvation of Israel in the last days, goes directly to show, that it consists in the work of the gathering.

Firstly, I shall begin by quoting from the prophecy of Enoch, speaking of the last days: "Righteousness will I send down out of heaven, and truth will I send forth out of the earth, to bear testimony of mine Only Begotten, his resurrection from the dead, [this resurrection I understand to be the corporeal body] yea, and also the resurrection of all men, righteousness and truth will I cause to sweep the earth as with a flood, to gather out mine own elect from the four quarters of the earth, unto a place which I shall prepare; a holy city, that my people may gird up their loins, and be looking forth for the time of my coming: for there shall be my tabernacle; and it shall be called Zion, a New Jerusalem."

Now I understand by this quotation, that God clearly manifested to Enoch, the redemption which he prepared, by offering the Messiah as a Lamb slain from before the foundation of the world: by virtue of the same, the glorious resurrection of the Savior, and the resurrection of all the human family,-even a resurrection of their corporeal bodies: and also righteousness and truth are agoing to sweep the earth as with a flood? I will answer:-Men and angels are to be co-workers in bringing to pass this great work: and a Zion is to be prepared; even a New Jerusalem, for the elect that are to be gathered from the four quarters of the earth, and to be established an holy city: for the tabernacle of the Lord shall be with them.

Now Enoch was in good company in his views upon this subject. See Revelations, 23:3 [21:3]-"And I heard a great voice out of heaven saying. Behold the tabernacle of God is with men, and he will dwell with them, and they shall be his people, and God himself shall be with them, and be their God." I discover by this quotation, that John upon the isle of Patmos, saw the same things concerning the last days, which Enoch saw. But before the tabernacle can be with men, the elect must be gathered from the four quarters of the earth.

And to show further upon this subject of gathering: Moses, after having pronounced the blessing and the cursing upon the children of Israel, for their obedience or disobedience, says thus:-"And it shall come to pass, when all these things are come upon thee, the blessing and the curse which I have set before thee; and thou shalt call them to mind, among all the nations whither the Lord thy God hath driven thee, and shalt return unto the Lord thy God, and shalt obey his voice, according to all that I command thee, this day, thou and thy children, with all thine heart, and with all thy soul, that then the Lord thy God, will turn thy captivity, and have compassion upon thee, and will return and gather thee from all the nations whither the Lord thy God hath scattered thee; and if any of thine be driven out unto the utmost parts of heaven; from thence will the Lord thy God gather thee; and from thence will he fetch thee."

It has been said by many of the learned, and wise men, or historians, that the Indians, or aboriginees [aborigines] of this continent, are of the scattered tribes of Israel. It has been conjectured by many others, that the aboriginees [aborigines] of this continent, are not of the tribes of Israel; but the ten tribes have been led away into some unknown regions of the north. Let this be as it may, the prophesy I have just quoted, "will fetch them" in the last days, and place them, in the land which their fathers possessed: and you will find in the 7th verse of the 30th chapt. quoted: "And the Lord thy God will put all these curses upon thine enemies and on them that hate thee, which persecuted thee."

Many may say that this scripture is fulfilled, but let them mark carefully what the prophet says: "If any are driven out unto the utmost parts of heaven;" (which must mean the breadths of the earth.) Now this promise is good to any, if there should be such, that are driven out, even in the last days: therefore, the children of the fathers have claim unto this day: and if these curses are to be laid over on the heads of their enemies, wo be unto the Gentiles: See book of Mormon, page 487, Wo unto the unbelieving of the Gentiles, saith the Father. Again see book of Mormon, page 497, which says: "Behold this people will I establish in this land, unto the fulfilling of the covenant which I made with your father Jacob: and it shall be a New Jerusalem." Now we learn from the book of Mormon, the very identical continent and spot of land upon which the new Jerusalem is to stand, and it must be caught up according to the vision of John upon the isle of Patmos. Now many will be disposed to say, that this New Jerusalem spoken of, is the Jerusalem that was built by the Jews on the eastern continent: But you will see from Revelations, 21:2, there was a New Jerusalem coming down from God out of heaven, adorned as a bride for her husband. That after this the Revelator was caught away in the Spirit to a great and high mountain, and saw the great and holy city descending out of heaven from God. Now there are two cities spoken of here, and as every thing cannot be had in so narrow a compass as a letter, I shall say with brevity, that there is a New Jerusalem to be established on this continent.-And also the Jerusalem shall be rebuilt on the eastern continent. See book of Mormon, page 566. Behold, Ether saw the days of Christ, and he spake also concerning the house of Israel, and the Jerusalem from whence Lehi should come: after it should be destroyed it should be built up again, a holy city unto the Lord: wherefore, it could not be a New Jerusalem, for it had been in a time of old. This may suffice upon the subject of gathering until my next.

I now proceed, at the close of my letter, to make a few remarks on the duty of elders with regard to their teachings parents and children, husbands and wives, masters and slaves, or servants, &c. as I said I would in my former letter. And firstly, it becomes an elder when he is travelling [traveling] through the world, warning the inhabitants of the earth to gather together, that they may be built up an holy city unto the Lord, instead of commencing with children or those who look up to parents or guardians, to influence their minds, thereby drawing them from their duties, which they rightfully owe to such, they should commence their labors with parents, or guardians, and their teachings should be such as are calculated to turn the hearts of the fathers to the children, and the hearts of the children to the fathers. And no influence should be used, with children contrary to the consent of their parents or guardians.-But all such as can be persuaded in a lawful and righteous manner, and with common consent, we should feel it our duty to influence them to gather with the people of God. But otherwise let the responsibility rest upon the heads of parents or guardians, and all condemnation or consequences, be upon (page 210) their heads, according to the dispensation which he hath committed unto us: for God has so ordained, that his work shall be cut short in righteousness, in the last days: therefore, first teach the parents, and then, with their consent, let him persuade the children to embrace the gospel also. And if children embrace the gospel, and their parents or guardians are unbelievers, teach them to stay at home and be obedient to their parents or guardians, if they require it; but if they consent to let them gather with the people of God let them do so and there shall be no wrong and let all things be done carefully, and righteously, and God will extend his guardian care to all such.

And secondly, it should be the duty of elders, when they enter into any house, to let their labors and warning voice be unto the master of that house: and if he receive the gospel, then he may extend his influence to his wife also, with consent, that peradventure she may receive the gospel; but if a man receive not the gospel, but gives his consent that his wife may receive it, and she believes, then let her receive it. But if the man forbid his wife, or his children before they are of age, to receive the gospel, then it should be the duty of the elder to go his way and use no influence against him: and let the responsibility be upon his head-shake off the dust of thy feet as a testimony against him, and thy skirts shall then be clear of their souls. Their sins are not to be answered upon such as God hath sent to warn them to flee the wrath to come, and save themselves from this untoward generation. The servants of God will not have gone over the nations of the Gentiles, with a warning voice, until the destroying angel will commence to waste the inhabitants of the earth; and as the prophet hath said. "It shall be a vexation to hear the report." I speak because I feel for my fellow-men: I do it in the name of the Lord, being moved upon by the Holy Spirit. O that I could snatch them from the vortex of misery, into which I behold them plunging themselves, by their sins, that I may be enabled, by the warning voice, to be an instrument of bringing them to unfeigned repentance, that they may have faith to stand in the evil day.

Thirdly, it should be the duty of an elder, when he enters into a house to salute the master of that house, and if he gain his consent, then he may preach to all that are in that house, but if he gain not his consent, let him go not unto his slaves or servants, but let the responsibility be upon the head of the master of that house, and the consequences thereof; and the guilt of that house is no longer upon thy skirts: Thou art free; therefore, shake off the dust of thy feet, and go thy way. But if the master of that house give consent; that they mayest preach to his family, his wife, his children, and his servants, his man-servants, or his maid-servants, or his slaves, then it should be the duty of the elder to stand up boldly for the cause of Christ, and warn that people with one accord, to repent and be baptized for the remission of sins, and for the Holy Ghost, always commanding them in the name of the Lord, in the spirit of meekness to be kindly affected one towards another; that the fathers should be kind to their children, husbands to their wives; masters to their slaves or servants; children obedient to their parents, wives to their husbands, and slaves or servants to their masters."

"Wives submit yourselves unto your own husbands, as unto the Lord. For the husband is the head of the wife, even as Christ is the head of the church: and he is the Savior of the body. Therefore as the church is subject unto Christ, so let the wives be to their own husbands in every thing. Husbands, love your wives even as Christ also loved the church and gave himself for it; that he might sanctify and cleanse it with the washing of water by the word, that he might present it to himself a glorious church, not having spot, or wrinkle, or any such thing; but that it should be holy and without blemish. So ought men to love their wives as their own bodies. He that loveth his wife loveth himself. For no man ever yet hated his own flesh: but nourisheth and cherisheth it, even as the Lord the church: for we are members of his body, of his flesh, and of his bones.-For this cause shall a man leave his father and mother, and shall be joined unto his wife, and they two shall be one flesh."-Ephesians, Chapt. 5. from the 22d to the end of the 21st. [31st] verse.

"Wives submit yourselves unto your own husbands, as it is fit in the Lord.

266

Husbands, love your wives, and be not bitter against them. Children, obey your parents in all things: for this is well pleasing unto the Lord. Fathers, provoke not your children to anger, lest they be discouraged. Servants, obey in all things your masters according to the flesh: not with eye service as men pleasers; but in singleness of heart, fearing God."-Colocians [Colossians], Chapt. III. from the 18th to the end of the 22d verse. (page 211) But I must close this letter and resume the subject in another number.

In the bonds of the new
and everlasting covenant
Joseph Smith, jr.
To J. Whitmer, Esq.

Joseph Smith letter to the *Messenger and Advocate*, December 1835

To the Elders of the Church of the Latter Day Saints.

I have shown unto you, in my last, that there are two Jerusalems spoken of in holy writ, in a manner I think satisfactorily to your minds. At any rate I have given my views upon the subject. I shall now proceed to make some remarks from the sayings of the Savior, recorded in the 13th chapter of his gospel according to St. Matthew, which in my mind affords us as clear an understanding, upon the important subject of the gathering, as any thing recorded in the bible. At the time the Savior spoke these beautiful sayings and parables, contained in the chapter above quoted, we find him seated in a ship, on the account of the multitude that pressed upon him to hear his words, and he commenced teaching them by saying: "Behold a sower went forth to sow, and when he sowed, some seeds fell by the way side, and the fowls came and devoured them up; some fell upon stony places, where they had not much earth, and forthwith they sprang up because they had no deepness of earth, and when the sun was up, they were scorched, and because they had not root they withered away; and some fell among thorns and the thorns sprang up and choked them; but other, fell into good ground and brought forth fruit, some an hundred fold, some sixty fold, some thirty fold: who hath ears to hear let him hear. And the disciples came and said unto him, why speakest thou unto them in parables, (I would remark here, that the "them," made use of, in this interrogation, is a personal pronoun and refers to the multitude,) he answered and said unto them, (that is the disciples,) it is given unto you to know the mysteries of the kingdom of heaven, but unto them (that is unbelievers) it is not given, for whosoever hath, to him shall be given, and he shall have more abundance; but whosoever hath not, shall be taken away, even that he hath."

We understand from this saying, that those who had previously been looking for a Messiah to come, according to the testimony of the Prophets, and were then, at that time, looking for a Messiah, but had not sufficient light on the account of their unbelief, to discern him to be their Savior; and he being the true Messiah, consequently they must be disappointed and lose even all the knowledge, or have taken away from them, all the light, understanding and faith, which they had upon this subject; therefore he that will not receive the greater light, must have taken away from him, all the light which he hath. And if the light which is in you, become darkness, behold how great is that darkness? Therefore says the Savior, speak I unto them in parables, because they, seeing, see not; and hearing, they hear not; neither do they understand: and in them is fulfilled the prophecy of Esias, which saith: by hearing ye shall hear and shall not understand; and seeing ye shall see and not perceive.

Now we discover, that the very reasons assigned by this prophet, why they would not receive the Messiah, was, because they did or would not understand; and seeing they did not perceive: for this people's heart is waxed gross; their ears are dull of hearing; their eyes they have closed, lest at any time, they should see with their eyes, and hear with their ears, and understand with their hearts, and should be converted and I should heal them.

But what saith he to his disciples: Blessed are your eyes, for they see, and your ears, for they hear; for verily I say nnto [unto] you, that many prophets and righteous men have desired to see those things which ye see, and have not seen them; and to hear those things which ye hear, and have not heard them.

We again make a remark here, for we find that the very principles upon which the disciples were accounted blessed, was because they were permitted to see with their eyes, and hear with their ears, and the condemnation which rested upon the multitude, which received not his saying, was because they were not willing to see with their eyes and hear with their ears; not because they could not and were not privileged to see, and hear, but because their hearts were full of iniquity and abomination: as your fathers did so do ye. The prophet foreseeing that they would thus harden their hearts plainly declared it; and herein is the condemnation of the world, that light hath come into the world, and men choose darkness rather than light because their deeds are evil: This is so plainly taught by the Savior, that a wayfaring man need not mistake it.

And again hear ye the parable of the sower: Men are in the habit, when the truth is exhibited by the servants of God, of saying, all is mystery, they are spoken in parables, and, therefore, are not to be understood, it is true they have eyes to see, and see not; but none are so blind as those who will not see: And although the Savior spoke this parable to such characters, yet unto his disciples he expounded it plainly; and we have reason to be truly humble before the God of our fathers, that he hath left these things on record for us, so plain, that, notwithstanding the exertions and combined influence of the priests of Baal, they have not power to blind our eyes and darken our understanding, if we will but open our eyes and read with candor, for a moment. But listen to the explanation of the parable: when any one heareth the word of the kingdom, and understandeth it not, then cometh the wicked one and catcheth away that which was sown in his heart. Now mark the expression; that which was before sown in his heart; this is he which received seed by the way side; men who have no principle of righteousness in themselves, and whose hearts are full of iniquity, and who have no desire for the principles of truth, do not understand the word of truth, when they hear it.-The devil taketh away the word of truth out of their hearts, because there is no desire for righteousness in them. But he that received the seed into stony places the same is he that heareth the word and, anon, with joy receiveth it, yet hath he not root in himself, but dureth for awhile; for when tribulation or persecution ariseth because of the word, by and by he is offended. He also that received seed among the thorns is he that receiveth the word, and the cares of this world, and the deceitfulness of riches choke the word, and he becometh unfruitful: but he that received seed into the good ground, is he that heareth the word and understandeth it which also beareth fruit and bringeth forth some an hundred fold, some sixty, some thirty. Thus the Savior himself explains unto his disciples the parable, which he put forth and left no mystery or darkness upon the minds of those who firmly believe on his words.

We draw the conclusion then, that the very reason why the multitude, or the world, as they were designated by the Savior, did not receive an explanation upon his parables, was, because of unbelief. To you, he says, (speaking to his disciples) it is given to know the mysteries of the kingdom of God: and why? because of the faith and confidence which they had in him. This parable was spoken to demonstrate the effects that are produced by the preaching of the word; and we believe that it has an allusion directly, to the commencement, or the setting up of the kingdom in that age: therefore, we shall continue to trace his sayings concerning this kingdom from that time forth, even unto the end of the world.

Another parable put he forth unto them, saying, (which parable has an allusion to the setting up of the kingdom, in that age of the world also) the kingdom of Heaven is likened unto a man which sowed good seed in his field, but while men slept an enemy came and sowed tares among the wheat and went his way; but when the blade was sprung up, and brought forth fruit, then appeared the tares also; so the servants of the householder came and said unto him, sir, didst not thou sow good seed in thy field? from whence then hath it tares? He said unto them, an enemy hath done this. The servants said unto him wilt thou then that we go and gather them up; but he said nay, lest while ye gather up the tares, ye root up also the wheat with them.-Let both grow together until the harvest, and in the time of harvest, I will say to the reapers, gather ye together first the tares, and bind them in bundles, to burn them; but gather the wheat into my barn.

Now we learn by this parable, not only the setting up of the kingdom in the days of the Savior, which is represented by the good seed, which produced fruit, but also the corruptions of the church, which is represented by the tares, which were sown by the enemy, which his disciples would fain (page 226) have plucked up, or cleansed the church of, if their views had been favored by the Savior; but he, knowing all things, says not so; as much as to say, your views are not correct, the church is in its infancy, and if you take this rash step, you will destroy the wheat or the church with the tares: therefore it is better to let them grow together until the harvest, or the end of the world, which means the destruction of the wicked; which is not yet fulfilled; as we shall show hereafter, in the Savior's explanation of the parable, which is so plain, that there is no room left for dubiety upon the mind, notwithstanding the cry of the priests, parables, parables! figures, figures! mystery, mystery! all is mystery! but we find no room for doubt here, as the parables were all plainly elucidated.

And again, another parable put he forth unto them, having an allusion to the kingdom which should be set up, just previous or at the time of harvest, which reads as follows:-The kingdom of heaven is like to a grain of mustard seed, which a man took and sowed in his field, which indeed is the least of all seeds, but when it is grown it is the greatest among herbs, and becometh a tree, so that the birds of the air come and lodge in the branches thereof. Now we can discover plainly, that this figure is given to represent the church as it shall come forth in the last days. Behold the kingdom of heaven is likened unto it. Now what is like unto it?

Let us take the book of Mormon, which a man took and hid in his field; securing it by his faith, to spring up in the last days, or in due time: let us behold it coming forth out of the ground, which is indeed accounted the least of all seeds, but behold it branching forth; yea, even towering, with lofty branches, and God-like majesty, until it becomes the greatest of all herbs: and it is truth, and it has sprouted and come forth out of the earth; and righteousness begins to look down from heaven; and God is sending down his powers gifts and angels, to lodge in the branches thereof: The kingdom of heaven is like unto a mustard seed. Behold, then, is not this the kingdom of heaven that is raising its head in the last days, in the majesty of its God; even the church of the Latter day saints,-like an impenetrable, immovable rock in the midst of the mighty deep, exposed storms and tempests of satan, but has, thus far, remained steadfast and is still braving the mountain waves of opposition, which are driven by the tempestuous winds of sinking crafts, have and are still dashing with tremendous foam, across its triumphing brow, urged onward with redoubled fury by the enemy of righteousness, with his pitchfork of lies, as you will see fairly represented in a cut, contained in Mr. Howe's "Mormonism Unveiled?"

And we hope that this adversary of truth will continue to stir up the sink of iniquity, that people may the more readily discern between the righteous and wicked. We also would notice one of the modern sons of Seeva, who would fain have made people believe that he could cast out devils by a certain pamphlet (viz. the "Millennial [Millennial] Harbinger,") that went the rounds through our country, who felt so fully authorized to brand Jo Smith, with the appellation of Elymus the sorcerer, and to say with Paul, O full of all subtilty [subtlety] and all mischief, thou child of the devil, thou enemy of all righteousness, wilt thou not cease to pervert the right ways of the Lord! We would reply to this gentleman-Paul we know, and Christ we know, but who are ye? And with the best of feelings, we would say to him, in the language of Paul to those who said they were John's disciples, but had not so much as heard there was a Holy Ghost, to repent and be baptised [baptized] for the remission of sins by those who have legal authority, and under their hands you shall receive the Holy Ghost, according to the scriptures.

Then laid they their hands on them, and they received the Holy Ghost.-Acts ch. 8 v. 17.

And, when Paul had laid his hands upon them, the Holy Ghost came on them; and they spake with tongues, and prophesied.-Acts ch. 19 v. 6.

Of the doctrine of baptisms, and of laying on of hands, and of resurrection of the dead, and of eternal judgment.-Heb. ch, 6 v. 2.

How then shall they call on him in whom they have not believed; and how shall they believe in him of whom they have not heard? and how shall they hear without a preacher? And how shall they preach except they be sent? as it is written, How beautiful are the feet of them that preach the gospel of peace, and bring glad tidings of good things!-Rom. ch. 10, v. 14-15.

But if this man will not take our admonition, but will persist in his wicked course, we hope that he will continue trying to cast out devils, that we may (page 227) have the clearer proof that the kingdom of satan is divided against itself, and consequently cannot stand: for a kingdom divided against itself, speedily hath an end. If we were disposed to take this gentleman upon his own ground and justly heap upon him that which he so readily and unjustly heaps upon others, we might go farther; we might say that he has wickedly and maliciously lied about, vilified and traduced the characters of innocent men. We might invite the gentleman to a public investigation of these matters; yea, and we do challenge him to an investigation upon any or all principles wherein he feels opposed to us, in public or in private.

We might farther say that, we could introduce him to "Mormonism Unveiled." Also to the right honorable Doct. P. Hurlburt, who is the legitimate author of the same, who is not so much a doctor of physic, as of falsehood, or by name. We could also give him an introduction to the reverend Mr. Howe, the illegitimate author of "Mormonism Unveiled," in order to give currency to the publication, as Mr. Hurlburt, about this time, was bound over to court, for threatening life. He is also an associate of the celebrated Mr. Clapp, who has of late immortalized his name by swearing that he would not believe a Mormon under oath; and by his polite introduction to said Hurlburt's wife, which cost him (as we have been informed) a round sum. Also his son Mathew testified that, the book of Mormon had been proved false an hundred times, by How's [Howe's] book: and also, that he would not believe a Mormon under oath. And also we could mention the reverend Mr. Bentley, who, we believe, has been actively engaged in injuring the character of his brother in-law, viz: Elder S. Rigdon.

Now, the above statements are according to our best information: and we believe them to be true; and this is as fair a sample of the doctrine of Campbellism, as we ask, taking the statements of these gentlemen, and judging them by their fruits. And we might add many more to the black catalogue; even the ringleaders, not of the Nazarenes, for how can any good thing come out of Nazareth, but of the far-famed Mentor mob: all sons and legitimate heirs of the same spirit of Alexander Campbell, and "Mormonism Unveiled," according to the representation in the cut spoken of above.

The above cloud of darkness has long been beating with mountain waves upon the immovable rock of the church of the Latter Day Saints, and notwithstanding all this, the mustard seed is still towering its lofty branches, higher and higher, and extending itself wider and wider, and the chariot wheels of the kingdom are still rolling on, impelled by the mighty arm of Jehovah; and in spite of all opposition will still roll on until his words are all fulfilled.

Our readers will excuse us for deviating from the subject, when they take into consideration the abuses, that have been heaped upon us heretofore, which we have tamely submitted to, until forbearance is no longer required at our hands, having frequently turned both the right and left cheek, we believe it our duty now to stand up in our own defence [defense]. With these remarks we shall proceed with the subject of the gathering.

And another parable spake he unto them: The kingdom of heaven is like unto leaven which a woman took and hid in three measures of meal, until the whole was leavened. It may be understood that the church of the Latter Day Saints, has taken its rise from a little leaven that was put into three witnesses. Behold, how much this is like the parable: it is fast leavening the lump, and will soon leaven the whole. But let us pass on.

All these things spake Jesus unto the multitudes, in parables, and without a parable spake he not unto them, that it might be fulfilled which was spoken by the prophet, saying: I will open my mouth in parables: I will utter things which have been kept secret from the foundation of the world: Then Jesus sent the multitude away and went into the house, and his disciples came unto him, saying, declare unto us the parable of the tares of the field. He answered and said unto them, he that soweth the good seed is the son of man; the field is the world; the good seed are the

273

children of the kingdom, but the tares are the children of the wicked one. Now let our readers mark the expression, the field is the world; the tares are the children of the wicked one: the enemy that sowed them is the devil; the harvest is the end of the world. Let them carefully mark this (page 228) expression also, the end of the world, and the reapers are the angels. Now men cannot have any possible grounds to say that this is figurative, or that it does not mean what it says; for he is now explaining what he had previously spoken in parables; and according to this language, the end of the world is the destruction of the wicked; the harvest and the end of the world have an allusion directly to the human family in the last days, instead of the earth, as many have imagined, and that which shall precede the coming of the Son of man, and the restitution of all things spoken of by the mouth of all the holy prophets since the world began; and the angels are to have something to do in this great work, for they are the reapers: as therefore the tares are gathered and burned in the fire, so shall it be in the end of this world; that is, as the servants of God go forth warning the nations, both priests and people, and as they harden their hearts and reject the light of the truth, these first being delivered over unto the buffetings of satan, and the law and the testimony being closed up, as it was with the Jews, they are left in darkness, and delivered over unto the day of burning: thus being bound up by their creeds and their bands made strong by their priests, are prepared for the fulfilment [fulfillment] of the saying of the Savior: The Son of man shall send forth his angels, and gather out of his kingdom all things that offend, and them which do iniquity, and shall cast them into a furnace of fire and there shall be wailing and gnashing of teeth.

We understand, that the work of the gathering together of the wheat into barns, or garners, is to take place while the tares are being bound over, and preparing for the day of burning: that after the day of burnings, the righteous shall shine forth like the sun, in the kingdom of their Father: who hath ears to hear let him hear.

But to illustrate more clearly upon this gathering, we have another parable. Again the kingdom of heaven is like a treasure hid in a field, the which when a man hath found, he hideth and for joy thereof, goeth and selleth all that he hath and buyeth that field: for the work after this pattern, see the church of the Latter Day Saints, selling all that they have and gathering themselves together unto a place that they may purchase for an inheritance, that they may be together and bear each other's affliction in the day of calamity.

Again the kingdom of heaven is like unto a merchant man seeking goodly pearls, who when he had found one pearl of great price, went and sold all that he had, and bought it. For the work of this example, see men travelling [traveling] to find places for Zion, and her stakes or remnants, who when they find the place for Zion, or the pearl of great prices; straightway sell all that they have and buy it.

Again the kingdom of heaven is like unto a net that was cast into the sea, and gathered of every kind, which when it was full they drew to shore, and sat down and gathered the good into vessels, and cast the bad away.-For the work of this pattern, behold the seed of Joseph, spreading forth the gospel net, upon the face of the earth, gathering of every kind, that the good may be saved in vessels prepared for that purpose, and the angels will take care of the bad: so shall it be at the end of the world, the angels shall come forth, and sever the wicked from among the just, and cast them into the furnace of fire, and there shall be wailing and gnashing of teeth.

Jesus saith unto them, have you understood all these things? they say unto him yea Lord: and we say yea Lord, and well might they say yea Lord, for these things are so plain and so glorious, that every Saint in the last days must respond with a hearty amen to them.

Then said he unto them, therefore every scribe which is instructed into the kingdom of heaven, is like unto a man that is an house holder; which bringeth forth out of his treasure things that are new and old.

For the work of this example, see the book of Mormon, coming forth out of the treasure of the heart; also the covenants given to the Latter Day Saints: also the translation of the bible: thus bringing forth out of the heart, things new and old: thus answering to three measures of meal, undergoing the purifying touch by a revelation of Jesus Christ, and the ministering of angels, who have already commenced this work in the last days, which will answer to the leaven which leavened the whole lump. Amen. So I close but shall continue the subject in another number.

In the bonds of the new and everlasting covenant.

Joseph Smith, jr.

To J. Whitmer Esq.

Joseph Smith letter to the *Messenger and Advocate*, April 1836

For the Messenger and Advocate

Brother O. Cowdery:

Dear Sir-This place having recently been visited by a gentleman who advocated the principles or doctrines of those who are called abolitionists; if you deem the following reflections of any service, or think they will have a tendency to correct the opinions of the southern public, relative to the views and sentiments I believe, as an individual, and am able to say, from personal knowledge, are the feelings of others, you are at liberty to give them publicity in the columns of the Advocate. I am prompted to this course in consequence, in one respect, of many elders having gone into the Southern States, besides, there now being many in that country who have already embraced the fulness [fullness] of the gospel, as revealed through the book of Mormon,-having learned, by experience, that the enemy of truth does not slumber nor cease his exertions to bias the minds of communities against the servants of the Lord, by stiring [stirring] up the indignation of men upon all matters of importance or interest.

Thinking, perhaps, that the sound might go out, that "an abolitionist" had held forth several times to this community, and that the public feeling was not aroused to create mobs or disturbances, leaving the impression that all he said was concurred in, and received as gospel and the word of salvation. I am happy to say, that no violence or breach of the public peace was attempted, so far from this, that all except a very few, attended to their own avocations and left the gentleman to hold forth his own arguments to nearly naked walls.

I am aware, that many who profess to preach the gospel, complain against their brethren of the same faith, who reside in the south, and are ready to withdraw the hand of fellowship because they will not renounce the principle of slavery and raise their voice against every thing of the kind. This must be a tender point, and one which should call forth the candid reflection of all men and especially before they advance in an opposition calculated to lay waste the fall States of the South, and set loose, upon the world a community of people who might peradventure, overrun our country and violate the most sacred principles of human society, chastity and virtue.

No one will pretend to say, that the people of the free states are as capable of knowing the evils of slavery as those who hold them. If slavery is an evil, who, could we expect, would first learn it? Would the people of the free states, or would the slave states? All must readily admit, that the latter would first learn this fact. If the fact was learned first by those immediately concerned, who would be more capable than they of prescribing a remedy?

And besides, are not those who hold slaves, persons of ability, discernment and candor? Do they not expect to give an account at the bar of God for their conduct in this life? It may, no doubt, with propriety be said, that many who hold slaves live without the fear of God before their eyes, and, and same may be said of many in the free states. Then who is to be the judge in this matter?

So long, then, as those of the free states are not interested in the freedom of the slaves, any other than upon the mere principles of equal rights and of the gospel, and are ready to admit that there are men of piety who reside in the South, who are immediately concerned, and until they complain, and call for assistance, why not cease their clamor, and no further urge the slave to acts of murder, and the master to vigorous discipline, rendering both miserable, and unprepared to pursue that course which might otherwise lead them both to better their condition? I do not believe that the people of the North have any more right to say that the South shall not hold slaves, than the South have to say the North shall.

And further, what benefit will it ever be to the slave for persons to run over the free states, and excite indignation against their masters in the minds of thousands and tons of thousands who understand nothing relative to their circumstances or conditions? I mean particularly those who have never travelled [traveled] in the South, and scarcely seen a negro in all their life. How any community can ever be excited with the chatter of such persons-boys and others who are too indolent to obtain their living by honest industry, and are incapable of pursuing any occupation of a professional nature, is unaccountable to me. And when I see persons in the free states signing documents against slavery, it is no less, in my mind, than an array of influence, and a declaration of hostilities against the people of the South! What can divide our Union sooner, God only knows!

After having expressed myself so freely upon this subject, I do not doubt but those who have been forward in raising their voice against the South, will cry out against me as being uncharitable, unfeeling and unkind-wholly unacquainted with the gospel of Christ. It is my privilege then, to name certain passages from the bible, and examine the teachings of the ancients upon this nature, as the fact is

277

uncontrovertable [incontrovertible], that the first mention we have of slavery is found in the holy bible, pronounced by a man who was perfect in his generation and walked with God. And so far from that prediction's being averse from the mind of God it remains as a lasting monument of the decree of Jehovah, to the shame and confusion of all who have cried out against the South, in consequence of their holding the sons of Him in servitude!

"And he said cursed be Canaan; a servant of servants shall he be unto his brethren. And he said, Blessed be the Lord God of Shem; and Canaan shall be his servant. God shall enlarge Japheth, and he shall dwell in the tents of Shem and Canaan shall be his servant."-Gen. 8:25, 26, 27.

Trace the history of the world from this notable event down to this day, and you will find the fulfilment [fulfillment] of this singular prophecy. What could have been the design of the Almighty in this wonderful occurrence is not for me to say; but I can say that the curse is not yet taken off the sons of Canaan, neither will be until it is affected by as great power as caused it to come; and the people who interfere the least with the decrees and purposes of God in this matter, will come under the least condemnation before him; and those who are determined to pursue a course which shows an opposition and a feverish restlessness against the designs of the Lord, will learn, when perhaps it is too late for their own good, that God can do his own work without the aid of those who are not dictate by his counsel.

I must not pass over a notice of the history of Abraham of whom so much is spoken in the scriptures. If we can credit the account, God conversed with him from time to time, and directed him in the way he should walk saying, "I am the Almighty God: walk before me and be thou perfect." Paul says that the gospel was preached to this man. And it is further said, that he had sheep and oxen, men servants and maid-servants, &c. From this I conclude, that if the principle had been an evil one, in the midst of the communications made to this holy man, he would have been instructed differently. And if he was instructed against holding men-servants and maid-servants, he never ceased to do it; consequently must have incurred the displeasures of the Lord and thereby lost his blessings-which was not the fact.

Some may urge, that the names, man-servant and maid-servant, only mean hired persons who were at liberty to leave their masters or employers at any time. But we can easily settle this point by turning to the history of Abraham's descendants, when governed by a law given from the mouth of the Lord himself. I know that when an Israelite had been brought into servitude in consequence of debt or otherwise, at the seventh year he went from the task of his former master or employer; but to no other people or nation was this granted in the law to Israel. And if, after a man had served six years, he did not wish to be free, then the master was to bring him unto the judges, boar his ear with an awl, and that man was "to serve him forever." The conclusion I draw from this, is that this people were led and governed by revelation and if such a law was wrong God only is to be blamed, and abolitionists are not responsible.

Now, before proceeding any farther, I wish to ask one or two questions:-Were the apostles men of God, and did they preach the gospel? I have no doubt but those who believe the bible will admit these facts, and that they also knew the mind and will of God concerning what they wrote to the churches which they were instrumental in building up.

This being admitted, the matter can be put to rest without much argument, if we look at a few items in the New Testament. Paul says:

"Servants, be obedient to them that are your masters according to the flesh, with fear and trembling, in singleness of your heart, as unto Christ: Not with eye service, as men pleasers; but as the servants of Christ, doing the will of God from the heart: With good will doing service, as to the Lord, and not to men. Knowing that whatsoever good thing may man doeth, the same shall he receive of the Lord, whether he be bond or free. And, ye masters, do the same things unto them, forbearing threatening: knowing that your Master also is in heaven; neither is there respect of persons with him." Eph. 6:5, 6, 7, 8, 9.

Here is a lesson which might be profitable for all to learn, and the principle upon which the church was anciently governed, is so plainly set forth, that an eye of truth might see and understand. Here, certainly are represented the master and servant; and so far from instructions to the servant to leave his master, he is commanded to be in obedience, as unto the Lord: the master in turn is required to treat them with kindness before God, understanding at the same time that he is to give an account.- The hand of fellowship is not withdrawn from him in consequence of having servants.

The same writer, in his first epistle to Timothy, the sixth chapter, and the five first verses, says:

"Let as many servants as are under the yoke count their own masters worthy of all honor, that the name of God and his doctrine be not blasphemed. And they that have believing masters, let them not despise them, because they are brethren: but rather do them service, because they are faithful and beloved, partakers of the benefit. These things teach and exhort. If any man teach otherwise, and consent not to wholesome words, even the words of our Lord Jesus Christ, and to the doctrine which is according to Godliness: he [He] is proud, knowing nothing but doting about questions and strifes of words, whereof cometh envy, strife, railings, evil surmisings, Perverse disputings of men of corrupt minds, and destitute of the truth, supposing that gain is Godliness: from such withdraw thyself."

This is so perfectly plain, that I see no need of comment. The scripture stands for itself, and I believe that these men were better qualified to teach the will of God, than all the abolitionists in the world.

Before closing this communication, I beg leave to drop a word to the travelling [traveling] elders: You know, brethren, that great responsibility rests upon you, and that you are accountable to God for all you teach the world. In my opinion, you will do well to search the book of Covenant, in which you will see the belief of the church concerning masters and servants. All men are to be taught to repent; but we have no right to interfere with slaves contrary to the mind and will of their masters. In fact, it would be much better and more prudent, not to preach at all to slaves, until after their masters are converted: and then, teach the master to use them with kindness, remembering that they are accountable to God, and that servants are bound to serve their master, with singleness of heart, without murmuring I do, most sincerely hope, that no one who is authorized from this church to preach the gospel, will so far depart from the scripture as to be found stirring up strife and sedition against our brethren of the South. Having spoken frankly and freely, I leave all in the hands of God, who will direct all things for his glory and the accomplishments of his work.

Praying that God may spare you to do much good in this life, I subscribe myself your brother in the Lord.

Joseph Smith, jr.

Appendix 6: William Smith in *The Prophet*

The Joseph Smith Papers provides a helpful biographical summary of William Smith.

Biographical summary: [150]

13 Mar. 1811–13 Nov. 1893.

Farmer, newspaper editor.

Born at Royalton, Windsor Co., Vermont.

Son of Joseph Smith Sr. and Lucy Mack.

Moved to Lebanon, Grafton Co., New Hampshire, 1811; to Norwich, Windsor Co., 1813; and to Palmyra, Ontario Co., New York, 1816–Jan. 1817.

Moved to Manchester, Ontario Co., 1825.

Baptized into LDS church by David Whitmer, ca. 9 June 1830, at Seneca Lake, Seneca Co., New York.

Ordained a teacher, by 5 Oct. 1830.

Lived at The Kingdom, unincorporated settlement near Waterloo, Seneca Co., Nov. 1830.

Moved to Kirtland, Geauga Co., Ohio, May 1831.

Ordained an elder by Lyman Johnson, 19 Dec. 1832, at Kirtland.

Served mission to Erie Co., Pennsylvania, Dec. 1832.

Attended organizational meeting of School of the Prophets, 22–23 Jan. 1833, in Kirtland.

Married Caroline Amanda Grant, 14 Feb. 1833, likely in Erie Co.

Ordained a high priest, 21 June 1833.

Participated in Camp of Israel expedition to Missouri, 1834.

Ordained member of Quorum of the Twelve, 15 Feb. 1835, at Kirtland.

Left Ohio for Far West, Caldwell Co., Missouri, May 1838.

Disfellowshipped, 4 May 1839.

---

[150] http://www.josephsmithpapers.org/person/william-b-smith.

Restored to Quorum of the Twelve, 25 May 1839.

Settled at Plymouth, Hancock Co., IL, ca. 1839, where he kept a tavern.

Member of Masonic lodge in Nauvoo, Hancock Co.

Member of Nauvoo City Council, 1842–1843.

Editor of Nauvoo newspaper the *Wasp,* 1842.

Represented Hancock Co. in Illinois House of Rep. 1842–1843.

Moved to Philadelphia to care for his sick wife, 1843.

Admitted to Council of Fifty, 25 Apr. 1844.

Participated in plural marriage during JS's lifetime.

Moved to Nauvoo, 4 May 1845.

Wife died, May 1845.

Ordained patriarch of church, 24 May 1845.

Married Mary Jane Rollins, 22 June 1845, at Nauvoo.

Excommunicated, 12 Oct. 1845.

Dropped from Council of Fifty, 11 Jan. 1846.

Sustained James J. Strang as successor to JS, 1 Mar. 1846.

Married Roxey Ann Grant, 19 May 1847, in Knox Co., Illinois.

Ordained patriarch and apostle of Strang's Church of Jesus Christ of Latter Day Saints, 11 June 1846, at Voree, Walworth Co., Wisconsin Territory.

Excommunicated from Strangite movement, 8 Oct. 1847.

Affiliated briefly with Lyman Wight, 1849–1850.

Initiated a new movement with Martin Harris and Chilton Daniels at Kirtland, likely 1855.

Married Eliza Elsie Sanborn, 12 Nov. 1857, at Kirtland.

Moved to Venango, Erie Co., Pennsylvania, by 1860, and to Elkader, Clayton Co., Iowa, shortly after.

Enlisted in U.S. Army during Civil War and apparently adopted middle initial *B* at this time. Spent active duty time in Arkansas.

Joined RLDS church, 1878.

Wife died, Mar. 1889.

Married Rosanna Jewitt Surprise, 21 Dec. 1889, at Clinton, Clinton Co., Iowa.

Moved to Osterdock, Clayton Co., 1890. Died there, 13 Nov. 1893.

Peter Crawley's description of *The Prophet* also discusses William's role there.[151]

At a conference in New York City, April 3–4, 1844, George T. Leach, the presiding elder in New York, raised the possibility of publishing a weekly newspaper in support of the Church. William Smith, late of The Wasp, spoke in favor of the idea, and the conference appointed A. E. Wright, G. T. Leach, William H. Miles, John Leach, and a member named Brocklebank to launch the paper. Henry J. Doremus, a physician and local branch member, bought a press and type, and on May 18, 1844, the committee issued the first number of The Prophet....

Who edited the early issues is not entirely clear, but the prospectus and the seventh number (June 29) suggest it was George T. Leach. Financial problems beset the paper from the outset, and after a few issues, Sam Brannan, apparently in partnership with A. E. Wright, assumed ownership of the press, the newspaper, and its debts. The seventh number (June 29) lists William Smith as editor, and after the ninth number, the Society for the Diffusion of Truth is replaced by S. Brannan & Co. as publisher. Although Smith is named as the editor for nos. 7–26 (June 29–November 16), it seems clear he held this position in name only, and that A. E. Wright and Brannan actually edited the paper.[note 32 below] Wright was excommunicated from the Church on October 25. The next day, G. T. Leach was excommunicated and replaced by Brannan as presiding elder in New York. *The Prophet* of November 9 (no. 25) carries a notice from Brannan and Wright of the dissolution of S. Brannan & Co. and a notice from Wright making over to Brannan the rights to and debts of The Prophet. From this number on, S. Brannan is given as the publisher. Issue 27 (November 23) prints the resignation of William Smith and lists S. Brannan as editor and publisher. This continues until the issue of May 10, 1845, (no. 51), which reports that George J. Adams and Sam Brannan had been disfellowshipped. The last two numbers designate Parley P. Pratt as the editor. The final issue was gotten out a week late, apparently because of Brannan's

---

[151] Entry 211, *The Prophet*, New York: May 18, 1844-May 24, 1845, in Peter Crawley, *A Descriptive Bibliography of the Mormon Church*, Vol. 1, https://rsc.byu.edu/archived/descriptive-bibliography-mormon-church-volume-1/entries-201-300.

departure for Nauvoo in an effort to clear himself.

[Note 32: *The Prophet*, 21 December 1844.]

I understand Crawley's point, but in my view, William was not only a nominal editor because he was soliciting authors, including Benjamin Winchester, and because much of the rhetoric in the editorials during his time as Editor reflects his personality.

The 21 December 1844 issue of *The Prophet* contains an editorial comment about the litigation between William and Winchester that includes an apology of sorts for something William wrote in a letter to Brannan, published in the 23 November 1844, issue of *The Prophet*. That was the first issue after William was last listed as Editor and I think it represents a change at the paper.

That said, it is consistent with Joseph's role at the *Times and Seasons* for William to have been the nominal editor of *The Prophet* at least for some period while his name was on the boilerplate.

The relationship between William and Winchester is discussed in my book *The Lost City of Zarahemla*. For purposes of understanding William's role as author and editor, here are some of his writings in *The Prophet*:

Bordentown, N. J. Nov. 1st, 1844.
BROTHER BRANNAN,
I ask pardon for obtruding the name of B. Winchester once more before the public, as I had considered him unworthy of further notice, and I still consider him so; but his manner of proceeding is calculated to give an air of importance and notoriety entirely unworthy of the MAN. (when we speak of man, we have reference to man in principle, not in shape.) And I should not have replied to his unholy attack and outrages upon the church, if circumstances had not rendered it necessary. Being in the city of Philadelphia last evening, I became more acquainted with his foul aspersions and base calumny, mingled with sophistry and subterfuges, to carry out his aspiring plans.

I stated in my last, that there was no law in this Church commending a plurality of wives; and I am bold to say, that B. Winchester is a wanton falsifier, and base calumniator, when he says a doctrine of this kind is tolerated or taught in the church!

It is plain to be seen then, that Benny is fighting nothing but the air; the belief and private opinion of men in or out of the church, is not the standard for church government, unless that opinion or belief is submitted to a law, and a church considered bound by it.

The first causes that have led to the late infraction, are not because (neither is it contended) there are deficiencies or immoralities in the laws of the church. But the difficulties pretended are in the Elders, or members of said church. What an argument is this? This would disorganize and unchristianize the whole religious world, allowing them to be christians as well as the old orthodox Mormon church. The only remeddy [remedy] to be applied is for bad men and members to repent and do their first works over again; if in error of doctrine—forsake it, and sin no more (especially where this doctrine that is false becomes a leading or a standard principle); otherwise the candlestick must be removed out of its place. But I do contend that all men have a right to their own opinion and belief, uncontrolled by church or state, provided that opinion does not interfere with church government, or the rights and privileges of others.

Who appointed Ben Winchester the Prophet, great dictator and regulator of this church, to direct and dictate to the saints, their faith and doctrine? Did Israel's God do it? If he did, I must confess that men of veracity and truth are getting rather scarce, judging from personal manifestations; but as he is ordained a King, when he is crowned, perhaps, there may be a different manifestation. It is singular, indeed, to see the low subterfuge resorted to by these Rigdonites, garbling the scriptures, Book of Doctrine and Covenants, revelations given to the saints concerning Jackson County, Mo., are made to apply to Nauvoo. Sayings spoken thousands of years ago, concerning Judea and Jerusalem are applied to the daughters of Nauvoo with their head dress, round ties, "nose jewels, and tinkling ornaments," when they have none— these few, if no more, are enough to show the saints the rottenness of a cause that has to be sustained by misapplying scriptures and revelations by false arguments.

An error of doctrine prevails in the churches concerning who shall and will stand at the head of the church. I will just say it is not B. Winchester nor Sidney Rigdon. It is well known that the following order is laid down in the Book of Doctrine and Covenants. 1. The Prophet Joseph and his council. 2. The Twelve. The next in order is the High Priesthood. First and second, seventies &c, elders, priests, teachers and deacons. The prophet and his first council being gone, the first quorum is dissolved. Hence the Twelve came next in order, and must take the presidency of the church. How was it when Christ left the church personally? The government devolved upon the Twelve; Peter was President, and we might say in connexion [connection], James and John. Did the church appoint a new Twelve?—No!

Rigdon was only appointed as counsellor [counselor] to the Prophet, and to be one of the three to preside, constituting what is called the first Presidency of the church. O. Cowd[e]ry was also called to the same office, also Wm. Law, Hyrum Smith, and various other individuals at different times. But say they God appointed Sidney Prophet, Seer, and Revelator, by revelation: this is not so! O. Cowd[e]ry, Hyrum, Marks, and Law, D Whitmer; and F, G. Williams and the others have all claims just as good as Rigdon; yet Cowd[e]ry has fallen! And where are all the rest?—mostly cut off. The body had to cut off Cowd[e]ry and Law, and the Lord displaced Hyrum and appointed him Patriarch of the Church. The Lord appointed Judas an Apostle, and he fell and was cut off. Lucifer fell, and heaven rejected him. And let it be remembered too, that Sidney Rigdon has been cut off, and rejected by the large body of the Saints. Hence if he has held the authority over the church has lost it now; and Cowd[e]ry, Law or Marks would have the same right to preside over the church as he has, they would have a body with many heads but this is not so; All and every man that arrives to the office of the High Priesthood, they are Prophets, Seers, Revelators and Apostles in their proper place, but not as heads. Thus the building, fitly framed and put togother [together], grows into a holy temple in the Lord, Let the Saints remember then, that Sidney Rigdon is not the Head of this church. God has placed in the church, fiirst [first], Apostles, secondly, Prophets, &c.

I do not wish any one to infer from my former communication, that B Winchester would or has stole a horse, or slept with bad women. But I would sooner be guilty of all these crimes and charges than to have my garments stained with innocent blood; for it is well known that this B. Winchester is now under bonds of $2,500, for slandering Elder Adams; and that he was more or less engaged in the Law-infraction at Nauvoo. **(p. 3 col. 1)** We are told that the partaker is as bad as the thief, and that "no murderer hath eternal life abiding in him." Benny, remember the blood of the Prophets is still crying for vengeance.

"Suspicion haunts the guilty mind.

The thief doth fear each bush and officer."

How is it with you Benny? Reflect on thy black deeds. O thou child of hell! Repent before thou die, and art called to judgment with thy sins upon thy head!

As ever your brother in Christ.

WM. SMITH

BORDENTOWN, N. J. Nov. 10th. 1844.

DEAR BROTHER W. W. PHELPS of Nauvoo. I take this method of addressing you through the columns of the Prophet, as it will save postage and is not so liable to be miscarried; hoping that it will receive due and immediate attention.

DEAR BROTHER.—Situated as I am in this Eastern land, and far from the great emporium of the West, (Nauvoo) and I might say my home, if there is any place on earth that I might with propriety call so. But, indeed, I could say with Abraham, I have no home this side the vale, but a pilgrim and sojourner here on earth; (not exactly in tents, as the good old Patriarch with flocks and herds) a stranger without purse and scrip among strangers to build up the kingdom of God, (a most unpopular theme) and bear some humble part of this last ministry to the nations of the earth. Can you tell, dear brother, why it is, the Saints of God in all ages, and especially in these last times, can have no more rest? persecuted as they are from city to city, and from place to place; I ask myself the question, Is anything criminal in Mormonism—in the divine pretensions of the prophet? this cannot be, other have professed the same; there has been hundreds of prophets, true ones too, and men have declared that if they had lived in their day, they would not have killed them, and yet, what have they not done?—("for if they will do these things in the green tree, what will they do in the dry?") But, they say, none of these signs have followed and proven him a prophet, that followed and proved them of old. What say ye, can you answer this? Tell us the crime, the time and place, when and where; was it finding the Nephite record?— revealing to the world the origin of a lost and scattered people, a knowledge of which and been hid for ages in midnight darkness; lost from the deepest research of modern antiquarians. Was it for revealing to the world a knowledge of whose lands, and by whom the foundation of these mighty cities had been laid, and since discovered by the Stephens and Carthewood. this none will doubt, yet a knowledge of the fact of these cities being built by skillful hands hundred of years ago, written in the Book of Mormon would be a 'humbug.' These discoveries, made by these men which are truly great and confirmatory of the truth of the Book of Mormon, and the inspiration of the prophet Joseph was made since this book was found and published to the world in 1830; then the prophecy was made that the Indians were a remnant of the house of Israel, "had wandered through the wilderness, and came over the sea," inhabited North and South America, built large cities, and were a warlike people; that many had fallen in battle and cities had been destroyed a remnant remained as the last vestige, to tell the sad tale and history of the fallen race. And who has proved this prophecy true?—Stephen and Carthewood! You will bear in mind, also, that Joseph was but a youth at this time, without any possible means of knowing as men naturally know of these things—a mere plough boy at the age of 17, 21 and 22, he never had by the aid of 'government friends, or wealthy parents the means to climb the Alpine mountains of the east—to traverse the holy land, and in Central America, stand and gaze upon the richly wrought Pyramids, and with wonder and amazement exclaim, Whose hands have laid these cities and reared those mighty monuments?—yet God had given him this knowledge; read the Book of Mormon and it will tell you; and mark, kind reader, that this book was published in 1830, and the discoveries and facts proved by Stephens and Carthewood in 1837, proving to a demonstration the inspiration of the prophet, and the divinity of the book. But it is said in Mormonism there is a charm—a mystery that the world cannot explain; I admit it; it has a charm more inviting than all the magicians' and sooth sayers' of Egypt and a mystery that sectarians cannot unravel;—Why? Because they have not the spirit of Christ, which is the spirit of prophecy. Mormonism has inferiors, but no superiors; it acknowledges no twin-sister but heaven; no superior but God; no king but Jesus; with uparallelled [unparalleled] rapidity it has rolled on, "out-vied the muttering crowd," and accumulated its thousands, who are now rejoicing in the fullness of the gospel revealed, and brought to light by the prophet Joseph. If it should be asked, then, is Mormonism true, a thousand intelligent voices reverberate yes! yes! yes! Again, who have gathered their thousands? built a city? two Temples? And embodied a code of morals garbed with immortality, that has made its way in the imperial thrones of the earth embosomed itself in the golden rays and unbounded glories of heaven, crowned with never fading laurels (is it not Joseph?) Men of sound minds (not Millerites nor bigots) of all ranks, from all societies of all the intelligence of the earth; combined in one word, the cream and salt of the same, and virtue of heaven; can this be, and Joseph Smith a false prophet?—again is heard form a thousand voices, no! no! no! Dear brother if the thousand and one testimonies, miracles, records, antiquities, facts, Bible truths, knowledge, revelation, fulfillment of prophecy, God, men and angels do not prove any thing but a fallen prophet, and Mormonism so far beneath the notice of the would be great and wise men of this age. I wish you would solve the mystery, for to me it is a mystery in deed.

And now, dear brother, I will come to the point having done with my preliminaries. As many faint and incorrect descriptions have been given of Nauvoo and the Temple, by travellers [travelers], passers-by, and others, until some have thought the Temple built upon moonshine, and the city a barbarian—ugly, formal with heads and horns, and stuck into the nethermost corner of the universe where none but Indians, Hottentots, Arabs, Turks, Wolverines and Mormons dwell; and if you can find time to reply, I wish you would give me an ungarnished [unvarnished] statement of facts respecting Nauvoo; its probable number on inhabitants and finally, a graphic description of the whole place; give us the number of distilleries, liquor venders, and what gross immoralities have corrupted Nauvoo, cursed the city, the temple, the Twelve, &c., **(p. 3 col. 2)** smote the daughters of Zion with scabby heads, and numbered the thousands of saints (that have gathered there to hear the word of the Lord, and be taught in his way) with goats, and cursed them above all horned cattle. An answer to these unaccountable problems, will, no doubt, be eagerly grasped after, and be very interesting to many in the east, as we have many braying animals which have become quite obnoxious to the quiet rest of the innocent, and bray to the discomfiture of many, not in account of the soundness of their doctrine. But on account of blasphemies the Twelve, the temple, the church at Nauvoo, and the great body of saints, their morals men and women, the abominable lies they tell, make people nervous sometimes when they do not know how things are; men who were once men of apparent intelligence, make these statements, the place must have become materially changed in its morals since last spring, when I was there a short time, indeed for such a mighty change.

I did not intend to argue the question, what is the difference between Millerism and Mormonism now Millerism is dead. Please to answer how high the Temple is to the ears and top of steeple, (if any at all) and how long, how many moons, suns, cars and heads, and what do they all represent, of what materials and workmanship, how antique and of what order the pillars and structure. Is it a pattern of church and priesthood? Show us the order; the fount with the length, the breadth, and the height thereof; the unity of the Saints, the proper age of my mother, and her birth place, also that of my father and his age at the time of his death, and the number of the family, (which you can obtain from the family records in my mother's possession) embodied in one, in as concise a manner as possible. This will correct many errors, and confer a favor on your old and tried friend. I must say, I wish I could think more of Nauvoo than I do, yet it is not Nauvoo! for when I reflect that there lie the silver locks of an aged and martyred father, martyred by a Missouri persecution, in the grave, numbered with the dead; and four brothers, two of whom in my vision appear with mangled bodies, and garments red with crimson gore. Oh! the fatal steal and barbarous murder! Their blood is still unavenged, and the cruel murderers are lounging about seeking for more; what have others to expect? Yet Nauvoo contains almost all that is near to me. My poor old mother, almost worn out with years and trouble, and three sisters that remain, with myself, are all of that family, who were the founders of Mormonism and the Church of Christ in these last days, through great persecution and trouble, having born the heat of the day; and how long the rest may be spared, God only knows. Brother Phelps, will you call and see my mother, and give her a word of consolation from me. I hope she will live till I can get to see her. She may live to see all her sons laid in the grave. Remember me also to my sisters Sophronia, Catherine, Lucy and their husbands, and the martyrs' widows—God bless them all forever, is my prayer. I wish also to be remember to all the Saints in Nauvoo, give them my prayer, that God may sustain them in all their trials, for truly they are great, and tell them to think of us their brother in affliction, and my sick family, which has kept me from their society in this their time of peril; and if the Lord does not interpose, they must ere long be numbered with the dead. Oh! that God would have mercy upon me and my sick family! Will you pray for us, dear brethren at Nauvoo? Remember me to your family. Mrs. Smith sends her love to your wife, and wishes to be remembered to all her friends in that country, as it will be a miracle if she ever sees them again. Write to me immediately.

With sentiments of respect and esteem, I subscribe myself your friend and brother in the Gospel of Christ.
WM. SMITH.

From T&S

CORRESPONDENCE.

Bordentown N. J. Nov. 10th, 1844.

Dear Brother W. W. Phelps of Nauvoo, I take this method of addressing you through the columns of the Prophet, as it will save postage and is not so liable to be miscarried; hoping that it will receive due and immediate attention.

Dear Brother:-Situated as I am in this eastern land, and far from the great emporium of the west, (Nauvoo) and I might say my home, if there is any place on earth that I might with propriety call so. But, indeed, I could say with Abraham, I have no home this side the vale, but a pilgrim and sojourner here on earth; (not exactly in tents, as the good old Patriarch with flocks and herds) a stranger without purse or scrip among strangers to build up the kingdom of God, (a most unpopular theme) and bear some humble part of this last ministry to the nations of the earth?

Can you tell, dear brother, why it is, the saints of God in all ages, and especially in these last times, can have no more rest? persecuted as they are from city to city, and from place to place; I ask myself the question, is anything criminal in Mormonism-in the divine pretensions of the prophet? this cannot be, others have professed the same; there has been hundreds of prophets, true ones too, and men have declared that if they had lived in their day, they would not have killed them; and yet, what have they not done? ("for if they will do these things in the green tree, what will they do in the dry?") But. they say, none of these signs have followed and proven him a prophet, that followed and proved them of old. What say ye, can you answer this?

Tell us the crime, the time and place, when and where; was it finding the Nephite record? revealing to the world the origin of a lost and scattered people, a knowledge of which had been hid for ages in midnight darkness; lost from the deepest research of modern antiquarians. Was it for revealing to the world a knowledge of whose lands, and by whom the foundation of these mighty cities had been laid, and since discovered by Stephens and Catherwood; this none will doubt, yet a knowledge of the fact of these cities being built by skillful hands, hundreds of years ago, written in the Book of Mormon would be 'humbug.'

These discoveries, made by the these men, which are truly great and confirmatory [confirmation] of the truth of the Book of Mormon, and the inspiration of the prophet Joseph, was made since this book was found and published to the world in 1830; then the prophecy was made that the Indians were a remnant of the house of Israel, "had wandered through the wilderness, and came over the sea," inhabited North and South America, built large cities, and were a warlike people; that many had fallen in battle and cities had been destroyed, a remnant remained as the last vestige, to tell the sad tale and history of their fallen race. And who has proved this prophecy true? 'Stephens and Catherwood!'

You will bear in mind, also, that Joseph was but a youth at this time, without any possible means of knowing, as men naturally know of these things-a mere plough [plow] boy at the age of 17, 21 and 22; he never had by the aid of 'government friends,' or wealthy parents, the means to climb the Alpine mountains of the east-to traverse the holy land, and in Central America, stand and gaze upon the richly wrought pyramids, and with wonder and amazement exclaim, whose hands have laid these cities and reared these mighty monuments? Yet God had given him this knowledge; read the Book of Mormon and it will tell you; and mark, kind reader, that this book was published in 1830, and the discoveries and facts proved by Stephens and Catherwood in 1837 proving to a demonstration the inspiration of the prophet, and the divinity of the book.

But it is said in Mormonism there is a charm a mystery that the world cannot explain; I admit it; it has a charm more inviting than all the magicians and sooth sayers of Egypt, and a mystery that sectarians cannot unravel. Why? Because they have not the spirit of Christ, which is the spirit of prophecy. Mormonism has inferiors, but no superiors; it acknowledges no twin-sister but heaven; no superior but God; no king but Jesus: with unparalleled rapidity it has rolled on, "out-vied the muttering crowd," and accumulated its thousands who are now rejoicing in the fulness [fullness] of the gospel, revealed and brought to light by the prophet Joseph.

If it should be asked, then, is Mormonism true? a thousand intelligent voices reverberate yes! yes! yes!

Again, who has gathered their thousands? built a city? two temples? and embodied a code of morals garbed with immortality, that has made its way to the imperial thrones of the earth, embosomed itself in the golden rays and unbounded glories of heaven, crowned with

293

(page 755)

never fading laurels, (is it not Joseph?) Men of sound minds (not Millerites nor bigots) of all ranks, from all societies, of all the intelligence of the earth; combined in one word, the cream and salt of the same, and virtue of heaven; can this be, and Joseph Smith a false prophet?-again is heard from a thousand voices, no! no! no!

Dear brother if the thousand and one testimonies, miracles, records, antiquities, facts, bible truths, knowledge, revelation, fulfilment [fulfillment] of prophecy, God, men and angels do not prove any thing but a fallen prophet, and Mormonism so far beneath the notice of the would be great and wise men, of this age, I wish you would solve the mystery, for to me it is a mystery indeed.

And now, dear brother, I will; come to the point, having done with my preliminaries.-As many faint and incorrect descriptions have been given of Nauvoo and the temple, by travellers [travelers], passers-by, and others, until some have thought the temple built upon moonshine, and the city a barbarian-ugly, formal with head and horns, and stuck into the nethermost corner of the universe, where none but Indians, Hottentots, Arabs, Turks, Wolverines and Mormons dwell; and if you can find time to reply, I wish you would give me an ungarnished statement of facts respecting Nauvoo; its probable number of inhabitants, and finally, a graphic description of the whole place; give us the number of distilleries, liquor venders, and what gross immoralities have corrupted Nauvoo, cursed the city, the temple, the Twelve, &c., smote the daughters of Zion with scabby heads, and numbered the thousands of saints (that have gathered there to hear the word of the Lord, and be taught in his way) with goats, and cursed them above all horned cattle. An answer to these unaccountable problems, will, no doubt be eagerly grasped after, and be very interesting to many in the east, as we have many braying animals which have become quite obnoxious to the quiet rest of the innocent, and bray to the discomfiture of many, not on account of the soundness of their doctrine; but on account of blasphemies, the Twelve, the temple, the church at Nauvoo, and the great body of saints, their moral men and women, the abominable lies they tell, make people nervous sometimes when they do not know how things are; men who were once men of apparent intelligence, make these statements The place must have become materially changed in its morals since last spring, when I was there, a short time indeed for such a mighty change.

I did not intend to argue the question, what is the difference between Millerism and Mormonism now Millerism is dead. Please to answer how high the temple is to the eaves and top of steeple, (if any at all,) and how long, how many moons, suns, ears and heads, and what do they all represent, of what material and workmanship, how antique and of what order the pillars and structure? Is it a pattern of church and priesthood? Show us the order, the font with the length, the breadth, and the height thereof; the unity of the saints, the proper age of my mother, and her birth-place, also that of my father and his age at the time of his death, and the number of the family, (which you can obtain from the family records in my mother's possession,) embodied in one, in as concise a manner as possible. This will correct many errors, and confer a favor on your old and tried friend I must say, I wish I could think more of Nauvoo than I do, yet it is not Nauvoo! for when I reflect that there he the silver locks of an aged and martyred father, martyred by a Missouri persecution, in the grave, numbered with the dead; and four brothers, two of whom in my vision appear with mangled bodies, and garments red with crimson gore. Oh! the fatal steel and barbarous murder! Their blood is still unavenged, and the cruel murderers are lounging about seeking for more; what have others to expect? Yet Nauvoo contains almost all that is near to me. My poor old mother, almost worn out with years and trouble, and three sisters that remain, with myself, are all of that family, who were the founders of Mormonism and the church of Christ in these last days, through great persecution and trouble, having borne [born] the heat of the day; and how long the rest may be spared, God only knows.

Brother Phelps, will you call and see my mother, and give her a word of consolation from me. I hope she will live till I can get to see her. She may live to see all her sons laid in the grave. Remember me also to my sisters

Sophronia, Catherine, Lucy and their husbands, and martyrs' widows-God bless them all for ever is my prayer. I wish also to be remembered to all the saints in Nauvoo, give them my prayer, that God may sustain them in all their trials, for truly they are great, and tell them to think of me their brother in affliction, and my sick family, which has kept me from their society in this their time of peril; and if the Lord does no interpose, they must ere long be numbered with the dead. Oh! that God would have mercy upon me and my sick family!

Will you pray for us, dear brethren at Nauvoo? Remember me to your family. Mrs. Smith sends her love to your wife, and wishes to be remembered to all her friends in that country,

(page 756)

as it will be a miracle if she ever sees them again. Write to me immediately.

With sentiments of respect and esteem I subscribe myself, your friend and brother in the gospel of Christ.

WM. SMITH

THE ANSWER.

Nauvoo, Ill., Dec. 25, 1844.

Remembered Brother William Smith:

Up to the reception of your excellent letter to me, (dated at Bordentown, N. J., Nov., 10, 1844, which you had the goodness to communicate through the columns of the "Prophet,") since we have been members together in the church of Jesus Christ of Latter-day Saints, I think it may be said we have been one in faith, one in love, and one in friendship, and like the often used key, we have grown brighter and brighter, as we have performed the great

296

service of opening and shutting the "lock" on religious understanding. As Jeremiah said, so say I: "The heritage of the Lord is like a lion in the forest ; yea, the heritage of the Lord is like a speckled bird:" every body is afraid, and every body is pecking at us. It is a great thing to be a messenger of salvation, and so I will begin to answer your questions.

You ask; "why is it that the saints of the last times, can have no rest!" and I answer, because the world loves darkness rather than light, and their deeds are evil. "popularity" now and ever, since the serpent was cursed to crawl upon his belly through the loss of his feet, is, has been, and will be, the best kind of religion in use. Talk about holiness, morality, temperance, humanity, brotherly kindness and charity among the refined polite nations of the world; why, ever since Cain built a city for the ungodly to revel in, for the polygamy of a Lamech; for the droving of a Jabul; for the music saloon of a Jubul; and for the brass and iron foundry, and bogus machine of a Tubal Cain, the majority of mankind, have made money their faith; popularity their works, and persecution their sincerest devotion of moral greatness.

They that live godly in Christ Jesus, shall suffer persecution, says Paul; and so it is-and it always comes first from him that professes godliness: Cain was a sectarian and could not admit revelation and hear God say: "well, Abel I have accepted thine offering:" and so he killed his brother because the devil slyly whispered in his ear:-it is blasphemy to talk with God.

Now the next generation could discover the wickedness of Cain, and the holiness of Abel, but the same evil spirit whispered that was in a day when revelation was necessary, but there is no need of it now, and it is done away. We have followed the rules and regulations of those good men, and O! if we had lived in their days, they should not have been killed! but as for this fellow he is "unpopular;" he blasphemes our God: he ought to die, but we being compassionate and charitable, and feeling a warm desire for the great cause of religion, will advise him to quit his folly, or delution [delusion]; and if he dont [don't], we will punish him a little by stripes, sword, dungeons, or banishment; and then if he does not stop, we will stop him!

297

Jonathan Neville

O Lord God Almighty, when the prison doors of Tophet, hell, and the horrible pit are unlocked; and the entrance into outer darkness opened, to bring the damned before the bar of the Judge of all the earth for the final judgment, I think some few christians in company with their father Cain and cousins of "popular" priesthood, from that day down to the judgment trumpet, will "grin horribly a ghastly smile'-YES, we killed the prophets and persecuted the saints, because they were not "popular." Then your question will be answered.

As to the "crime, time, and place, &c., of finding the Nephite record," its revelation is the very thing that produces an earthquake to this generation. It explains the bible: it opens the vision of the prophets; it unravels the mystery who first settled this country, and it shows the old paths wherein if a man walk he shall live. It copes with the boasted knowledge of the world; it glitters through the combined fog of ages; shows that God who eat [ate] of a calf with Abraham, will eat and drink again on the earth with his saints, when the wolf and the lamb, and the lion and the ox, will be as friendly as the saints and seraphs, in the full fruition of bliss; it cuts the gordian knot of priestcraft, and reveals the priesthood of the Son of God which is "without beginning days or end of years;" whereby it shows that prophets were ordained in eternity, when the "morning stars sang together, and all the sons of God shouted for joy:" and it speaks from the dead, whereby the living can hear from their friends, who have fought the good fight of faith, and passed from life unto death, and from death unto life! and Stevens [Stephens] with his incidents of travels in Central America; and others who are opening the bowels of the earth, and rolling "ruins' into being; and tend thousand elders of Israel filled with the Holy Ghost, declaring the everlasting gospel with irresistable [irresistible] power and economy, that surpasses understanding; the great persecutions and murders which are dealt out without measure to its believers; and the distress of nations and the

(page 757)

298

signs that Jesus Christ said should be, like the sound of many waters, or of a great thunder, declare that it is eternal truth! and that your brother Joseph Smith was one of the Lord's anointed! That he now sits with God in the heavens, and laughs at the calamities that will speedily wrap the world in wo! and that he will mock when their fear seizes the last hope of a crude existence!

Joseph Smith was a Captain General and this world will be introduced to him as such, when the epitaph of its great men's greatness will be written within and without on the gates of the lower prisons, and entrance into outer darkness: "we were, and are not, and yet are!"

But I must not go to preaching to an apostle as I know you are, lest I enter into the rich treasure of knowledge too, and cause you to exclaim:-cast not thy precious jewels to strangers, lest greediness and covetousness seize them and they like the avaricious steward, with his goose that laid a golden egg a day, kill her in order to obtain the whole litter at once, and so destroy the fountain!

Mormonism is the wonder of this world, and the great leveling machine of creeds, constitutions, kingdoms, countries, divisions, notions, notorieties [notoriety's] and novelties; and praise it, talk about it, lie about it, exalt it, degrade it, blow at it, sneer at it, fear it, love it, hate it, persecute it, or laugh at it, still it is Mormonism, true as heaven, powerful as Jesus, eternal as element, going on conquering and to conquer!

Have the mightiest men on earth reared monuments of grandeur? of glory? of splendor? of fame? of utility? or of admirations?-Joseph Smith has exceeded all their wisdom and greatness. He has brought back the past and rolled up the future, whereby the past, present, and future, exhibit their images like the skies over the ocean.

Mormonism! O Mormonism! Nimrod, Homer, Pharoah, Cadmus, Alexander, Nebuchadnezzar, Holofornes, Herod, Bonaparte, and an immense retinue of other dignitaries, who have burst into being with pomp and glory, and made a trembling world wonder at their cruelty and cunning:-Where are the pillars, the records, and the approvals of heaven, of all your greatness?

"A heap of dust alone remains of thee,

'Tis all thou art and all the proud shall be,"

while Mormonism, from an Abel, though dead, yet speaketh; from an Elijah though translated in a fiery chariot to heaven, yet, returns in glory with Moses, and blesses Jesus at the transfiguration on the mount! O Mormonism! Thy father is God, thy mother is the Queen of heaven, and so thy whole history, from eternity to eternity, is the laws, ordinances and truth of the "Gods"-embracing the simple plan of salvation, sanctification, death, resurrection, glorification and exaltation of man, from infancy to age, from age to eternity, from simplicity to sublimity: from faith, repentance, baptism, reception of the Holy Ghost by the laying on of the hands, to washing, anointing, holy conversation, baptism for the dead, to the presence of angels, the general assembly and church of the first born; to the unspeakable glory of seeing God and the Lamb, and to spirits of just men, made perfect, and to be ordained unto eternal life!

And again, we exclaim, O Mormonism! No wonder that Lucifer, son of the morning, the next heir to Jesus Christ, our eldest brother, should fight so hard against his brethren; he lost the glory, the honor, power, and dominion of a God: and the knowledge, spirit, authority and keys of the priesthood of the son of God.

Christ kept his first estate-Lucifer lost his by offering to save men in their sins on the honor of a God, or on his father's honor.-Christ hated sin, and loved righteousness, therefore he was anointed with holy oil in heaven, and crowned in the midst of brothers and sisters, while his mother stood with approving virtue, and smiled upon a Son that kept the faith as the heir of all things! In fact the Jews thought so much of his coronation among Gods and Goddesses; Kings and Queens of heaven, that they broke over all restraints and actually began to worship the "Queen of heaven," according to Jeremiah.

Well, now, Brother William, when the house of Israel begin to come into the glorious mysteries of the kingdom, and find that Jesus Christ, whose goings forth, as the prophets said, have been from of old, from eternity: and that eternity, agreeably to the records found in the catacombs of Egypt, has been going on in this system, (not this world) almost two thousand five hundred and fifty five millions of years: and to know at the same time, that deists, geologists and others are trying to prove that matter must have existed hundreds of thousands of years;-it almost tempts the flesh to fly to God, or muster faith like Enoch to be translated and see and know as we are seen and known!

O Mormonism! no wonder the earth groans with the blood of thy martyrs! But there is one sweet consolation: death hath power on a saint, but once! the righteous rise triumphant over death, hell, and the grave! The wicked, thanks be to God, have to go through the agonies of the grim monster, twice! and the "second

(page 758)

death," will be long enough, excruciating enough, and woful [woeful] enough, to satisfy the "uttermost farthing" for murdering the Lord's anointed! and the punishment still is eternal.

But I must begin to talk about Nauvoo, for I think I have said enough to prove the "mystery," whether the perishing philosophy of the age credit it, or not; so you may set me down as a living monument of Mormonism, and with the Twelve, there will then be thirteen united saints, bearing this testimony to the world that God, man, and Mormonism, are not only material, but eternal, and therefore, like Jesus, when martyred they come to life again.

I shall not describe the localities of Nauvoo, now, because I shall not have room; but as to the facilities, tranquilities [tranquillity's], and virtues of the city, they are not equalled [equaled] on the globe. The saints, since Sidney, the great "Anti-Christ" of the last days and his sons of 'Sceva,' have left Nauvoo, together with some other Simon Maguses, or foolish virgins, and wicked men who had crept in to revel on the bliss of Jehovah, have gone also, peace, union and harmony prevail.

I speak advisedly when I say Nauvoo is the best place in the world. No vice is meant to be tolerated: no grog shops allowed: nor would we have any trouble, if it were not for our lenity in suffering the world, as I shall call them, to come in and trade and enjoy our society as they say: which thing has made us the only trouble of late. These pretended friends, too frequently like old Baalam's girls, when let in among the young men of Israel, find admirers, and break the ordinances of the city, and then "Phineas' javelin," touches the heart.

The temple is up as high as the caps of the pilasters, and it looks majestic, and especially to me, when I know that the tithing, "the mites of the poor," thus speaks of the glory of God. All the description that is necessary to give you now, is that this splendid model of Mormon grandeur, exhibits thirty hewn stone pilasters which cost about $3,000 apiece.-The base is a crescent new moon: the capitols, near fifty feet high, the sun, with a human face in bold relief, about two and a half feet broad, ornamented with rays of light and waves, surmounted by two hands holding two trumpets. It is always too much trouble to describe an unfinished building. The inside work is now going forward as fast as possible. When the whole structure is completed it will cost some five or six hundred thousand dollars; and as Captain Brown of Tobasco, near the ruins of Palenque, said, "it will look the nearest like the splendid remains of antiquity in Central America of any thing he had seen, though not half so large."

The temple is erected from white limestone, wrought in a superior style: is 128 by 88 feet square; near 60 feet high: two stories in the clear, and two half stories in the recesses over the arches; four tiers of windows; two gothic and two round. The two great stories will each have two pulpits, one at teach end; to accommodate the Melchisedek [Melchizedek] and Aaronic priesthoods; graded into four rising seats: the first for the president of the

302

elders, and his two counsellors [counselors]; the second for the president of the high priesthood and his two counsellors [counselors]; the third for the Melchisedek [Melchizedek] president and his two counsellors [counselors], and the fourth for the president over the whole church, (the first president) and his two counsellors [counselors]. This highest seat is where the scribes and pharisees used to crowd in "to Moses' seat" The Aaronic pulpit at the other end the same.

The fount in the basement story is for the baptism of the living, for health, for remission of sin, and for the salvation of the dead, as was the case in Solomon's temple, and all temples that God commands to be built. You know I am no Gentile, and of course, do not believe that a monastery, cathedral, chapel, or meeting house erected by the notions and calculations of men, has any more sanction from God than any common house in Babylon.

The steeple of our temple will be high enough to answer for a tower:- between 100 and 200 feet high. But I have said enough about the temple; when finished it will show more wealth, more art, more science, more revelation, more splendor, and more God, than all the rest of the world, and that will make it a Mormon temple:-"God and Liberty;" patterned somewhat after the order of our fore fathers', which were after the order of eternity.

The other public puildings [buildings] in Nauvoo, besides the temple, are the Seventies Hall, the Masonic Hall, and Concert Hall; all spacious, and well calculated for their designated purposes.

There is no licensed grocery to sell or give away liquors of any kind in the city; drunkards are scarce. Probable number of inhabitants, 14,000: nine-tenths Mormons.

Now for the welfare of your relatives. I have seen your mother and she cried for joy over your letter. Though in her 69th year, her heart was big with hope for her "darling son, William:"-and she blessed you in the name of the Lord.

The rest, I think, enjoy good health, and especially Emma, who amid her great affliction, has given birth to a son, and like David

(page 759)

of old, may he yet be a terror to evil doers; one that will light his candle in the same great fire where his father's was lit, and search the world by the light of it, till the last stain of his father's blood, is made white by righteousness.

The record of your father's family presents the following summary of life and death:

Joseph Smith Sen., born in Topsfield, Mass., July 12, 1722. Died in Nauvoo, Ill., Sept. 14, 1840, aged 68. His grey [gray] hairs were brought down to the grave by being driven from the State of Missouri in the dead of winter by Gov. Boggs and his murderous banditti.

Lucy Smith (Mack) born in Gilsum, N. H. July 8, 1776, now in her 69th year; mourns the loss of a husband and six sons, the most of whom fell by the tender mercies of a Christian Republic, bestowed by the Herods of the land in civilized exile and murder.

Joseph Smith and Lucy Mack, married in Tunbridge, Vt. June 24, 1796.

Alvin Smith, born in Tunbridge, Vt., February 11, 1798. Died in Palmyra, N. Y., November 19, 1829, aged nearly 32.

Hyrum Smith born in Tunbridge, Vt., February 9, 1800, was murdered in Carthage jail, on the 27th of June, 1844, (by a mob,) aged 44. Thus fell a martyr, against whom not even one crime had ever been known.

Sophronia Smith born in Tunbridge, Vt. May 10, 1803, aged 41.

Joseph Smith Jr. born in Sharon Vt., December 23, 1805. Murdered in Carthage jail on the 27th of June, 1844, (by a mob,) on account of his religion as allmost [almost] all holy men had been before him;-aged 39. Thus fell a martyr, to gratify the cupidity of a priestly thirst for innocent blood; and shows the weakness of our government to protect her citizens: this first prophet of the last dispensation, whose godly works, whose virtuous deeds, and whose innocent blood will entitle him to a fame, a name, a glory, an honor, power, and dominion, with Gods, when his persecutors and murderers will mutter, groan, gnash their teeth, and sigh among the damned, where "their worm dieth not, and the fire is not quenched."

Samuel Harrison Smith, born in Tunbridge, Vt., March 13, 1808. Died July 30th, 1844, broken hearted, and worn out with persecution. Aged 36. The righteous are removed from the evils to come.

Ephraim Smith, born in Royalton, Vt., March 13, 1810. Died March 24, 1810; aged 11 days.

William Smith, born in Royalton Vt., March 13, 1811; aged (soon) 34; the only male (living) of the family, and one of the "Twelve." Lord, while I write the "the fire burns for the mighty of Israel, to come up like a lion from the swelling of Jordan."

Katharine Smith, born in Lebanon N. H. July 28, 1813, aged 31.

Don Carlos Smith, born in Norwich Vermont, March 25, 1815. Died August 7, 1841, aged 26. His untiring vigilance for his parents and the persecutions of Missouri, brought him to the grave, just as he was stepping upon the threshhold [threshold] of life and usefulness.

Lucy Smith, born in Palmyra, N. Y. July 15, 1821; aged 23.

So here you have your history-without painting. The females all married, all Mormons and live in this vicinity.

How think ye this little sketch will fit the refinement of christendom? I believe the next generation will say, O, if we had only lived with those good men, we would not have murdered them! Do you think that this benevolent world, with all their priests, piety, pulpits and philanthropy, will call to mind that through their exertion or silence, one mother, born four days after our independence was declared, and four daughters-in-law, weep over the tombs of their mob-murdered husbands, while their innocent blood stains the land, the law, liberty and religion of the whole nation?

Our pseudo-President says in his last message: "The great moral spectacle has been exhibited of a nation, approximating in numbers to 20,000,000, of people, having performed the high and important duty of electing their chief magistrate for the term of four years, without the commission of any acts of violence, or a manifestation of a spirit of insubordination to the laws."

Now what says the people about the "riots in Philadelphia," the murder at Carthage of one of the candidates for that high office, and shooting a man dead in Tennessee for carrying a poke stalk? was their "any acts of violence" in all these manifestations of murder? Wo unto the hypocrite!

Governor Edwards of Missouri, in his message to the legislature, after regretting mob law or disobedience in other states, says, "but in our State, the great majority of the people are sober and discreet, mild and prudent, industrious and frugal, honest and virtuous, and above all, the lovers of good order and peace in society."

Such mock virtue; such hypocritical eulogy, is enough to merit an earthquake! Great God!! 15,000 people exiled, robbed, mobbed and murdered by executive authority, and now the people are all lovers of good order, and peace in society!

(page 760)

306

This out Herods Herod! and out Bogges Boggs! O wrath of God! where art thou?

But I must begin to draw to a close, or my letter will be long enough for a pamphlet. I cannot leave the subject, however, till I bring in the "Twelve." They were known from before the foundation of the world, and are thus noticed in the prophecy of Zenos, in the Book of Mormon; I mean in that masterly parable of the "olive tree:" All men, acquainted with revelation and the spirit of God, have agreed that the "servant" spoken of in that parable, was Joseph Smith, and when the Lord commanded him "to go to and call other servants," and "they did go to it with their mights,"-as the whole has been backed up by revelations in the Book of Doctrine and Covenants, it would require more than "mortal" to prove that allusion to the "servants," meant any body but the "Twelve."

I know the Twelve, and they know me.-Their names are Brigham Young, the lion of t he Lord; Heber C. Kimball, the herald of grace; Parley P. Pratt, the archer of paradise; Orson Hyde, the olive branch of Israel; Willard Richards, the keeper of the rolls: John Taylor, the champion of right; William Smith, the entablature of truth; Orson Pratt, the gauge of philosophy; John E. Page, the sun dial; and Lyman Wight, the wild ram of the mountain. And they are good men; the best the Lord can find; they do the will of God, and the saints know it.

As to Sidney Rigdon and his clique of dissatisfied being-there was to be "another beast," and unclean spirits, like frogs, were to come out of the mouth of the dragon, beast, and false prophet, and time will reveal all about him-and eternity will settle it. The seed by the way side, among thorns, and stony places, belongs to the wicked one, and he will have it. Let the dead bury their dead.

So now, dear brother, while I respect you and the "Twelve," and all their kin, as my own blood relations, shall we, as the legal heirs of salvation, enlightened by the voice of God; by revelation upon revelation; by the gift of the Holy Ghost bringing all things to our remembrance; shall we, who have witnessed the power of God in the spread of the everlasting gospel; in the

307

manifestations of the gift of tongues; the miraculous healing of the sick by the laying on the hands of the elders; shall we, who have spent so many sweet hours under the holy dropping of the prophets' golden fountain; who have been delighted at his heavenly knowledge combating the errors of generations; teaching senators wisdom; judges justice; priests piety, and mankind mercy; shall we, who have beheld prophecies fulfilled knowing that the very bowels of the earth have hove up her "stony ruins," to establish the validity of the Book of Mormon, beyond a doubt; shall we, who have heard the echo of glad tidings from the islands of the sea, and from all quarters of the earth; shall we, who now gaze upon the blood stained prairies of the west; where bleaches the bones of the prophets, patriarchs, elders, men, women, and children, who all gave up the ghost in full faith; shall we, who have tasted of the good word of God, and seen the mysteries of the world to come, shall we turn to the beggarly elements of the world, to work our passage back to popularity and hell, for a "mess of portage," like Hinkle, Bennett, Laws, Rigdon and Co? No! Eternally no!-While water runs and grass grows, while eternity goes and eternity comes we will go on, knowing that it is written in heaven; published on earth, and muttered in hell, that Mormonism is ETERNAL TRUTH, and God Almighty is the author of it!

All the friends and saints greet you and your wife and family, with prayer and love.

As ever,

W. W. PHELPS
To ELDER WM. SMITH.
TIMES AND SEASONS.
CITY OF NAUVOO,
JANUARY 1, 1845.

Appendix 7: Editorial Draft, circa 1 March 1842

The Joseph Smith Papers have released a draft of editorial content that never appeared in the *Times and Seasons*. This is very interesting because it is in the handwriting of Willard Richards, not Joseph Smith, suggesting it was dictated.

Source Note
JS, Editorial draft, Nauvoo, IL, ca. 1 Mar. 1842; handwriting of Willard Richards; two pages; JS Collection, CHL. Includes endorsements.

http://www.josephsmithpapers.org/paper-summary/editorial-draft-circa-1-march-1842/1

Document Transcript

Times & Seasons

A considerable quantity of the matter in the last paper. was in type, before the establishment come into ~~our~~ My hands,— Some of which went to press. without our my recivecd, ~~or~~ knowledge ~~Thh~~ and a multiplicity of business= while enteri[n]g on the additional care of the editorial departmet of the Times & Seasons. mu[s]t be my apology for what is past.—

In future, I design to furnish much original matter, which will be found of enestimable adventage to the saints, – & to all who — desire a knowledge of the kingdom of God.— and as it is not practicable to bring forthe the new translation of the Scriptures. & varies records of ancint date. & great worth to this genration in ~~book~~ <the usual> form. by books. I shall prenit [print] specimens of the same in the Times & Seasons as fast. as time & space will admit. so that the honest in heart may be cheerd & comforted and go on their way rejoi[ci]ng.— as their souls become expanded.— & their undestandi[n]g enlightend, by a knowledg of ~~what~~ Gods work through the fathers. in former days, as well as what He is about to do in Latter Days—

To fulfil the words of the fathers.—

    In the p[r]enst no. will be found the Commencmet of the Records discovered in Egypt. some time since, as penend by the hand. of Father Abraham. which I shall contin[u]e to t[r]anslate & publish as fast as possible till the whole is completed.— and as the saints have long been anxious to obtain a copy of these rec[o]rds, those [p. [1]] are now taking this times & Seasons. will confer a sp[e]cial favor on their brethren, who do not take the paper, by infor[m]ing them that. they can now obtain their hearts

    Joseph Smith to the Times & Seasons
    about, 1842 [p. [2]]

Appendix 8: Church Printing Offices

The Joseph Smith Papers include useful background on the main Church printing offices.

Printing office, Independence, Missouri[152]
Summary

JS revelations, dated 20 July and 1 Aug. 1831, directed establishment of LDS church's first printing office in Independence, Missouri. [1] Dedicated by Bishop Edward Partridge, 29 May 1832. [2] Located on Lot 76, on Liberty Street just south of courthouse square. [3] Westernmost press in U.S. [4] Housed on top floor of two-story brick building, with family of church printer, William W. Phelps, residing on first floor. [5] Established to print revelations, to facilitate communication between church bodies in Ohio and Missouri, and to educate public about church. [6] Printed fourteen issues of first church periodical, *The Evening and the Morning Star,* June 1832–July 1833. [7] W. W. Phelps & Co. also published *Upper Missouri Advertiser,* featuring community and national news, in printing office. [8] Mob damaged press, scattered type, and leveled building, 20 July 1833. [9] Some printed sheets of Book of Commandments recovered by church members and later collated and bound. [10]

Printing office, Kirtland Township, Ohio
Summary

Following destruction of church printing office in Independence, Missouri, July 1833, JS and other church leaders determined to set up new printing office in Kirtland under firm name F. G. Williams & Co. [1] Oliver Cowdery purchased new printing press in New York, Oct. 1833, and Kirtland printing office was opened and dedicated in John Johnson inn, Dec. 1833. [2] JS revelation, dated 23 Apr. 1834, gave Williams and Cowdery joint stewardship of office. [3] Publication of Missouri newspaper *The Evening and the Morning Star* soon resumed. [4] In Dec. 1834, printing office was moved to second story of newly built

---

[152] Information on these sites is from this web page: http://www.josephsmithpapers.org/place/printing-office-independence-missouri.

schoolhouse, immediately west of temple lot. Press later launched new periodical,*Latter Day Saints' Messenger and Advocate* (Oct. 1834–Sept. 1837), followed by *Elders' Journal*(Oct.–Nov. 1837). Also published local political paper *Northern Times* (Feb. 1835–ca. Feb. 1836), first LDS church hymnal, first edition of Doctrine and Covenants (1835), and second edition of Book of Mormon (1837). Printing office destroyed when schoolhouse was torched by arsonist, 16 Jan. 1838.

Printing office, Nauvoo, Illinois

Summary

Located at four different sites from 1839–1846: cellar of warehouse on bank of Mississippi River, June–Aug. 1839; frame building on northeast corner of Water and Bain streets, Nov. 1839–Nov. 1841; newly built printing establishment on northwest corner of Water and Bain streets, Nov. 1841–May 1845; and part of three-building brick complex on northwest corner of Main and Kimball streets, May 1845–Mar. 1846. Shop sold by first proprietor, Ebenezer Robinson, to JS, 4 Feb. 1842. Leased by JS to John Taylor and Wilford Woodruff, Nov. 1842. Published third and fourth editions of Book of Mormon, three editions of Doctrine and Covenants, church hymnal, and newspapers *Times and Seasons, Wasp,* and *Nauvoo Neighbor.* Printing shop sold, Jan. 1844, to John Taylor, who ran it until operations ceased, Mar. 1846. JS often conducted church business at printing office.

Appendix 7: Benjamin Winchester to Parley P. Pratt

This is the text of a letter Winchester wrote to Pratt on January 14, 1845.[153]

New York Jan 14th 1845

PP Pratt

    Sir you will do me a favor by writing the letter to R. Hadlock on the subject of an account that I have standing against him for books as soon as you can so that it ~~will~~ <can> be sent by the next mail steamer because that my circumstances are such that it is necessary I should have returns from there as soon as possible I let him have three hundred dollars worth and if they are not all sold I think they can be and as I do not intend to do anything in future that will injure the church or cause of truth there will be no impropriety in disposing of them in England hence without doing himself or the cause any injustice he can remit to <me> the full amount It can be done by a bill of exchange on some good house in the city or Philadel. In my name directed to your care at the Prophet Office then I think it will come safe and when I receive it I will give you a receipt for it for him I wish you would particularly ~~state~~ urge ~~upon~~ the immediate payment of this bill by stating to him the circumstances as I detailed them to you and my intentions at the present time and I assure you I shall act in good faith so I rely on you to write soon and knowing your influence with Hadlock I shall certainly expect the money

    Yours Respectfully

    B. Winchester

---

[153] The letter is available in MS 897, *Letter from Wilford Woodruff*, 1845, under MS 897_f0002_d0004_0001.jpg, at this link:

    https://dcms.lds.org/delivery/DeliveryManagerServlet?dps_pid=IE1738087.

Brief Index

The Editors: Joseph, William and Don Carlos Smith

NOTES: